AF245576

RUSSIAN WEAPONS
OF WORLD WAR II

RUSSIAN WEAPONS OF WORLD WAR II

DAVID PORTER

Published by
Amber Books Ltd
United House
North Road
London N7 9DP
United Kingdom
www.amberbooks.co.uk
Instagram: amberbooksltd
Facebook: www.facebook.com/amberbooks
Twitter: @amberbooks

ISBN: 978-1-78274-630-0

Project Editor: Michael Spilling
Designer: Brian Rust
Picture Researcher: Terry Forshaw

Printed in China

ILLUSTRATION CREDITS
PHOTOGRAPHS
Art-Tech: 126–128, 135, 153
Cody Images: 131, 147, 198, 202, 205
Nik Cornish/STAVKA: 8, 56–64, 78, 87, 91 (top), 92, 93, 96, 100, 119–123, 142, 158–170, 172–192
Public Domain: 204
Ukrainian State Archive: 7, 10–54, 65–74, 80–84, 89, 90, 91 (bottom), 95, 97, 99, 102–113, 124, 133, 140, 145, 150, 154, 171, 196, 200, 211–213

ARTWORKS
Alcaniz Fresno's: 144, 152, 193 (bottom)
Amber Books: 25 (top)
Art-Tech: 63 (top), 66 (top), 94, 106–143, 146–151, 155, 168, 182–190, 193 (top), 203
Oliver Missing (www.o5m6.de): 11–23, 25–50, 63 (bottom), 65, 66 (bottom), 68, 69, 71–90, 96, 98, 161–167, 173–181, 206–210

Contents

Introduction

'Lies, damned lies and statistics.' Although every care has been taken to check the figures quoted in the following chapters, Soviet sources were notorious for faking statistics for just about everything. This practice originated with the rapid industrialization of Russia under Stalin's Five-Year Plans, which set impossibly high production targets. Failure to meet these quotas was regarded as treasonous; those held to be responsible were either shot or sent to a living death in the labour camps of the Gulag.

In mid-1941, Stalin's Russia was truly a 'stumbling colossus', with at least 5 million men under arms and a further 14 million more or less trained reserves. Armoured Fighting Vehicle (AFV) strengths included 23,000 tanks, of which only 14,700 were combat-ready, and 4800 assorted armoured cars. Although many of these AFVs were at least as good as their German counterparts, their combat value was markedly inferior due to poor maintenance and crew training. Maintenance problems were worsened by dire shortages of both spare parts and fully qualified mechanics.

Similar problems bedevilled the artillery; although there were 117,600 guns and mortars of all calibres in service in June 1941, their mobility was severely limited by a lack of artillery tractors and even horses. Even with the vast influx of lend-lease vehicles, much Soviet artillery was horse-drawn throughout the war.

The shortage of support vehicles drastically reduced the effectiveness of Soviet weapons in the opening stages of the German invasion. Inexperienced Russian commanders rapidly discovered that, without these vehicles, there was no fuel and ammunition resupply and no tank recovery. Lacking adequate transport, potentially powerful armoured formations were crippled even before they went into action, their tanks reduced to static defences or scrap metal.

Opposite:
On watch
Spring 1945: crews of T-34/85s of 3rd Guards Tank Army still keep watch for German aircraft on the approaches to Berlin. Even as late as February 1945, the *Luftwaffe* claimed the destruction of over 800 Soviet AFVs and support vehicles in a two-week period.

Any weapons are only as good as the troops who use them – despite the impressive military hardware regularly paraded through Red Square, the wartime Red Army was essentially an army of peasant conscripts, drawn largely from isolated villages in which living conditions had changed little for centuries. (In 1945, civilians in newly-conquered German towns were amazed to see some Russian troops carefully removing light bulbs and taps in the belief that they would give light and water anywhere.) Adequately training huge numbers of conscripts drawn from across the vast Soviet empire – many of whom spoke little or no Russian – was one of the Red Army's greatest achievements.

SELF-INFLICTED WOUND

A further factor that reduced the combat efficiency of even the best-equipped Red Army units was the self-inflicted wound of Stalin's purges of the officer corps. The rationale for these purges is uncertain – Stalin was always paranoid and may have suspected that able commanders such as Marshal Tukhachevsky represented a threat to his power.

In any event, between 1937 and 1939, three out of five Marshals of the Soviet Union (Tukhachevsky, Blyukher and Yegorov) were shot. By the time that the main waves of arrests ended in 1939, 90 per cent of all generals, 80 per cent of colonels and 30,000 officers of lower rank had been executed or sent to the Gulag. Unsurprisingly, this slaughter meant that, throughout the war, many Soviet officers were too terrified of arrest to do anything other than follow orders to the letter, even in cases where this was virtually suicidal.

Chapter 1

Armoured Fighting Vehicles

In June 1941, the Red Army fielded a bewildering variety of AFVs, ranging from ultra-modern T-34s and KV-1s to worn-out twin-turreted T-26s dating back to 1932. By 1945, its armoured units had been transformed, with formidable tanks developed under the pressures of four years of war.

The Red Army's first armoured fighting vehicles (AFVs) were a strange mixture of armoured cars inherited from the Tsar's army and small numbers of Medium Mark Vs, Whippets and Renault FTs that had been captured from the White forces in the Russian Civil War. Many of these were in poor condition, but they provided a small cadre of personnel with experience of operating AFVs until Soviet tank production began in the late 1920s.

The first Soviet-designed tank, the T-18, did not enter service until 1929, and was little more than a modernized Renault FT, but it marked the beginning of a rapid development of the Red Army's armoured force. This development was made possible by Stalin's 'Five-Year Plans' – ruthless programmes of industrialization that began to transform a largely agrarian nation into an industrial superpower.

Under the direction of Mikhail Tukhachevsky, who served as Chief of

Opposite:
JS-2 heavy tank
The crew of a battered JS-2 take a break in a German town. A DT machine gun has been mounted on the commander's cupola for defence against infantry anti-tank teams.

Field maintenance
Keeping AFVs serviceable in the depths of a Russian winter posed a major challenge. Here the turret is hoisted from a BT-5 in a field workshop during the winter of 1941/42.

Staff of the Red Army (1925–1928) and as Deputy Commissar for Defence, the Red Army's cavalry began to be replaced by powerful armoured forces. An experimental Mechanized Brigade was formed during the summer of 1929; this demonstrated the potential of such formations, and Tukhachevsky was given a chance to put his ideas into practice.

Annual tank production figures soared during this period. This allowed the new theories of warfare to be tested in ever-larger annual manoeuvres, culminating in the huge 1935 exercises held in the Kiev Military District, where Western observers were staggered to see hundreds of AFVs. They would have been even more amazed had it been known that the Russians had more tank units (and, indeed, more AFVs) than the rest of the world's armies combined.

Just as it seemed that the Red Army was establishing an unassailable technological lead over other European armies, that lead was swept away by Stalin's paranoia: Tukhachevsky and the most able senior officers were killed or imprisoned in the purges launched in 1937. Thousands of more junior officers were also shot or imprisoned, and the wave of terror widened to include the heads of the defence industries and even weapons' design teams.

Spanish Civil War

At the same time, the Spanish Civil War provided an invaluable opportunity to test Soviet military equipment in combat conditions, including a sizeable Soviet armoured contingent, which included 300 T-26s and 50 BT-5s, operating in support of the Republicans. Although there were no large-scale tank battles, a number of actions proved that these machines were technically far superior to the Panzer Is and Italian tankettes fielded by the Nationalist forces.

Despite this technological superiority, there were worrying signs of problems with Russian tank designs. The petrol engines of the T-26s and BT-5s were found to be a significant fire hazard when Nationalist infantry began to use 'Molotov cocktail' improvised incendiary grenades. There was even greater concern at the ease with which the Nationalists' German-supplied 37mm (1.46in) anti-tank guns could penetrate the tanks' thin armour.

Reports from Spain helped to frame the requirements for the new tank designs, including the need for armour immune to 37mm (1.46in) anti-tank guns at point-blank range and to 76mm (3in) guns at ranges over 1000m (3280ft). The poor fuel efficiency of contemporary petrol engines and their inherent fire risk led to the decision that diesel engines should be used if possible. These requirements formed the starting point for the development of the T-34, which was arguably the 'tank that saved Russia', not only due to its battlefield capabilities, but also its suitability for manufacture in the most appalling conditions when factories had to be hastily evacuated. Despite primitive factory conditions, production times were halved by the end of 1942, even though most experienced factory workers had been conscripted and replaced by a workforce of 50 per cent women, 15 per cent boys and 15 per cent invalids and old men.

T-26 LIGHT INFANTRY TANKS

The T-26 was derived from the British Vickers 6-ton tank. It proved to be a

T-26TU Model 1931

This was the command tank version of the Model 1931, fitted with radio and the distinctive 'clothes line' aerial. The right-hand turret was armed with a low-velocity 37mm (1.46in) gun derived from the French Puteaux SA 18, while the left-hand turret retained its single DT machine gun.

T-26 Model 1931
Crew: 3
Production: 1931–33
Weight: 8.6 tonnes (8.46 tons)
Length: 4.88m (16ft)
Width: 3.41m (11ft 2in)
Height: 2.08m (6ft 10in)
Engine: 66kW (88hp) GAZ-T26 4-cylinder petrol
Road speed: 35km/h (22mph)
Range: 130km (81 miles)
Armament: 1 x 37mm (1.46in) gun and 1 x 7.62mm (.3in) DT machine gun
Armour: 6–15mm (0.24–0.59in)

highly successful design, with more than 12,000 examples of all versions built during the period 1931–1941. The initial production type was the T-26 Model 1931 with two turrets, each fitted with a single DT machine gun. Just over 2000 examples were completed between 1931and 1934.

It was soon realized that the twin-turret concept was outdated, and the design of a single-turret version began in 1932. This resulted in the Model 1933, fitted with a two-man turret armed with a 45mm (1.77in) gun and a coaxial DT machine gun. Production of this version continued until 1936. A total of 5500 were completed, more than any other Soviet tank until 1941.

During the mid-1930s, skirmishes between Soviet and Japanese forces along the Mongolian/Manchurian border highlighted the poor quality of the T-26s' riveted armour. Production was suspended until welded armour could be incorporated in the new Model 1936, which also had an additional DT machine gun in the turret rear.

By the late 1930s, the vulnerability of the T-26 to light anti-tank guns such as the 37mm (1.46in) Pak 36 had been demonstrated in the Spanish Civil War. Simply increasing the armour would have severely reduced battlefield mobility and risked overloading the suspension. The solution adopted was to fit a new turret incorporating the

T-26 Model 1933

The Model 1933 was the first single-turret version of the T-26. Its 45mm (1.77in) main armament was far more powerful than any other tank gun of the early 1930s.

T-26 M1933

Crew: 3
Production: 1933–35
Weight: 9.4 tonnes (9.25 tons)
Length: 4.88m (16ft)
Width: 3.41m (11ft 2in)
Height: 2.41m (7ft 11in)
Engine: 67kW (90hp) GAZ-T26 4-cylinder petrol
Road speed: 28km/h (17mph)
Range: 175km (108 miles)
Armament: 1 x 45mm (1.77in) gun and 1 x coaxial 7.62mm (.3in) DT machine gun
Armour: 6–15mm (0.23–0.59in)

T-26 Model 1938
The Model 1938 featured a new welded turret with sloped armour and increased fuel capacity. This example is fitted with a DT machine gun on a P-40M AA mount, which was retrofitted to many earlier T-26s.

T-26 M1938
Crew: 3
Production: 1938–39
Weight: 8.6 tonnes (8.46 tons)
Length: 4.88m (16ft)
Width: 3.41m (11ft 2in)
Height: 2.41m (7ft 11in)
Engine: 676kW (90hp) 4-cylinder petrol
Road speed: 30km/h (18.6mph)
Range: 225km (140 miles)
Armament: 1 x 45mm (1.77in) gun and up to 3 x 7.62mm (.3in) DT machine guns (1 coaxial, 1 in turret rear and 1 x AA)
Armour: 6–20mm (0.24–0.79in)

same thickness of sloped armour; this offered greater protection without any weight penalty. This Model 1938 was in turn developed into the Model 1939, in which a modified Model 1938 turret was combined with a modernized hull with a new wider upper superstructure protected by thicker sloped armour.

Large numbers of T-26s saw action in the Winter War against Finland, where losses were staggering: 7th Army lost 930 during operations in the Karelian Isthmus between 30 November 1939 and 13 March 1940. (This figure includes 463 that were repaired during the war, many of which had simply broken down.) This emphasized the urgent need to improve the armour of even the latest T-26s; a number were hastily fitted with additional armour, bringing the maximum thickness up to 50mm (1.96in). These were designated T-26E ('E' standing for *ekranami* – appliqué armour).

The T-26 comprised 39.5 per cent of the Red Army's tank strength at the time of the German invasion. There were 4875 in the western military districts, of which 3100 were operational. This almost matched the total German tank strength deployed at the start of Operation 'Barbarossa'.

T-26E

The weight of the appliqué armour degraded the automotive performance and mechanical reliability of the T-26, but was accepted as a necessary evil to improve survivability.

Once in action, it was soon found that dire shortages of recovery vehicles and spares meant that the majority of damaged or broken-down tanks had to be destroyed or abandoned. Although the later versions of the T-26 were at least equal to the majority of Axis tanks of 1941, they were hamstrung by poor infantry and artillery support. When German air superiority and their infinitely superior tactics were added to the equation, they resulted in horrendous Soviet losses. The experience of the 12th Mechanized Corps defending the Baltic Special Military was typical.

On 22 June 1941, it deployed 449 T-26s, 2 OT-130 flamethrowing tanks and 4 T-26T artillery tractors; by 7 July, it had lost 201 T-26 tanks and all the OT-130s and artillery tractors. Significantly, a further 186 T-26 tanks were lost to mechanical failures.

Surviving T-26s fought throughout the war, with more than 1000 taking part in the Soviet offensive that defeated the Japanese Kwantung Army and overran Manchuria in August 1945.

T-27 'TANKETTE'

This was a very basic armoured machine-gun carrier developed from the British Carden Loyd tankette, 20 of which were bought for trials in 1930. The T-27 was little more than an enlarged Carden Loyd, fitted with a more powerful engine and armed with a single 7.62mm (0.3in) DT machine gun with 2520 rounds. More than 2500 T-27s were completed between 1931 and 1933; barely half of these remained in service by June 1941, when they were still listed on the strengths of the 1st, 4th, 9th, 10th, 15th, 18th and 24th Mechanized Corps. Some of the few survivors took part in the defence of Moscow in December 1941.

T-37, T-38 AND T-40 AMPHIBIOUS LIGHT TANKS

By 1933, it was clear that the little T-27 'tankettes' were just too small and vulnerable to be effective

T-37 Amphibious Light Tank
A T-37 in Finland during the Winter War. The thin armour was no more than bulletproof; one unlucky T-37 was destroyed on the ice of Lake Ladoga at a range of 1700m (5580ft) by a 37mm (1.46in) Bofors gun of the Finnish 7th Anti-Tank Detachment.

T-37A
Crew: 2
Production: 1933–36
Weight: 3.2 tonnes (3 tons)
Length: 3.75m (12ft 4in)
Width: 2.1m (6ft 10in)
Height: 1.82m (6ft)
Engine: 30kW (40hp) GAZ-AA petrol
Road speed: 35km/h (22mph)
Range: 185km (115 miles)
Armament: 1 x 7.62mm (0.3in) DT machine gun
Armour: 3–9mm (0.12–0.39in)

T-38 Amphibious Light Tank
Although the T-38 was an improvement on the T-37, only a few were fitted with radios, which severely limited their effectiveness in the reconnaissance role. The limitations of the type led to the development of the T-40.

T-38
Crew: 2
Production: 1936–39
Weight: 3.3 tonnes (3.25 tons)
Length: 3.78m (12ft 5in)
Width: 3.33m (10ft 11in)
Height: 1.63m (5ft 4in)
Engine: 30kW (40hp) GAZ-AA petrol
Road speed: 40km/h (25mph)
Range: 170km (109 miles)
Armament: 1 x 7.62mm (0.3in) DT Model 1929 machine gun
Armour: 3–9mm (0.12–0.35in)

T-40 Amphibious Light Tank

The T-40 was a more thickly armoured amphibious light tank with improved armament – a 12.7mm (0.5in) DShK heavy machine gun and a coaxial 7.62mm (0.3in) DT machine gun.

T-40

Crew: 2
Production: 1939–41
Weight: 5.9 tonnes (5.8 tons)
Length: 4.11m (13ft 6in)
Width: 2.33m (7ft 8in)
Height: 1.95m (6ft 5in)
Engine: 52.2kW (70hp) GAZ-202 petrol
Road speed: 45km/h (28mph)
Range: 450km (280 miles)
Armament: 1 x 12.7mm (.5in) DShK machine gun and 1 x coaxial 7.62mm (.3in) DT machine gun
Armour: 3–13mm (0.12–0.51in)

reconnaissance vehicles. They were rapidly phased out of front-line service in favour of a succession of larger, more powerful, amphibious light tanks, starting with the T-37, which was armed with a single DT machine gun in a small one-man turret.

A total of 1200 T-37s were produced between 1933 and 1937, but the type's performance in the water was not impressive and a major redesign was ordered. This was so extensive that the new tank received the designation T-38. It was wider and lower than the T-37 and had a higher road speed. Approximately 1300 were completed between 1937 and 1939, but concern was expressed at the lack of firepower, and the single 7.62mm (0.3in) machine gun was sometimes replaced with a 20mm ShVAK cannon.

The T-40 represented a significant advance on the T-37 and T-38 when it entered service in 1940. The coil-spring suspension of the earlier tanks was replaced by a modern torsion-bar suspension with four pairs of road wheels. Firepower was improved and the welded, conical turret offered better protection, although the armour was still very thin.

No more than 222 had been completed at the time of the German invasion; production was then switched to the simpler T-60. The design marked the end of the line for Soviet amphibious light tanks until the PT-76 entered service in 1951.

T-60 LIGHT TANK

The T-60 originated as a 'non-amphibious' version of the T-40, but the design evolved into a more heavily armoured light tank retaining only the lower hull and running gear of the T-40. The type was initially intended to be fitted with the same armament as the T-40; however, it was soon realized that this was inadequate, and all production vehicles were armed with the 20mm (0.79in) TNSh cannon and a coaxial 7.62mm (0.3in) DT machine gun.

The first vehicles were completed in July 1941 and output was rapidly increased to meet the desperate need for tanks to replace the huge losses inflicted by the Germans in the opening stages of Operation 'Barbarossa'.

Once in action, the type proved to be highly vulnerable to even the lightest Axis anti-tank weapons. It soon became known as *Bratskaya Mogila na Dovoikh*, literally: 'a brother's grave for two'. Attempts were made to improve battlefield survivability by thickening the turret and frontal armour, but this worsened the T-60's already poor battlefield mobility. (This was largely due to increased ground pressure that resulted from the retention of the original narrow tracks.)

It also proved to be impossible to increase firepower; trials with the more powerful 23mm (0.9in) VYa-23 cannon were abandoned after it was found that its recoil jammed the turret traverse mechanism.

T-60
Crew: 2
Production: 1941–43
Weight: 5.8 tonnes (5.7 tons)
Length: 4.1m (13ft 5in)
Width: 2.3m (7ft 6in)
Height: 1.74m (5ft 8in)
Engine: 63.4kW (85hp) GAZ-203 petrol
Road speed: 45km/h (27mph)
Range: 450km (280 miles)
Armament: 1 x 20mm (.79in) TNSh cannon and 1 x coaxial 7.62mm (.3in) DT machine gun
Armour: 7–35mm (0.28–1.38in)

T-60 Light Tank
Early-production T-60s had spoked road wheels; later up-armoured examples such as this had solid road wheels to cope with the greater weight.

Despite the type's undoubted problems, Major General Katukov acknowledged that with intelligent deployment, the T-60 did prove valuable in the desperate fighting of 1941: 'In this fateful hour, when the Germans had almost defeated us, those ridiculous tanks saved our positions. It was lucky that the rye in the area was almost a metre high, as it hid the T-60s. Using the rye field, both of our T-60 tanks were able to infiltrate the rear of German infantry and open fire on them. After several minutes of intense fire, the German attack was halted.'

Such occasional successes could not compensate for the inherent weaknesses of the design, its vulnerability and poor cross-country performance that made it difficult to operate effectively in tank brigades alongside T-34s and KVs.

General Rotmistrov reported to Stavka that: 'The difficulty was that while there wasn't much difference between the T-60 and the T-34 on the roads, when moving across country, the light tanks were quickly left behind. The KVs were already behind and often crushed bridges, cutting off units behind them. Under battlefield conditions, this meant that too often the T-34s arrived alone; the light tanks had difficulty in fighting the Germans anyway, and the KVs were delayed in the rear.'

Well over 6000 T-60s were produced, but combat experience showed that they were incapable of taking on any but the lightest German AFVs; the type was phased out during 1943 in favour of the T-70.

T-70 LIGHT TANK

The T-70 was the final Soviet light tank to enter service in significant numbers during the war, with more than 8000 being completed between 1942 and 1943. Initial attempts to speed up production by using existing assemblies caused endless problems, the worst being the adoption of a powerplant comprising two GAZ-202 lorry engines, one on each side of the hull. Each engine drove one track through separate, unsynchronized transmissions, but trials showed that this arrangement was impractical and it was rapidly redesigned so that the engines were fitted in-line with a conventional transmission and differential assembly. At the same time, the original conical turret was replaced by a more easily produced welded turret mounting a 45mm (1.77in) gun and a coaxial DT machine gun. The new version was officially designated T-70M, but was almost always simply referred to as the T-70.

Main gun

Although the 45mm (1.77in) main armament was a welcome improvement on the ineffective 20mm (0.79in) cannon of the T-60, by 1942/43 it was unable to penetrate most contemporary German tanks at normal battle ranges. A further design flaw was the retention of a one-man turret, which imposed an excessive workload on the commander. A two-man turret was designed for the T-70; about 120 tanks were fitted with this under the designation T-80 before production was halted in favour of the SU-76, which utilized many of the same components.

T-70 Light Tank

Despite its limitations, the T-70 could be a useful reconnaissance vehicle when used intelligently: it was much smaller than a T-34 and its petrol engines had a much less conspicuous 'signature' than the clouds of exhaust fumes emitted by the T-34's diesel.

T-70M

Crew: 2
Production: 1941–43
Weight: 9.2 tonnes (9.05 tons)
Length: 4.29m (14ft 1in)
Width: 2.04m (7ft 7in)
Height: 1.74m (6ft 7in)
Engine: 2 x 52kW (70hp) GAZ-202 6-cylinder petrol
Road speed: 45km/h (28mph)
Range: 360km (224 miles)
Armament: 1 x 45mm (1.77in) gun and 1 x coaxial 7.62mm (.3in) DT machine gun
Armour: 10–60mm (0.39–2.36in)

The type did score occasional spectacular successes, although these were few and far between. On 26 March 1944, Sergeant Alexander Pegov ambushed a column of Panthers and knocked out two with flank shots from less than 200m (660ft) using APCR ammunition. Amazingly, Pegov survived to be promoted and decorated as a Hero of the Soviet Union.

The T-70 did have the advantage that it could be produced in small factories

BT-2
One of the few surviving BT-2s in roughly applied winter camouflage during the defence of Moscow, December 1941.

BT-2
Crew: 3
Production: 1932–34
Weight: 10.2 tonnes (9.8 tons)
Length: 5.58m (18ft 3in)
Width: 2.23m (7ft 3in)
Height: 2.2m (7ft 2in)
Engine: 298kW (400hp) M5 petrol
Road speed: 100km/h (62mph)
Range: 200km (124 miles)
Armament: 1 x 37mm (1.46in) Model 1930 gun; 1 x 7.62mm (0.3in) DT machine gun
Armour: 6–13mm (0.24–0.51in)

that could not manufacture medium or heavy tanks, and the type remained in service until 1948.

BT FAST TANKS

The BT (*Bystrokhodny* tank – high-speed tank) series was developed from the US M1930 convertible tank designed by the eccentric Walter Christie, who recognized that tank tracks of the period were not only unreliable, but severely restricted tank speed. His solution to the problem was to make the tracks readily removable and to fit a chain drive to the rear road wheels. The tracks could be removed in about 30 minutes and stowed on the track guards, allowing the tank to run at very high road speeds – up to 100km/h (62mph) in the wheeled mode.

The Russians bought two of Christie's prototypes in 1931; these were designated BT-1 and provided the basis for the first BT-2 tanks, which entered service in 1932. The BT-2 was powered by the 300kW (400hp) M5-400 that was a licence-built copy of the American Liberty aircraft engine. Early versions were difficult to maintain, although the high power-to-weight ratio delivered exceptional performance when everything worked properly.

All BT-2s had simple cylindrical turrets; most were armed with a 37mm (1.46in) B-3 (5-K) tank gun, which was essentially a Russian version of the German 3.7cm (1.46in) KwK 36, and a single ball-mounted DT machine gun. Shortages of the 37mm gun (1.46in)

BT-5 Model 1933
This radio-equipped company or platoon commander's vehicle, seen in disruptive winter camouflage, would be a priority target for German tank gunners.

BT-5 Model 1933
Crew: 3
Production: 1933–35
Weight: 11.5 tonnes (11 tons)
Length: 5.58m (18ft 3in)
Width: 2.23m (7ft 3in)
Height: 2.2m (7ft 2in)
Engine: 298kW (400hp) M-5 petrol
Road speed: 72km/h (45mph)
Range: 200km (124 miles)
Armament: 45mm (1.77in) 20K Model 1932 gun; 1 x 7.62mm (0.3in) coaxial DT machine gun
Armour: 6–13mm (0.24–0.51in)

BT-7 Model 1937
Crew: 3
Production: 1937–39
Weight: 14 tonnes (13.2 tons)
Length: 5.58m (18ft 3in)
Width: 2.29m (7ft 6in)
Height: 2.42m (7ft 10in)
Engine: 373kW (500hp) Milukin M17-T V-12 petrol
Road speed: 86km/h (53mph)
Range: 250km (155 miles)
Armament: 45mm (1.77in) 20K Model 1932 gun; 1 x 7.62mm (0.3in) coaxial DT machine gun
Armour: 6–13mm (0.23–0.51in)

BT-7 Model 1937
This is the mass-production version of the BT-7. It has been painted in a three-tone camouflage and served in eastern Poland in 1939.

forced the completion of the earliest BT-2s with three DTs.

By 1933, it was clear that the BT-2 needed to be up-gunned with the 45mm (1.77in) 20-K tank gun that was already the standard main armament of the latest T-26s. This requirement led to the introduction of the BT-5 armed with the 45mm (1.77in) and a coaxial DT in a turret closely resembling that of the T-26.

Although the BT-5 was formidable by the standards of the early 1930s, the need for improved protection from the increasing numbers of light anti-tank guns led to the BT-7, which entered large-scale production in 1937. The principal feature of the type was a new conical turret, derived from that of the T-26 Model 1937. The turret's sloped armour gave greater protection and increased space for ammunition stowage, plus a rear-mounted DT machine gun.

In addition to the standard BT-7s, a batch of 154 BT-7A artillery tanks was produced between 1936 and 1938. These tanks were armed with the 76.2mm (3in) KT howitzer in a large cylindrical turret derived from that of the T-28 medium tank.

The heavier armament increased the tank's weight to a point at which it was impracticable to retain the convertible wheel/track drive, and this became the only service version of the BT to run solely on tracks.

The BT series remained in production until 1941, by which time almost 7000 vehicles had been completed. Many fought in the opening

BT-7A

The BT-7A's 76.2mm (3in) KT howitzer fired a 6.23kg (13.73lbs) HE shell to a maximum range of 7100m (23,300ft), although the tank was primarily intended to support the 45mm (1.77in) armed BTs with close-range direct fire against enemy strongpoints and anti-tank guns.

BT-7A Artillery Tank

Crew: 3

Production: 1936–38

Weight: 14.5 tonnes (13.8 tons)

Length: 5.66m (18ft 3in)

Width: 2.29m (7ft 6in)

Height: 2.52m (8ft 1in)

Engine: 373kW (500hp) Milukin M17-T V-12 petrol

Road speed: 86km/h (53mph)

Range: 200km (124 miles)

Armament: 76.2mm (3in) KT-28 Model 1932 howitzer; 1 or 2 7.62mm (0.3in) DT machine guns (1 turret roof, 1 turret rear)

Armour: 6–15mm (0.24–0.59in)

T-28 Model 1934
Crew: 6
Production: 1934–40
Weight: 28 tonnes (27.4 tons)
Length: 7.44m (248ft 5in)
Width: 2.87m (9ft 5in)
Height: 2.82m (9ft 3in)
Engine: 373kW (500hp) V-12 Milukin-M17 petrol
Road speed: 37km/h (23mph)
Range: 220km (137 miles)
Armament: 1 x 76.2mm (3in) howitzer; 5 x 7.62mm (.3in) DT machine guns (1 x AA, 1 in turret front, 1 in turret rear and 1 in each of the two forward sub-turrets)
Armour: 10–30mm (0.39–1.18in)

T-28
At the time of its service debut, the T-28 was one of the world's best medium tanks: the 76.2mm (3in) howitzer fired an effective 6.2kg HE shell, ideal for its infantry support role. More than 8000 rounds of machine-gun ammunition were carried, allowing a high volume of suppressive fire.

stages of Operation 'Barbarossa', but losses were horrendous and the type virtually disappeared from the Eastern Front during 1942. Some reports indicate that significant numbers remained in service in the Far Eastern Military Districts and took part in the invasion of Japanese-occupied Manchuria in 1945.

T-28 MEDIUM TANK

The T-28 was developed in response to a 1929 requirement for an infantry support tank and entered production in 1933. By the standards of the time, it was well protected with 20–30mm (0.79–1.18in) armour and had impressive firepower divided between three turrets. Two small turrets each mounted a single DT machine gun, while the main turret of early-production vehicles carried a 76.2mm (3in) KT-28 howitzer and a third ball-mounted DT machine gun.

In 1938, production switched to an improved version with the longer, higher-velocity 76.2mm (3in) L-10 tank gun and an additional DT machine gun in the rear of the main turret. Many were later fitted with a P-40 AA mount for a further DT machine gun.

Losses to Finnish anti-tank guns during the Winter War were high – possibly as many as 90 T-28s. This prompted an emergency programme to fit 50mm (1.97in) appliqué armour panels to the hull front and main turret, but as the engine was not uprated, battlefield mobility and top speed were dramatically reduced.

The final production batch delivered in 1940 was fitted with the main turret of the T-35 Model 1939, whose sloped armour gave improved protection. By the time of the German invasion, perhaps 400 remained in service, but most had been lost by the end of 1941.

T-34

The T-34's origins can be traced back to the BT fast tanks. In 1937, the talented designer Mikhail Koshkin was appointed to supervise work on an improved version of the BT. His initial design studies led to the A-20, which retained the 45mm (1.77in) gun and the convertible wheel/track drive of the BT series. However, the type broke new ground with the introduction of all-round sloped armour on both hull and turret and a new V12 diesel engine. By this time, it was recognized that the wheel/track drive was increasingly outdated; it added significant weight and complexity and, in practice, commanders in the field were reluctant to employ BT tanks in the wheeled mode. The A-20 was therefore abandoned in favour of the more heavily armoured A-32 of 1939, which only ran on tracks and was armed with the 76.2mm (3in) L-10 gun.

Good as the A-32 was, Koshkin was convinced that further improvements were essential and he updated the design to produce the A-34 with 45mm (1.77in) armour and the new L-11 76.2mm (3in) gun. The tracks were widened from 400 to 550mm (15.74 to 21.6in) – a feature that greatly improved battlefield mobility, especially in deep mud and snow. After prolonged trials, including a 3000-km (1864-mile) round trip from Kharkov to Moscow in March

Berlin 1945

A T34/85 and supporting infantry advance cautiously through a remarkably undamaged Berlin suburb. Their caution was fully justified – the Russians lost at least 108 tanks in the city to weapons ranging from 128mm AA guns to hand-held panzerfausts.

T-34 Model 1940

Early-production T-34s were notoriously unreliable. Units learned to carry as many spares as possible, such as the complete transmission lashed to the engine deck of this T-34 Model 1940.

T-34 Model 1940
Crew: 4
Production: 1940–41
Weight: 26 tonnes (26.08 tons)
Length: 5.95m (19ft 6in)
Width: 3m (9ft 10in)
Height: 2.4m (7ft 10in)
Engine: 373kW (500hp) Model V-2-34 diesel
Road speed: 55km/h (34mph)
Range: 300km (186 miles)
Armament: 1 x 76.2mm (3in) L-11 L/30.5; 2 x 7.62mm (0.3in) DT machine gun, 1 coaxial, 1 hull front
Armour: 15–45mm (0.59–1.77in)

T-34 Model 1941

The crew's poor vision when closed down could be lethal – German infantry soon learned to take advantage of the T-34's numerous blind spots to wedge a demolition charge or time-fused anti-tank mine under the turret's rear overhang. Either was sufficient to blow the turret off – a feat that could only be equalled by the 88mm gun.

T-34 Model 1941
Crew: 4
Production: 1940–41
Weight: 28.12 tonnes (27.7 tons)
Length: 6.68m (21ft 11in)
Width: 3m (9ft 10in)
Height: 2.4m (7ft 10in)
Engine: 373kW (500hp) Model V-2-34 diesel
Road speed: 55km/h (34mph)
Range: 300km (186 miles)
Armament: 1 x 76.2mm (3in) L-11 L/30.5; 2 x 7.62mm (0.3in) DT machine gun, 1 coaxial, 1 hull front
Armour: 15–45mm (0.59–1.77in)

T-34 Stalingrad production

In 1941/42, dire shortages of rubber forced the adoption of simplified road wheels with resilient steel rims. As the supply situation gradually improved, priority was given to providing rubber-rimmed road wheels for the first and fifth positions, as all-steel wheels in these positions set up severe vibrations at high speeds that could cause serious mechanical damage.

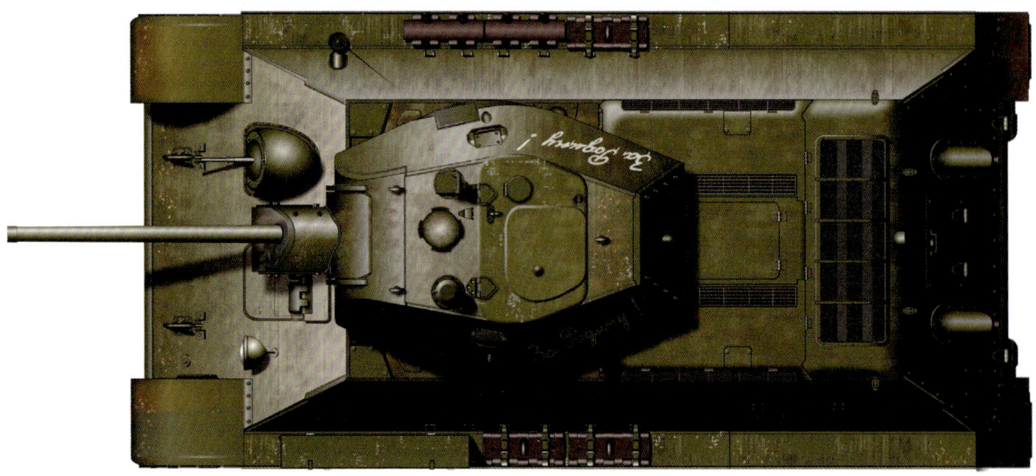

T-34 Model 1942

Crew: 4
Production: 1942–43
Weight: 28.5 tonnes (28.05 tons)
Length: 6.68m (21ft 11in)
Width: 3m (9ft 10in)
Height: 2.4m (7ft 10in)
Engine: 373kW (500hp) Model V-2-34 diesel
Road speed: 55km/h (34mph)
Range: 300km (186 miles)
Armament: 1 x 76.2mm (3in) F-34 L/40.5 gun; 2 x 7.62mm (0.3in) DT machine guns; 1 coaxial, 1 hull front
Armour: 20–70mm (0.79–2.76in)

1940, the type was accepted for service as the T-34 Model 1940. The relatively few T-34s in service at the time of the German invasion shocked the confident panzer crews. One sergeant commented: 'Numbers – they don't mean much, we're used to that. But better machines, that's terrible.... The Russian tanks are so agile, at close range they climb a slope or cross swampy ground faster than you can traverse the turret. And through the noise and vibration, you keep hearing the clang of shot against armour. When they hit one of ours there is so often a deep, long explosion, a roar as the fuel burns, a roar too loud, thank God, to let us hear the cries of the crew.'

Although the T-34 had impressive firepower, its accuracy was not so impressive, as Russian AFV sighting equipment was far cruder than that produced by German firms such as Zeiss. Matters were not helped by the two-man turret crew: the commander/gunner was overworked and could not operate efficiently in either role. Rate of fire was restricted by the ammunition stowage. Only 9 of the 77 main armament rounds were stowed in readily accessible clips in the turret and hull; the rest were carried in bins covered by neoprene matting that formed the fighting compartment floor. In any action where more than a few rounds were fired, the loader had to work at a furious pace amid a tangled mass of open bins and discarded matting, while each time the main armament fired, another very hot cartridge case was ejected onto the floor. The 76.2mm (3in) L-11 gun was

T-34 Model 1943
Crew: 4
Production: 1943–44
Weight: 30.9 tonnes (30.41 tons)
Length: 6.68m (21ft 11in)
Width: 3m (9ft 10in)
Height: 2.4m (7ft 10in)
Engine: 373kW (500hp) Model V-2-34 diesel
Road speed: 55km/h (34mph)
Range: 300km (186 miles)
Armament: 1 x 76.2mm (3in) F-34 L/40.5 gun; 2 x 7.62mm (0.3in) DT machine guns; 1 coaxial, 1 hull front
Armour: 20–70mm (0.79–2.76in)

T-34 Model 1943
The operational range of the Model 1943 was improved by the addition of 90-litre (20-gallon) cylindrical auxiliary fuel tanks, which became commonplace fittings on most late-war Soviet AFVs.

an effective weapon by the standards of 1941, but the more powerful 76.2mm (3in) F-34 was ready for production, although its adoption had been blocked by the incompetent Marshal Kulik. Combat experience with the T-34 Model 1940 showed that improvements were needed – a new welded turret was combined with the F-34 gun to produce the T-34 Model 1941.

Although crews appreciated greater firepower, some features of this version were far less popular, such as the poor-quality sights and periscopes. Perhaps the worst single feature was the large, forward-opening turret hatch that was heavy and prone to jamming. Even when the hatch could be opened, it blocked the commander's forward view, forcing him to lean around it and make himself a prime target for sniper fire.

By 1942, it was clear that the T-34's cramped two-man turret needed updating. The ideal solution of fitting an enlarged three-man turret was rejected as too complex and likely to disrupt production at a time when every tank was desperately needed. As an interim measure, a new two-man turret was introduced with separate loader's and commander's hatches. This still failed to improve the commander's very limited field of vision when closed down; later Model 1943s were fitted with a 360-degree vision commander's cupola.

The 85mm (3.35in) gun of the T-34/85 that entered service in 1944 dramatically increased firepower,

T-34/85, Berlin 1945

As Red Army AFVs advanced into the urbanized terrain of central Europe in 1944/45, they took increasing losses from German infantry armed with panzerfaust and panzershreck anti-tank weapons. The threat from these 'faustniks' became so acute that many tank units added improvised stand-off armour in an attempt to improve protection. This vehicle shows a typical set of such 'armour' – wire mesh screens, probably improvised from bedsprings – welded to the hull and turret sides.

T-34/85 Model 1944

Crew: 5
Production: 1944–45
Weight: 32 tonnes (31.49 tons)
Length: 8.15m (26ft 8in)
Width: 3m (9ft 10in)
Height: 2.6m (8ft 6in)
Engine: 373kW (500hp) Model V-2-34 diesel
Road speed: 55km/h (34mph)
Range: 350km (217 miles)
Armament: 1 x 85mm (3.35in) ZiS-53 or ZiS-S-53 L/51.5 gun; 2 x 7.62mm (0.3in) DT machine guns
Armour: 20–90mm (0.79–3.54in)

T-35 Model 1938
The T-35 was never mechanically reliable, largely due to the use of the same engine and transmission as the far lighter T-28. These problems became even more acute with the introduction of the 49-tonne (54-ton) up-armoured Model 1938.

T-35 (Model 1936)
Crew: 11
Production: 1935–39
Weight: 45 tonnes (44.3 tons)
Length: 9.72m (31ft 10in)
Width: 3.2m (10ft 6in)
Height: 3.43m (11ft 4in)
Engine: 373kW (500hp) M-17M petrol
Road speed: 30km/h (19mph)
Range: 150km (93 miles)
Armament: 1 x 76.2mm (3in) Model 1927/32 gun; 2 x 45mm (1.77in) 20K Model 1932 gun; 2 x 7.62mm (0.3in) DT machine guns
Armour: 11–30mm (0.43in–1.18in)

giving the new tank a reasonable chance of destroying Panthers and Tiger Is at normal combat ranges. The more powerful main armament required a new enlarged turret. This allowed space for a three-man turret crew (loader, gunner and commander) that significantly increased combat effectiveness.

Despite its limitations, the T-34 was well suited to mass production in the appalling conditions that followed the mass evacuation of Soviet war industries in 1941 in the face of the German invasion. The evacuation of the huge Kharkov tank factory to the Urals was typical – the last shipments left Kharkov on 19 October and the first batch of 25 T-34s completed in the most primitive conditions left the new site on 8 December. More than 34,900 T-34s and 18,650 T-34/85s were completed by the end of the war.

T-35 HEAVY TANK

Design studies for a multi-turreted heavy tank began in 1930, and a first prototype was completed in July 1932. This was armed with a main turret mounting a 76.2mm (3in) howitzer and four sub-turrets, two with 37mm (1.46in) guns and two with machine guns. Problems with the transmission led to the decision to drop the type in favour of a simpler design with an improved automotive system. A further prototype incorporating these improvements was completed in 1933 using the main and sub-turrets of the T-28. Two further sub-turrets each mounted a 37mm (1.46in) gun. An initial batch of 20 was completed over the next two years. Production then switched to the Model 1935, in which the 37mm (1.46in) sub-turrets were replaced with larger turrets similar to those of the BT-5, each mounting a 45mm (1.77in) gun and a coaxial DT machine gun. A final batch of six was completed in 1938/39 as the Model 1938 with redesigned turrets, incorporating sloped armour.

T-35s served with the 5th Separate Heavy Tank Brigade in Moscow, primarily for parade duties, from 1935 until 1940. All serviceable vehicles were then assigned to the 67th and 68th Tank Regiments of the 34th Tank Division, which served with the 8th Mechanized Corps in the Kiev Special Military District. Most were lost in the opening stages of Operation 'Barbarossa', mainly due to mechanical failures.

SMK AND T-100

In 1938, a requirement was issued for a five-turreted 'anti-tank gun destroyer' with armour capable of resisting 37mm (1.46in) and 45mm (1.77in) rounds at any range and 76.2mm (3in) artillery fire at ranges greater than 1200m (3940ft). The two design teams working on the project objected to the five-turret specification and this was altered to three turrets before serious work began. When models of both tanks were shown to Stalin, he supposedly ripped a turret off one model, joking: 'Why turn a tank into a department store?' and ordered that the prototypes should be completed with only two turrets.

As finally completed, the two tanks closely resembled each other, both mounting a 76.2mm (3in) L-11 gun and a coaxial DT machine gun in the main turret, firing over a forward sub-turret armed with a 45mm (1.77in) gun and a coaxial DT. The T-100 had thicker armour (70mm/2.75in maximum against 60mm/2.36in maximum for the SMK), but there was otherwise little to choose between them in terms of performance.

A total of four prototypes (two of each design) were sent to Finland for battlefield trials as part of the 91st Tank Battalion of the 20th Heavy Tank Brigade. In December 1939, they took part in an attack on the Mannerheim Line near Summa. As expected, they proved to be invulnerable to 37mm (1.46in) anti-tank guns, but one of the SMKs was knocked out by Finnish anti-tank mines that had been packed in TNT to boost their effect.

Both the SMK and T-100 were dead ends in heavy tank design, but a single-turret version of the SMK had also been developed. Two prototypes, designated Kliment Voroshilov (KV), were completed in time for deployment to Finland alongside the SMKs and T-100s. In action, they proved to be superior to the twin-turreted designs and were approved for production as the KV-1.

KV HEAVY TANKS

Although armour up to 90mm (3.54in) thick gave the early KV-1s virtual invulnerability to most weapons of

KV-1 Model 1939
The distinctive mantlet of the 76.2mm (3in) L-11 gun is the primary recognition feature of the Model 1939.

KV-1 Model 1939
Crew: 5
Production: 1939–40
Weight: 43 tonnes (42.3 tons)
Length: 6.75m (22ft 2in)
Width: 3.32m (10ft 10in)
Height: 2.71m (8ft 9in)
Engine: 450kW (600hp) V-2 diesel
Road speed: 35km/h (22mph)
Range: 160km (99 miles)
Armament: 1 x 76.2mm (3in) L-11 L/32 gun; 3 x 7.62mm (0.3in) DT machine guns, 1 coaxial, 1 turret rear, 1 hull front
Armour: 25–90mm (0.98–3.54in)

KV-1 Model 1940
Crew: 5
Production: 1940–41
Weight: 45 tonnes (44.3 tons)
Length: 6.75m (22ft 2in)
Width: 3.32m (10ft 10in)
Height: 2.71m (8ft 9in)
Engine: 450kW (600hp) V-2 diesel
Road speed: 35km/h (22mph)
Range: 335km (208 miles)
Armament: 1 x 76.2mm (3in) L-11 L/32 or F-32 gun; 3 x 7.62mm (0.3in) DT machine guns, 1 coaxial, 1 turret rear, 1 hull front
Armour: 25–75mm (0.98–2.95in)

KV-1 Model 1940
This green, brown and sand camouflage scheme was mainly applied to AFVs in the relatively static conditions of the front around Leningrad, spring 1942.

KV-1 Model 1941

This Model 1941 has a cast turret, standard monochrone camouflage, and is equipped with an F-34 gun.

KV-1 Model 1941

Crew: 5

Production: 1941–42

Weight: 45 tonnes (44.3 tons)

Length: 6.75m (22ft 2in)

Width: 3.32m (10ft 10in)

Height: 2.71m (8ft 9in)

Engine: 450kW (600hp) V-2 diesel

Road speed: 35km/h (22mph)

Range: 335km (208 miles)

Armament: 1 x 76.2mm (3in) F-34 gun; 3 x 7.62mm (0.3in) DT machine guns, 1 coaxial, 1 turret rear, 1 hull front

Armour: 30–90mm (1.18–3.54in)

1940/41, their mobility was poor. The driver's field of vision was very restricted and his controls were so unreliable that a mallet was frequently carried to free stubborn jams. A weak clutch, combined with a transmission designed 20 years earlier, virtually guaranteed frequent breakdowns.

As series production began at a slow rate in 1940, only 500 or so KV-1s, spread across a total of 30 Mechanized Corps, were in service at the time of the German invasion. Many Corps had none, although the six Corps in the Special Western Military District fielded a total of 313, most of which were captured or destroyed in the first two months of fighting.

In the summer of 1941, even isolated KV-1s occasionally caused massive disruption to the seemingly unstoppable German advance. There are several accounts of the following action, but this seems to be the most plausible: near Raseiniai in Lithuania, 6th Panzer Division was halted for 24 hours by a lone KV-1 that had been cut off by the German advance and now blocked the division's supply route. Four 50mm anti-tank guns were brought up and scored several hits without any effect before all were silenced by the KV's fire. An 88mm (3.4in) AA gun from the divisional Flak battalion was then manoeuvred into position behind the KV, but was destroyed before it could open fire. During the night, combat engineers attacked the tank with demolition charges, but only succeeded in damaging the tracks and running gear. Next morning, several German tanks fired from surrounding woodland to distract the KV's attention while another 88mm (3.4in) gun was deployed behind it. This time, the 88 was able to score at least two penetrating hits, but as German infantry moved in to ensure that the KV was indeed knocked out, it brought them under machine-gun fire. The tank was finally destroyed when the infantry worked their way behind it, climbed onto the engine decks and lobbed grenades through the hatches.

Although the KV-1's protection was impressive, its firepower was criticized. At a time when the T-34 mounted the higher-velocity F-34 gun, there was no justification for continuing production of the KV-1 armed with the distinctly inferior L-11. Initially, production switched to the F-32 that armed the KV-1 Model 1940. However, this had an armour-piercing capability little better than that of the L-11, so the F-34 was finally adopted for the Model 1941 and the very similar Model 1942.

In parallel with improving the type's firepower, efforts were made to ensure that its armour kept pace with increasingly formidable German tank and anti-tank guns. Early work concentrated on adding appliqué armour; panels of 35mm (1.38in) plate were bolted to the hull and turret to produce the KV1E. As production picked up again following the mass evacuation of war industries, the Model 1942 was produced with thicker hull and turret armour (90mm/3.54in and 120mm/4.72in respectively).

KV-1 Model 1942
Crew: 5
Production: 1942
Weight: 47 tonnes (46.26 tons)
Length: 6.75m (22ft 2in)
Width: 3.32m (10ft 10in)
Height: 2.71m (8ft 9in)
Engine: 450kW (600hp) V-2 diesel
Road speed: 28km/h (17mph)
Range: 250km (155 miles)
Armament: 1 x 76.2mm (3in) F-34 or ZiS-5 L/40.5 gun; 4 x 7.62mm (0.3in) DT machine guns, 1 coaxial, 1 turret rear, 1 turret roof, 1 hull front
Armour: 30–120mm (1.18–4.72in)

KV-1 Model 1942
KV-1 Model 1942, showing the new cast turret fitted with a P-40 AA mount for a DT machine gun.

Although this extra protection was welcome, the increased weight worsened the KV's already poor automotive performance. General Katukov, commanding 1st Guards Tank Brigade, reported that: 'The T-34… has proven itself in action. But the soldiers don't like the KV. It is very heavy, clumsy and not very agile. It surmounts obstacles with great difficulty, often damages bridges and becomes involved in other accidents. More to the point, it is armed with the same 76mm gun as the T-34. This raises the question, to what extent is it superior to the T-34? If the KV had a more potent gun, or one of greater calibre, it might be possible to excuse its weight and other shortcomings.'

In an attempt to improve the type's mobility, the decision was taken to lighten the KV by reducing the armour thickness in less vulnerable areas and to make long overdue improvements to the transmission. The opportunity was also taken to redesign the turret with a 360-degree vision commander's cupola and a better crew layout. The KV-1S that resulted from these changes certainly improved matters, but it still left the Red Army with a heavy tank that was no better protected or armed than the T-34.

As an interim solution to the lack of firepower, a small batch of KV-85s was completed using KV-1S hull mated with a new turret intended for the Josef Stalin 1 mounting the 85mm (3.35in) gun. Almost 150 were produced in late 1943.

A unique member of the KV family was the KV-2 'heavy artillery tank' developed in late 1939 to meet an emergency requirement for a 'bunker

KV-1S

A few KV heavy tanks remained in service until the end of the war, often as command vehicles in JSU-122 and JSU-152 units.

KV-1S
Crew: 5
Production: 1942–43
Weight: 42.5 tonnes (41.83 ton)
Length: 6.8m (22ft 4in)
Width: 3.25m (10ft 8in)
Height: 2.64m (8ft 8in)
Engine: 485kW (650hp) V-2K 12-cylinder diesel
Road speed: 43km/h (26mph)
Range: 250km (155 miles)
Armament: 1 x 76.2mm (3in) ZiS-5 gun; 4 x 7.62mm (0.3in) DT machine guns, 1 coaxial, 1 hull front, 1 turret rear, 1 turret roof
Armour: 20–82mm (0.79in–3.2in)

KV-2

KV-2, with pre-production turret, 2nd Tank Division, 3rd Mechanized Corps, summer 1941. Marshal Rokossovsky recalled that: 'They withstood the fire of every type of gun that the German tanks were armed with, but what a sight they were returning from combat. Their armour was pock-marked all over and sometimes even their barrels were pierced.'

KV-2 Model 1939
Crew: 5
Production: 1939–40
Weight: 52 tonnes (51.18 tons)
Length: 6.95m (22ft 10in)
Width: 3.32m (10ft 10in)
Height: 3.25m (10ft 8in)
Engine: 373kW (500hp) V-2 diesel
Road speed: 25km/h (12mph)
Range: 200km (120 miles)
Armament: 1 x 152mm (6in) M-10T howitzer; 2 x 7.62mm (.3in) DT machine guns; 1 x bow and 1 in turret rear)
Armour: 30–110mm (1.18–4.3in)

buster' to deal with the Finnish fortifications of the Mannerheim Line. Several designs were mooted, but the simplest was finally adopted – a 152mm (5.98in) howitzer and two DT machine guns in a huge 'box' turret on a standard KV-1 hull. Two prototypes were swiftly completed and sent for highly successful battlefield trials on the Karelian Isthmus.

The type was ordered into production, but proved to be less successful in action in the summer of 1941. It had stupendous firepower and was immune to anything less than 88mm (3.4in) or medium artillery fire, but the huge turret brought the tank's weight up to at least 47 tonnes (52 tons),

KV-1S, 6th Guards Tank Regiment, 1943

A propaganda photograph of the sort beloved by Red Army political officers, complete with the regimental standard. The unit was one of the earliest Guards Tank Regiments to be formed in October 1942 and first saw action at Stalingrad in late 1942.

compared to the 40 tonnes (45 tons) of contemporary KV-1s. This extra load put even more strain on the inadequate transmission, which was unchanged from that of the KV-1, with the result that breakdowns occurred even more frequently. The traversing mechanism could barely cope with the turret's weight. According to some reports, it could not traverse if the tank was on anything more than a very shallow side slope; to add to the problems, the recoil of the 152mm (5.98in) howitzer was liable to jam the turret. Just over 200 KV-2s were completed, but the type's limitations led to the decision to cease production in October 1941.

JOSEF STALIN (JS) HEAVY TANKS

The JS series marked the culmination of a line of heavy tank development that had begun with the design of the SMK back in 1938. The JS-1 used the same turret as the KV-85, but had an entirely new hull with better armour protection than any KV series tanks. The type was powered by a new V2-IS 12-cylinder diesel, which improved automotive reliability. Just over 200 JS-1s were completed between October 1943 and January 1944, when production switched to the far more formidable JS-2.

By late 1943, it was clear that a more powerful weapon than the 85mm (3.35in) was needed to cope with the increasing numbers of Panthers and Tigers being deployed on the Eastern Front. Both 100mm (3.94in) and 122mm (4.8in) guns were considered as potential replacements for the 85mm (3.345in). Although the 100mm (3.94in) had a better armour-piercing performance, the 122mm (4.8in) was adopted for the new JS-2 as there were already surplus stocks of the gun and production facilities were more readily available.

Early-production JS-2s were armed with the 122mm (4.8in) A-19 gun, but the heavy, separate-loading ammunition, combined with a relatively slow-action interrupted screw breech mechanism, restricted the rate of fire to less than 2rpm. The situation was not helped by a small turret, which also limited ammunition stowage to 28 rounds (generally 20 HE and 8 AP). However, the gun was certainly effective: during firing trials against a captured Panther at close range, it penetrated the frontal armour, passed straight through the length of the tank and came out through the rear plate. The hull front closely resembled that of the KV series, but was more carefully shaped to improve ballistic protection.

During 1944, an improved JS-2, sometimes referred to as the Model 1944, entered service. A 12.7mm (0.5in) DShK AA machine gun was added to the commander's cupola and the main armament was changed to the 122mm (4.8in) D-25T that had a faster-action semi-automatic breech, allowing a practical rate of fire of up to 3rpm. The hull's armour protection was also improved, with the adoption of a 100mm (3.94in) glacis plate sloped at 60 degrees.

Initially, crews were critical of the JS-2, claiming that AP rounds failed to penetrate the Panther's frontal armour under 700m (2300ft). Ironically, HE rounds were often found to be more effective in the anti-tank role, as their blast would often jam turrets, shatter

JS-1
A JS-1 of 1st Guards Heavy Tank Regiment in the Ukraine, autumn 1943. The type was quickly replaced by the JS-2, as combat experience showed that its gun was barely adequate against the heavy armour of newer German AFVs.

JS-1
Crew: 4
Production: 1943–44
Weight: 44.2 tonnes (43.5 tons)
Length: 8.56m (28ft 1in)
Width: 3m (9ft 10in)
Height: 2.74m (9ft)
Engine: 473kW (600hp) V-2-IS 12-cylinder diesel
Road speed: 37km/h (23mph)
Range: 150km (93 miles)
Armament: 1 x 85mm (3.35in) D-5T L/51.6 gun; 3 x 7.62mm (0.3in) DT machine guns, 1 coaxial, 1 turret rear, 1 hull front
Armour: 30–120mm (1.18in–4.72in)

JS-2
During the assault on Berlin, JS-2s often fought in ad hoc units of five tanks supported by a company of infantry, including sappers and flamethrowers. At least 67 JS-2s were destroyed in the fierce street fighting, mainly by panzerfausts.

JS-2
Crew: 4
Production: 1943–45
Weight: 46 tonnes (45.27 tons)
Length: 9.9m (32ft 6in)
Width: 3.09m (10ft 2in)
Height: 2.73m (8ft 11in)
Engine: 473kW (600hp) V-2-IS 12-cylinder diesel
Road speed: 37km/h (23mph)
Range: 240km (149 miles)
Armament: 1 x 122mm (4.8in) A-19 or D-25T L/48 gun; 2 x 7.62mm (0.3in) DT machine guns, 1 coaxial, one turret rear; sometimes 1 x 12.7mm (0.5in) DShK machine gun on turret roof
Armour: 30–120mm (1.18–4.72in)

sights or rip off tracks. As crews gained experience, their anti-tank performance improved, aided by a deterioration in the quality of German armour, which became increasingly brittle as manganese shortages became more acute.

At least 3800 JS-2s had been completed by 1945, when production ceased in favour of the JS-3.

FLAMETHROWER TANKS

The first Soviet flamethrower tank to enter service in 1932 was the OT-26, a rebuilt T-26 Model 1931. The left-hand turret was removed and a 400-litre (88-gallon) flame fuel tank was installed in the hull below its position, together with three compressed air cylinders. Flame fuel was fed through a flexible hose to a KS-24 flamethrower in the heavily modified right-hand turret, which was also fitted with a ball-mounted DT machine gun. Service trials showed that the turret's traverse had to be restricted to 270 degrees to avoid tangling and damaging the hose. Apart from this restriction, the system worked well, allowing for repeated five-second bursts of flame out to a maximum range of about 35m (115ft).

OT-130 and OT-133

A total of about 600 OT-26s were completed before production switched to the OT-130 in 1938. The new tank was a rebuilt T-26 Model 1933 with the 45mm (1.77in) gun replaced by a KS-24 flamethrower. Later OT-130s

OT-133

The OT-133's thin armour made it especially vulnerable, as the short range of its short-barrelled flame gun meant that it had to open fire at less than 35m (115ft) to stand any chance of hitting its target.

OT-133

Crew: 3
Production: 1938–40
Weight: 9.75 tonnes (9.6 tons)
Length: 4.55m (14ft 11in)
Width: 2.31m (7ft 7in)
Height: 2.3m (7ft 7in)
Engine: 67.1kW (90hp) 4-cylinder petrol
Road speed: 35km/h (22mph)
Range: 220km (140 miles)
Armament: 1 x short-barrelled flame device; 1 x 7.62mm (0.3in) DT machine gun, turret rear
Armour: 6–15mm (0.24–0.59in)

were armed with the new KS-25 flamethrower, with 360 litres (80 gallons) of fuel, enough for 40 six-second bursts of flame at ranges of up to 50m (164ft). (A few tanks may have been fitted with a more powerful compressor that increased the maximum range to 100m/328ft.) Production of the OT-130 ended in 1939, after 400 had been completed.

The final flamethrower versions of the T-26 were the OT-133 and OT-134. Both were based on the Model 1939. The OT-133 had the armament layout of the OT-130 – KS-25 flamethrower and coaxial DT machine gun, while the OT-134 retained the 45mm (1.77in) gun and carried a fixed forward-firing flamethrower in the hull front alongside the driver.

All these tanks were vulnerable to even light anti-tank weapons. This vulnerability first became apparent during clashes with Japanese forces at Khalkhin Gol in the summer of 1939, but losses there were trivial in comparison with those suffered in Finland during the Winter War. More than 440 Soviet flamethrower tanks saw action in Finland, 124 of which were knocked out. All too often, these were totally destroyed. A contemporary combat report refers to '...the inevitable ignition of the fuel for the flamethrower, tanks often burned for between 15 and 20 hours and were so hot that the hulls cracked and melted.'

Many of the surviving T-26-based flamethrower tanks were lost in the first few months of Operation 'Barbarossa'. The survivors were mainly deployed in the defence of Leningrad until 1944, by which time they were worn out.

OT-34

The desperate defensive fighting of 1941 gave little scope for the effective use of flamethrower tanks. However, interest revived in 1942 and a new flamethrower, the ATO-41, was developed. This was fitted to the T-34, as the OT-34, in which it replaced the hull machine gun. The 100-litre (22-gallon) flame fuel tank was mounted internally, which made the fighting compartment even more cramped than that of conventional T-34s. The same flamethrower was fitted to the turret of the KV-1, as the KV-8, replacing the 76.2mm (3in) gun. A coaxial 45mm (1.77in) gun was mounted in a false barrel to simulate the 76.2mm (3in).

The final Soviet AFV flamethrower was the ATO-42. This was fitted to the T-34, T-34/85 and KV-1S in the same mountings as those used for the ATO-41. The new weapon could fire four or five bursts in 10 seconds. The theoretical maximum range was 120m (394ft), but the effective range was probably closer to 60m (197ft).

SU-76 SELF-PROPELLED GUNS

Design studies for a light self-propelled gun mounting the 76.2mm (3in) ZiS-3 gun began in early 1942. Initial attempts to use the hull of the T-60 light tank were quickly abandoned in favour of a design based on the larger T-70. Amazingly, the first production vehicles that entered service in early 1943 used the powerplant of the early T-70: two GAZ-202 lorry engines, one on each side of the hull, with each engine driving one track through separate, unsynchronized transmissions.

SU-76i

The SU-76i was in many respects a superior design to the SU76 and the SU-76M and was certainly more popular with its crews.

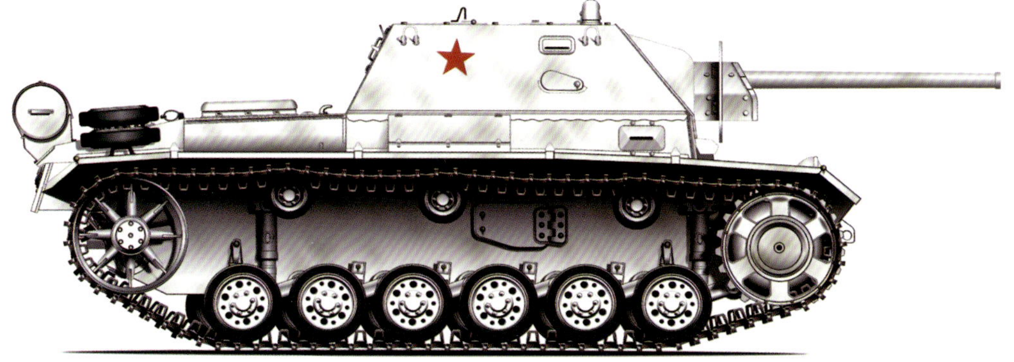

SU-76i

Crew: 4
Production: 1943
Weight: 23.9 tonnes (23.5 tons)
Length: 6.77m (22ft 2in)
Width: 2.95m (9ft 8in)
Height: 2.38m (7ft 10in)
Engine: 223.5kW (300hp) 12-cylinder Maybach petrol
Road speed: 40km/h (25mph)
Range: 180km (112 miles)
Armament: 1 x 76.2mm (3in) S-1 gun
Armour: 15–35mm (0.59–1.38in)

SU-76M

When operating in the indirect fire role, the SU-76M's ZiS-3 gun had a maximum range of 13,000m (42,650ft). The SU-76's problems led to the type being dubbed 'Suka' (bitch) by its crews, a nickname also applied to the SU-76M.

SU-76M

Crew: 4
Production: 1943–45
Weight: 10.2 tonnes (10.04 tons)
Length: 5m (16ft 5in)
Width: 2.7m (8ft 10in)
Height: 2.1m (6ft 10in)
Engine: 2 x 63.4kW (85hp) GAZ 203 petrol
Road speed: 45km/h (28mph)
Range: 320km (199 miles)
Armament: 1 x 76.2mm (3in) ZiS-3Sh L/42.6 gun
Armour: 16–35mm (0.59–1.38in)

This impractical arrangement had been abandoned with the introduction of the T-70M almost a year earlier. Despite these problems, 360 vehicles were completed under the designation SU-76, but protests from their crews were so vehement that production was halted so a complete redesign could be undertaken.

The SU-76's mechanical problems were so severe that it had to be withdrawn from service, leaving a dire need for an interim light self-propelled gun. This was met by rebuilding at least 200 captured Panzer IIIs and Sturmgeschütz IIIs as the SU-76i ('i' standing for '*inostrannaya*' – foreign). These were fitted with a new fully enclosed fighting compartment and were rearmed with the 76.2mm (3in) S-1 tank gun, a slightly modified version of the F-34 that armed the T-34. The type remained in front-line service until it was replaced by the SU-76M in early 1944.

The SU-76M adopted the engine and transmission layout of the T-70M, which certainly improved its automotive performance and mechanical reliability. However, it was never as popular with its crews as the SU-76i, largely because of its open-topped fighting compartment, which had only a canvas cover to giver shelter from the worst of a Russian winter. This also made it vulnerable to air-burst artillery fire (and grenades when fighting in urban areas).

Its thin armour could easily be penetrated by contemporary German tank and anti-tank guns. This was especially serious, as it was primarily used for direct fire in the infantry support role, and only rarely deployed as a self-propelled gun to provide indirect fire. Despite these shortcomings, it had good firepower for its size and was easy to manufacture; almost 14,000 were completed before production ended in 1945.

SU-122

The SU-122 originated with a requirement issued in April 1942 for a range of assault guns. One of the first to be produced was a 122mm (4.8in) M-30S howitzer that was mounted

SU-122
Crew: 5
Production: 1943
Weight: 30.9 tonnes (30.4 tons)
Length: 6.95m (22ft 9in)
Width: 3m (9ft 10in)
Height: 2.32m (7ft 7in)
Engine: 373kW (500hp) V-2 diesel
Road speed: 55km/h (34mph)
Range: 300km (186 miles)
Armament: 1 x 122mm (4.8in) M-30S howitzer
Armour: 20–45mm (0.79–1.77in)

SU-122
An SU-122 in an exceptionally elaborate snow camouflage scheme with red air recognition markings, Volkhov Front, winter 1943.

SG-122

Despite some sophisticated features such as a loading tray, which gave the 122mm (4.8in) howitzer a maximum rate of fire of up to 7rpm, production of the SG-122 was halted in favour of the simpler SU-122.

on a modified Sturmgeschütz III. This was designated SG-122. Around 20 were completed in mid-1942 before production was halted, as the type was judged too complex and difficult to maintain.

Design studies were already under way for an assault gun based on the T-34, and it was decided to combine the 122mm (4.8in) howitzer with the hull of the T-34. The new SU-122 entered service in early 1943. The fully enclosed fighting compartment and well-sloped frontal armour offered good protection, while its 21.7kg (47.84lbs) HE round was highly effective in the close support role. About 1150 SU-122s had been completed by the time production ended in mid-1944.

SU-85 AND SU-100 TANK DESTROYERS

The SU-85's origins can be traced back to the SU-122. The appearance of the first Tiger Is on the Eastern Front in September 1942 emphasized the need for a more powerfully armed AFV than the T-34. The SU-122 provided an ideal basis for the rapid development of a very similar 85mm (3.35in)-armed version, the SU-85. The first examples reached operational units in August 1943 and demonstrated excellent anti-tank capabilities. More than 2000 were completed before the type became obsolescent with the introduction of the T34/85 in mid-1944. Production then switched to the SU-100, and many SU-85s were passed on to Polish and Czech units fighting alongside the Red Army.

The 100mm (3.94in) D10S gun that was selected to arm the SU-100 had a spectacular anti-tank performance, being able to penetrate 120mm (4.72in) of armour at up to 2000m (6560ft). It proved to be so effective that its derivatives were fitted to the postwar T-54 and T-55 main battle tanks. Protection was significantly improved; the frontal armour was well sloped and thickened to 75mm (2.95in), compared to the 45mm (1.77in) of the SU-85's front plate.

The SU-100 entered production in September 1944 and the first units were equipped with the type the following month. It rapidly became popular with its crews, as it was easily able to deal with all German AFVs at combat ranges except for the rarely encountered Tiger II, which was always a difficult opponent. In March 1945, it was instrumental in defeating the

SU-85
Crew: 5
Production: 1943
Weight: 29.2 tonnes (28.74 tons)
Length: 8.25m (26ft 8in)
Width: 3m (9ft 10in)
Height: 2.45m (8ft)
Engine: 373kW (500hp) V-2 diesel
Road speed: 47km/h (29mph)
Range: 300km (186 miles)
Armament: 1 x 85mm (3.35in) D-5S gun
Armour: 20–45mm (0.79–1.77in)

SU-85
The SU-85 was an effective tank destroyer that was well suited to mass production, as it used 80 per cent of the components of the standard T-34.

SU-100
Crew: 4
Production: 1944–45
Weight: 31.6 tonnes (31.1 tons)
Length: 9.45m (31ft)
Width: 3m (9ft 10in)
Height: 2.25m (7ft 5in)
Engine: 373kW (500hp) V-2 diesel
Road speed: 48km/h (30mph)
Range: 320km (199 miles)
Armament: 1 x 100mm (3.94in) D-10S L/53.5 gun
Armour: 20–75mm (0.78in–2.95in)

SU-100
More than 2300 SU-100s had been completed when production ended in July 1945. The type had a remarkably long service life – it remained in first-line Soviet service until 1957, and Egyptian examples fought in the 1973 Yom Kippur War. In 2016, significant numbers remained in service with North Korea, Vietnam and Yemen.

last German offensive on the Eastern Front – *Unternehmen Frühlingserwachen* (Operation Spring Awakening) – near Lake Balaton in Hungary. The SU-100 also played an important role in the assault on East Prussia, the Vistula-Oder Offensive and in the Battle of Berlin.

SU-152 AND JSU-152

In November 1942, a requirement was issued for a heavy self-propelled gun armed with the 152.4mm (5.98in) ML-20 gun-howitzer. Learning from the KV-2's stability problems, it was tacitly accepted that the main armament would have to be hull-mounted. A design with a fully enclosed fighting compartment based on the KV-1 was accepted as the SU-152 and entered production in February 1943. The ML-20 was fitted with slightly modified controls and a large muzzle brake to reduce recoil, and redesignated as the ML-20S. The only other weapons carried by early-production vehicles were two PPSh submachine guns and 25 F1 grenades for close-quarter defence. From mid-1943, new SU-152s received DShK 12.7mm (0.5in) AA machine guns; these were fitted to earlier vehicles as they were returned to maintenance depots for repair.

The Battle of Kursk marked the SU-152's combat debut, where it earned the nickname of 'animal killer' due to its successes against Tigers, Elefants and Panthers. This exceptional anti-tank capability ensured that the type was in constant demand. This caused rapid mechanical deterioration and imposed a massive strain on the maintenance system. Around 700 were completed, with later vehicles based on the KV-1S hull, before production ended in favour of the JSU-152 in December 1943.

The first JSU-152s were based on JS-1 hulls, but production soon switched to vehicles based on the JS-2. These all had the DShK 12.7mm (0.5in) AA machine guns as standard and thicker armour than

SU-152

Although the SU-152's 43.5kg (95.9lbs) HE shell would not always penetrate heavy armour, its massive blast effect was capable of blowing the turret off a Tiger I.

SU-152
Crew: 5
Production: 1943
Weight: 45.5 tonnes (44.78 tons)
Length: 8.95m (29ft 4in)
Width: 3.25m (10ft 8in)
Height: 2.45m (8ft)
Engine: 473kW (600hp) V-2 12-cylinder diesel
Road speed: 43km/h (27mph)
Range: 220km (137 miles)
Armament: 1 x 152.4mm (5.98in) ML-20S Model 1938 L/29 gun-howitzer; sometimes 1 x 12.7mm (0.5in) DShK heavy machine gun
Armour: 20–75mm (0.78–2.95in)

JSU-152
A relatively rare example of a JSU-152 in a four-colour camouflage scheme adopted for the Lvov-Sandomierz operation, July–August 1944.

JSU-152
Crew: 4 or 5
Production: 1943–44
Weight: 46 tonnes (45.27 tons)
Length: 9.18m (30ft 1in)
Width: 3.07m (10ft 1in)
Height: 2.48m (8ft 1in)
Engine: 447kW (600hp) V-2 diesel
Road speed: 40km/h (25mph)
Range: 220km (137 miles)
Armament: 1 x 152.4mm (5.98in) ML-20S Model 1938 L/29 gun
Armour: 30–120mm (1.18–4.72in)

the SU-152 – a maximum of 120mm (4.72in), compared to 76mm (3in). A 48.78kg (107.5lbs) 152mm APHE round was issued, which could penetrate 125mm (4.9in) of armour at 500m (1640ft), but in practice, the blast effect of the HE shell was equally effective in the anti-tank role.

The JSU-152 rapidly became as highly valued as its predecessor, despite some shared shortcomings – notably the limited ammunition stowage of 20 rounds (usually 13 HE and 7 APHE), although some crews took the risk of stowing extra ammunition on the engine decks. Although the 152.4mm (5.98in) gun had a maximum range of 7000m (23,000ft) in the indirect fire role, this capability was rarely used: the JSU-152's heavy armour and limited on-board ammunition made the type better suited to short-range direct fire that could be sustained at a rate of about 2rpm.

Production of the JSU-152 continued until 1947, by which time at least 4600 had been built. The type remained in service with the Red Army well into the 1960s.

JSU-122 AND JSU-122S

The JSU-122 originated due to the production of 152.4mm (5.98in) ML-20S gun-howitzers failing to keep pace with the output of JSU-152 hulls. At the same time, there was a substantial surplus of 122mm (4.8in) A-19S guns, and design studies indicated that these could be fitted to the JSU-152 hulls with minimal modifications. This combination was approved for service as the JSU-122 and the first production vehicles were completed in April 1944.

Although the new type was a formidable tank destroyer, able to penetrate 160mm (6.3in) of armour at 1000m (3280ft), it was less popular than the JSU-152 due to its smaller HE shell. The manual breech of the A-19S was another unpopular feature: combined with the separate loading ammunition, it restricted the rate of fire to less than 2rpm – slower than that of the JSU-152.

The obvious answer was to replace the A-19S with the 122mm (4.8in) D-25. The latter had a semi-automatic breech that increased the practical rate of fire to 2–3rpm; it also benefitted from a muzzle brake that reduced recoil and a new mantlet that allowed greater traverse. Vehicles fitted with the D-25 were designated JSU-122S. A total of 2410 of both versions (1735 JSU-122 and 675 JSU-122S) were completed by the time production ended in late 1945.

SOVIET ARMOURED CARS

Pre-war Red Army armoured cars were categorized as light and heavy, the distinction between the two being based on armament rather than weight. Light armoured cars were armed solely with machine guns, while heavies had a 45mm (1.77in) gun as their main armament. The most important pre-war armoured types were the BA-3/BA-6/BA-10 series of heavy armoured cars. These were all 6x4 vehicles fitted with a turret very similar to that of the T-26, mounting a 45mm (1.77in) gun and a coaxial DT machine gun. A second, ball-mounted DT was fitted in the co-driver's position.

JSU-122

A JSU-122 finished in two-tone camouflage took part in the assault on Berlin in April 1945.

JSU-122
Crew: 4 or 5
Production: 1944–45
Weight: 45.5 tonnes (44.78 tons)
Length: 9.85m (32ft 3in)
Width: 3.07m (10ft 1in)
Height: 2.48m (8ft 1in)
Engine: 447kW (600hp) V-2 diesel
Road speed: 37km/h (23mph)
Range: 220km (137 miles)
Armament: 1 x 122mm (4.8in) A-19S Model 1931/37 L/46.5 gun; sometimes 1 x 12.7mm (0.5in) DShK heavy machine gun
Armour: 30–90mm (1.18–3.54in)

BA-6
A BA-6 of 12th Mechanized Corps, Northwestern Front, 1941.

BA-6 Armoured Car
Crew: 4
Production: 1936–38
Weight: 5.1 tonnes (5.02 tons)
Length: 4.65m (15ft 3in)
Width: 2.1m (6ft 10in)
Height: 2.2m (7ft 2in)
Engine: 29.8kW (40hp) GAZ-A petrol
Road speed: 55km/h (34 mph)
Range: 200km (136.71 miles)
Armament: 1 x 45mm (1.77in) 20-K gun and 2 x 7.62mm (.3in) DT machine guns (1 x bow and 1 x coaxial)
Armour 20–75mm (0.78–2.95in)

Early-production BA-3s were based on the Ford-Timken chassis, a 6x4 version of the Ford AA 4x2 truck; later examples (together with the BA-6 and BA-10) used the GAZ-AAA chassis. A novel feature (also shared with the BA-6 and BA-10) was the provision of removable tracks stowed on the rear mudguards that could be fitted around the rear wheels to convert the armoured car into a halftrack. The conversion could be made in around 10 minutes, and the tracks improved cross-country performance. Despite this ingenuity, service trials showed that the car's off-road performance was poor, mainly due to excessive weight that strained the front suspension. Due to these limitations, only 180 were completed between 1933 and 1935.

In 1936, the BA-6 entered production. This was essentially a modernized version of the BA-3 with a reinforced suspension and better engine cooling. In an attempt to reduce vulnerability to small arms fire and shell splinters, 'bulletproof' tyres filled with sponge rubber were fitted, although these reduced the car's speed and range. A total of 386 were completed by the time production ended in 1939.

The BA-6M incorporated sloped armour and served as the prototype for the BA-10. This became the most prolific pre-war Soviet armoured car, with more than 3300 completed between 1938 and 1941.

The BA-6 and BA-10 saw action in the Spanish Civil War, the Winter War, and the opening stages of Operation 'Barbarossa', with a few remaining operational as late as 1943.

BA-64

By mid-1941, the Red Army's pre-war light armoured cars were obsolescent, and studies were undertaken for a new vehicle based on the chassis of the GAZ-64 jeep. The BA-64 that resulted from these studies entered service in late 1942 with an armour layout and open-topped turret loosely based on the SdKfz 221. It had better armour, speed, range and off-road capability than any other Soviet wheeled AFV, although, due to the limitations of the chassis, it could only carry a single DT machine gun. In service, some shortcomings became apparent – the type was top-heavy and unstable, requiring caution when driving off-road. These problems were solved when production switched to the BA-64B in September 1943. This utilized the chassis of the wider GAZ-67B jeep, which dramatically improved stability and cross-country performance. More than 9000 were completed by the time production ended in 1946.

IMPROVISED AFVS

Soviet losses in the opening stages of Operation 'Barbarossa' were horrendous: by August 1941, von Bock's Army Group Centre had destroyed more than 5000 tanks, almost 25 per cent of the total Red Army

BA-64B

BA-64, Bucharest, summer 1944. Some units replaced the single DT machine gun with a PTRS/PTRD anti-tank rifle or captured 2cm (0.79in) KwK 30 cannon.

BA-64B

Crew: 2

Production: 1942–46

Weight: 2.3 tonnes (2.26 tons)

Length: 3.66m (12ft)

Width: 1.74m (5ft 8in)

Height: 1.9m (6ft 3in)

Engine: 37kW (50hp) GAZ-MM petrol

Road speed: 80km/h (50mph)

Range: 500km (310 miles)

Armament: 1 x 7.62mm (0.3in) DT machine gun

KhTZ-16

In many respects, the KhTZ-16 was better than most other improvised AFVs as it had a fully enclosed fighting compartment and was relatively well protected with 25mm/10mm (.98in/.39in) armour.

KhTZ-16
Crew: 2
Production: 1941
Weight: 7 tonnes (6.89 tons)
Length: 4.2m (13ft 9in)
Width: 1.9m (6ft 3in)
Height: 2.4m (7ft 10in)
Engine: 38.78kW (52hp) petrol
Road speed: 20km/h (13mph)
Range: 120km (75 miles)
Armament: 1 x 45mm (1.77in) 20-K gun and 1 x coaxial 7.62mm (.3in) DT machine gun

tank strength. In response to the crisis, an order was issued in July 1941 for the production of improvised AFVs. It is likely that small batches of wildly different vehicles were produced by factories and workshops across Russia. As with the improvised 'tanks' and 'armoured cars' built in Britain during the invasion scare of 1940, standards of construction ranged from competent to appalling. Many were mechanically unreliable death traps with hopelessly overloaded chassis, high silhouettes and inadequate armour and armament. The following summary is almost certainly incomplete, but covers a selection of the more important types.

In Leningrad, GAZ-AA, ZIS-5 and ZIS-6 truck chassis were partially armoured at the Izhorsky factory before being armed with a variety of weapons, including 45mm (1.77in) anti-tank guns and quadruple Maxim AA machine guns. Production of what was officially the Medium Armoured Car IZ ran from August to December 1941 and may have totalled 100 or so vehicles.

Odessa was besieged by Romanian and German forces from 8 August to 16 October 1941. The relatively small armoured forces supporting the garrison were rapidly depleted during the siege, and the January Uprising tank repair plant proposed the use of surplus STZ-5 artillery tractors and obsolete tank turrets as the basis for an improvised tank. Three prototypes

ZiS-30

The 57mm (2.24in) ZiS-2 anti-tank gun had an impressive armour-piercing performance, but there was only stowage space for a few rounds of ammunition. The gun's weight and recoil made the Komsomolets unstable, while the open mounting left the crew vulnerable to small-arms fire and shell splinters.

ZiS-30 tank destroyer

Crew: 4
Production: 1941
Weight: 4 tonnes (4.4 tons)
Length: 3.45m (11ft 4in)
Width: 1.86m (6ft 1in)
Height: 2m (6ft 6in)
Engine: 37kW (50hp) GAZ-M 4-cylinder
Road speed: 40km/h (25mph)
Range: 250km (155 miles)
Armament: 1 x 57mm (2.24in) ZiS-2 gun; 1 x 7.62mm (0.3in) DT machine gun
Armour: 7–10mm (0.28–0.39in)

of these 'Na Ispug' – 'Terror Tanks' – were ready by 20 August. Production continued until just before the city fell, by which time as many as 40 may have been completed.

In July/August 1941, the KHZ tractor factory in Kharkov began the design of the KhTZ-16 tank destroyer based on the chassis of the STZ-3 artillery tractor. It was armed with a 45mm (1.77in) gun and coaxial DT machine in a limited traverse mounting. It seemed so promising that more than 800 were ordered. However, due to the rapid German advance, no more than 90 were completed before Kharkov was overrun in October 1941.

The ZiS factory in Gorki proposed a self-propelled version of their 57mm (2.24in) ZiS-2 anti-tank gun. Trials were undertaken with guns mounted on both the Komsomolets tractor and the GAZ-AAA truck. The truck-mounted version (ZiS-31) proved to have greater accuracy, as the mounting was more stable, but the Komsomolets variant (ZiS-30) was selected due to its superior cross-country performance.

Production finally began in September 1941, as no new Komsomolets were available, forcing the factory to wait for vehicles to be returned from the front line for repair. A total of about 100 were completed by the end of October 1941, when production ceased as no more Komsomolets could be made available for conversion.

SOVIET AFV ARMAMENTS

7.62mm (0.3in) Degtyaryov DT machine gun

The DT (a derivative of the infantry's DP light machine gun) armed the vast majority of Russian wartime AFVs. Modifications included a heavy barrel and 60-round drum magazine together with a retractable metal stock and wooden pistol grip. Changing drums was awkward in the confined space of AFV turrets and restricted the practical rate of fire to about 125rpm.

12.7mm (0.5in) DShK machine gun

This gun became the Soviet equivalent of the .5 inch M2 Browning, and was used in an equally wide variety of roles. It formed the main armament of the T-40 light tank and was fitted as a pintle-mounted AA weapon on the IS-2, ISU-122 and ISU-152.

20mm (0.79in) TNSh cannon

This modified version of the ShVAK aircraft cannon was fitted to the T-60. Its theoretical performance was akin to that of the KwK 38 that armed the Panzer II and many German armoured cars. However, in practice, its muzzle velocity was often drastically reduced due to the frequent issue of cartridge cases loaded with the much smaller propellant charge of the DShK machine gun. When full-charge API ammunition was available, the weapon's anti-tank capability was quite good for its calibre – 35mm (1.38in) at 50m (164ft) – but the panzers rarely allowed the thinly armoured T-60 to close to this sort of range.

45mm (1.77in) 20-K tank gun

By the standards of the 1930s, the Soviet 45mm (1.77in) anti-tank gun was an exceptionally powerful weapon, and was rapidly adapted to become the main armament of many AFVs. A later version, the 45mm (1.77in) tank gun model 1938, had an electric firing system and a stabilized gun sight, which theoretically allowed accurate fire on the move. However, the gyro stabilizer was of limited practical value. It was phased out of production in 1941, as it proved too complex for inadequately trained conscript tank crews.

57mm (2.24in) ZiS-4 tank gun

In early 1940, rumours that German designers were working on heavily

T-40 amphibious tank

The T-40 amphibious light tank (left) was armed with a 12.7mm (0.5in) DShK Model 1938 machine gun.

armoured tanks led General Kulik, head of the Red Army's Main Artillery Directorate, to order the development of a new generation of tank and anti-tank guns. The first of these was the 57mm (2.24in) ZiS-2 anti-tank gun, which entered service in mid-1941 and had a remarkably good armour-piercing performance by the standards of the time. A tank gun variant, the ZiS-4, was rapidly developed and fitted to a batch of T-34s in an attempt to improve on the poor anti-tank capability of the type's standard 76.2mm (3in) L-11 gun. Although these T-34/57 tanks were efficient tank destroyers, the poor lethality of the 57mm (2.24in) HE shell led to the decision to adopt the 76.2mm (3in) F-34 as the standard armament of the T-34. In 1943, it was again proposed to replace the F-34 with 57mm (2.24in) in response to the increasing numbers of Panthers and Tigers being encountered. A further small batch of T-34/57s were completed, but these were soon superseded by the T34/85.

76.2mm (3in) L-11 and F-34 guns

The L-11 was designed in 1938 by the SKB-4 design bureau at the Kirov Plant in Leningrad. It was 30.5 calibres long (L/30.5), had a semi-automatic vertical sliding-wedge breech, and used ammunition originally developed for the 76.2mm (3in) AA gun M1914/15. The type was selected as the main armament for early versions of both the T-34 and KV-1 tanks. However, it quickly became clear that it was barely adequate against the German tanks of 1941 and would have to be replaced. During 1941, new production T-34s were fitted with the L/42.5 F-34. At first, KV-1s received the L/31.5 F-32, but this had virtually the same anti-tank performance as the L-11 and had to be replaced by the ZiS-5, a modified version of the F-34.

76.2mm (3in) ZIS-3Sh gun

Although the towed version of the ZiS-3 was designed in 1940, it was another victim of the prejudices of the incompetent Marshal Kulik, who delayed its introduction until his hand was forced by the enormous losses of Soviet artillery in the opening stages of the German invasion. The ZiS-3 was a high-velocity gun with a good anti-tank capability; it was the obvious choice for arming the light self-propelled gun that entered service as the SU-76 in 1943. Although the SU-76 was vulnerable due to its thin armour, it had excellent battlefield mobility and was highly successful.

85mm (3.35in) D5-T tank gun

By 1942, it was becoming clear that the F-34 and ZiS-5 were on the point of being outclassed by the improved armour of the latest Stug IIIs, Panzer IVs and Tiger Is. The solution was to adapt the 85mm (3.35in) AA gun M1939 (52-K). The resulting 85mm (3.35in) D-5T was too large to fit into the cramped turret of the T-34, but its anti-tank performance was so good that the SU-122 was hastily modified to take the new gun and was fielded as the SU-85. The T-34 was finally redesigned to take the 85mm (3.35in) in 1943, and the first examples of the T34/85 reached front-line units in spring 1944.

100mm (3.94in) D-10S tank gun

The appearance of the Panther in 1943 raised fears that even the 85mm (3.35in) gun might be inadequate against future German AFVs. Various possibilities were investigated, including the naval 100mm (3.94in) B-34, which was modified to produce the D-10S. Firing trials showed that it could penetrate the Panther's glacis plate at up to 1500m (4920ft) and the type was ordered into production to arm the SU-100 tank destroyer. Attempts were made to adapt the gun to fit various tanks, including the T-34, T-44 and IS-2, but the first successful tank version was that fitted in the postwar T-54.

122mm (4.8in) D-25T howitzer

This weapon was a modified 122mm (4.8in) M-30S howitzer that armed the SU-122 assault gun. It proved to be highly effective

Heavy assault gun
The JSU-152 assault gun's 152mm (5.98in) ML20S howitzer was capable of penetrating the thickest armour.

in its primary role of destroying enemy strongpoints with direct fire. Although it was too inaccurate for anti-tank use, except at very short ranges, a direct hit by its 21.7kg HE round was capable of blowing the turret off even a Tiger I. A new BP-460A HEAT projectile was introduced in May 1943, but design faults meant that it was only marginally more effective against AFVs than the brute power of the original HE round.

122mm (4.8in) A-19S and D-25 tank guns

The 122mm (4.8in) gun M1931/37 (A-19) was another of the options considered in 1943 as a means of countering the latest German tanks. Adapting the weapon for AFVs proved to be challenging: its separate-loading ammunition slowed the rate of fire, and the first design of muzzle brake had to be hastily reworked after one shattered during firing trials, almost killing Marshal Voroshilov. Under intense pressure from Stalin, the gun was developed into a series of successful weapons that armed the ISU-122 tank destroyer and the ISU-2 heavy tank.

152mm (5.98in) ML-20S gun-howitzer

An urgent requirement was issued in November 1942 for a heavy self-propelled gun with a 152mm (5.98in) main armament. Within six weeks, a slightly modified 152mm (5.98in) ML-20 gun-howitzer (designated ML-20S) was mounted on a KV-1S hull and accepted for service as the SU-152. The design proved to be highly successful in its intended role as a close-support weapon and also as a close-range tank destroyer – a direct hit by its 43.5kg HE shell could wreck any German AFV.

Chapter 2

Artillery, Rockets and Mortars

The Red Army inherited the Imperial Russian Army's respect for artillery, informally dubbing it the 'God of War'. The upheavals of the Revolution prevented any significant updating of the stocks of World War I vintage weapons until the 1930s. Stalin's Five-Year Plans provided the resources for modernizing the Red Army, and much effort went into providing new artillery, rockets and mortars.

Although much of the new equipment was excellent, the loss of so many of the most capable Red Army officers in Stalin's purges meant that it was not used to full effect until well into the war. The first indications of the damage caused by the purges were seen during the Winter War against Finland: camouflage was condemned as a sign of cowardice and guns were deployed in the open, in full view of Finnish artillery observers, who brought down counter-battery fire that inflicted horrendous casualties. There were also reports of Soviet artillery opening fire without orders 'to help the infantry keep its spirits up' and causing mass panic among the very infantry they were supposedly supporting.

The first six months of Operation 'Barbarossa' confirmed the dire state of the Red Army's artillery: estimated

Opposite:
Action front!
A 203mm (8in) Howitzer Model 1931 (B-4) is brought into action – its 100kg (220lb) VG-625 anti-concrete shells proved to be devastating against even the strongest bunkers.

losses for 1941 totalled 25,000 guns. Losses of mortars and small arms were on a similar scale; this meant that the Soviet counteroffensives launched during the winter of 1941/42 were crippled by acute shortages of the most basic weapons and ammunition. General Zhukov recalled that this was a time of acrimonious Stavka meetings at which furious discussions were held to decide which units should be allotted a dozen or so anti-tank rifles or mortars. Debates on the allocation of artillery ammunition were even more heated – at times, batteries were limited to one or two rounds per gun per day. Gradually, the arms factories evacuated to the Urals in late 1941 began to increase production. By the spring of 1942, 10,000 guns and mortars were assembled to support Timoshenko's Kharkov offensive. However, the defeat of this offensive again inflicted staggering equipment losses on the Red Army, including 1600 guns and 3200 mortars. Nonetheless, with ever-increasing lend-lease supplies, the numerical odds had swung in the Red Army's favour by early 1943, when it fielded 33,000 guns against an Axis total of 6360 guns.

By 1945, the Russians had overwhelming numerical superiority. The Vistula-Oder offensive of January

Heave!

A 76.2mm (3in) Regimental Gun Model 1927 is manhandled by its crew. The gun was highly effective against infantry in the open as detonation of its UOF-354A HE Fragmentation round produced at least 200 lethal fragments.

1945 was launched with massive artillery support from 2513 assault guns, 13,763 guns, 14,812 mortars, 4936 anti-tank guns and 2198 Katyusha salvo rocket launchers. The logistic support needed to supply this mass of weaponry was staggering – 2,500,000 shells and mortar bombs were stockpiled in the Magnuszew bridgehead, with a further 1,300,000 held in the Pulawy sector. In comparison, the Don Front had fired less than 1,000,000 shells at Stalingrad. The effect of such firepower was devastating. A German battalion commander recalled that he '...began the operation with an under-strength battalion... after the smoke of the Soviet preparation cleared... I had only a platoon of combat effective soldiers left.'

BATTLE FOR BERLIN

Even at this stage of the war, brute force did not always work. During the second week of April 1945, a massive Soviet force was assembled in the small bridgehead on the west bank of the Oder near Kustrin. Zhukov's 1st Belorussian Front was preparing to attack the Seelow Heights, the last natural defence line before Berlin. It deployed 3155 AFVs, 16,934 guns and had stockpiled more than 7,000,000 rounds of artillery ammunition. Zhukov's forces were opposed by General Gotthard Heinrici's Army Group Vistula. Its 9th Army, which would bear the brunt of the assault on the Seelow Heights, fielded only 512 AFVs, 344 guns and 300 to 400 AA guns.

At 05.00 on 16 April, the offensive began with a massive bombardment by thousands of guns and Katyushas before the main assault went in. Almost immediately, things started to go wrong – the debris and smoke from the shelling meant that the glare of the 140-plus searchlights intended to blind the Germans was reflected and blinded the attackers. It also turned them into easy targets, silhouetted against the light. Worse still, the bombardment had largely been wasted on empty defences – a Russian prisoner had revealed the timing of the attack and Heinrici had pulled his forces back to their second defensive line.

Taking advantage of the slow and confused Soviet advance, the Germans reoccupied their forward defences and brought down a murderous fire on the attackers. By the next day, 1st Belorussian Front had advanced no more than 8km (5 miles) and was still bogged down in the German defences. An enraged Zhukov overruled the protests of his army commanders and committed the 1337 AFVs of his two tank armies to the attack, but the huge number of vehicles deployed on a narrow front caused a massive traffic jam, providing more targets for the German artillery. Zhukov's forces finally broke through the last defences on the Seelow Heights on 19 April and were on their way to Berlin, but the cost had been appalling – more than 700 Soviet AFVs had been destroyed in the battle for the Heights and the Red Army had sustained at least 30,000 casualties (three times the German total).

The Battle of Berlin was very much an artillery battle. On 26 April, Zhukov and Konev's forces completed the encirclement of Berlin – the city had been under artillery bombardment since 20 April and attacks on the suburbs had begun on 24 April. The initial attack was made by 1st Guards Tank Army under cover of a barrage from 3000 guns and heavy mortars – 650 guns per kilometre of front.

As Chuikov ruefully remarked, 'A battle within a city is a battle of firepower.' Units quickly developed special assault teams comprising an infantry platoon or company, a tank platoon, a section of self-propelled guns, a section of Katyushas and a detachment of assault engineers. The assault drills almost invariably involved artillery and Katyushas smothering the objective with smoke and close-range direct fire before the infantry attacked.

A Soviet war correspondent described how the gunners '…sometimes fired a thousand shells on to one small square, a group of houses, or even a tiny garden.' As the Red Army reached the city centre, the larger government buildings proved to have been turned into 'improvised fortresses', which were supported by fire from Berlin's three enormous flak towers. These were six storeys high, each with a thousand-strong garrison to man the tower's four twin 128mm (5in) and 12 quadruple 20mm (0.79in) guns. Dealing with these demanded exceptional measures; at one stage, 500 Soviet guns were firing from a one-kilometre section of the Unter den Linden.

Despite such massive firepower, Russian losses continued to rise. At least 108 tanks were destroyed in the city centre by weapons ranging from 128mm (5in) AA guns to the ubiquitous panzerfaust. As always, infantry casualties were the heaviest: between 19 and 30 April, one infantry company was reduced from 104 men to just 20 exhausted survivors. By the time that the last German units surrendered on 2 May after Hitler's suicide and the capture of the battered shell of the Reichstag, the losses on both sides had been horrendous. Soviet casualties totalled more than 352,000, including more than 78,000 dead. In addition, the 1st and 2nd Polish Armies lost almost 9000 men.

Load, fire!
A 120mm (4.72in) mortar about to be fired amidst the ruins of Berlin, 1945. A well-trained crew could fire up to 12 bombs per minute for limited periods.

MARSHAL GRIGORY KULIK, HEAD OF THE MAIN ARTILLERY DIRECTORATE

Apart from Stalin himself, few individuals had such a disastrous influence on the pre-war Red Army as Grigory Kulik. He began his military career as a junior artillery NCO in the Imperial Russian Army before joining the Red Army as commander of 1st Cavalry Army's artillery. This dramatic promotion was probably due to the influence of his friend, Kliment Voroshilov, who together with Josef Stalin jointly commanded 1st Cavalry Army.

Despite what was, at best, a mediocre performance as an artillery commander, Kulik's unquestioning loyalty impressed Stalin and made him secure from any future criticism. Years later, Khrushchev questioned his competence only to provoke a tirade from Stalin: 'You don't even know Kulik! I know him from the civil war when he commanded the artillery in Tsaritsyn. He knows artillery!'

In 1937, Kulik's impeccable political credentials led to his appointment as Head of the Main Artillery Directorate of the Red Army, responsible for weapons systems research and development. Kulik's near-total ignorance of weapons technology and his tendency to condemn military innovations as 'bourgeois sabotage' contributed to the Soviet humiliation in the Winter War against Finland and the Red Army's catastrophic defeats in 1941/42. A few of his pronouncements give a feel for his almost unerring ability to get things wrong:

- He convinced Stalin that Marshal Tukhachevsky's theories of armoured warfare showed a dangerous ideological sympathy with the 'degenerate fascist ideology' of feint and deception rather than the revolutionary doctrine of frontal attack.
- Kulik distrusted the whole concept of AFVs, arguing that they were inferior to horses and would 'never replace them'.
- He condemned the use of mines, deriding them as 'a weapon of the weak'.
- The German use of the MP-40 submachine gun was derided as a 'bourgeois fascist affectation' that encouraged inaccurate fire and excessive ammunition consumption. He forbade the issue of the PPD-40 submachine gun to the Red Army, stating that it was only fit to be a 'pure police weapon'.

During Kulik's term in office, weapons production was constantly disrupted by his bizarre and unpredictable decisions, which led even senior colleagues to regard him as 'a murderous buffoon'. He was prone to ordering the mass arrests of weapons design teams and senior staff at major arms factories on fabricated charges and sending them to the Gulag. All too often, their replacements were Kulik's political cronies, who were totally unqualified for their new jobs.

Kulik's incompetence finally caught up with him in August 1941, when he was given command of the newly formed 54th Army fighting in the defence of Leningrad. His dismal battlefield performance led to his swift dismissal and demotion to major general, although Stalin's patronage saved him from execution or the Gulag.

Artillery general
Marshal Kulik poses for the camera, his awards and medals prominently displayed on his chest.

MORTARS

The Red Army relied heavily on mortars, which were far easier to produce than conventional artillery in the chaotic conditions of 1941–42.

37mm (1.46in) Spade Mortar

This oddity was apparently an attempt to give every infantryman his own mortar. When folded, it was effectively a short-handled entrenching spade, but pulling a monopod leg from the handle locked the 'spade' at an angle so that it acted as a baseplate. Each infantryman carried 15 rounds in a fabric ammunition belt. When committed to action for the first time in the Winter War, the small bombs proved to be ineffective, especially in deep snow. Although the type was still in service at the time of the German invasion, it was rarely encountered after 1941.

50mm (1.96in) 50-PM 38, 50-PM 39, 50-PM 40 and 50-PM 41 mortars

The 50mm (1.96in) Model 38 (50-PM 38) was the first of a succession of light infantry mortars. The barrel could only be set at elevations of 45 degrees and 75 degrees, with intermediate ranging being carried out by adjusting a sleeve around the base of the barrel that opened a series of gas ports to bleed off firing gases. In service, it was found to be too complex and was rapidly phased out in favour of the Model 1939. Some fell into German hands in 1941 and were used as the 5cm (1.96in) Granatwerfer 205/1(r).

The Model 1939 (50-PM 39) was an attempt to produce a cheaper and simpler replacement for the Model 1938. It incorporated the baseplate and sight of the Model 1938, but had conventional elevation controls Ironically, it was rapidly replaced by an even cheaper version, the Model 1940. In German use, the Model 1939 was designated the 5cm (1.96in) Granatwerfer 205/2(r).

50-PM 38 in action

A 50-PM 38 mortar in action during the winter of 1941/42 – the small bombs were relatively ineffective in deep snow, which 'smothered' their fragmentation.

50-PM 38

Calibre: 50mm (1.96in)
Barrel length: 780mm (30.7in)
Bore length: 553mm (21.77in)
Weight in action: 12.1kg (26.6lb)
Elevation (fixed): 45° and 75°
Traverse: 6°
Muzzle velocity (max): 96m/sec (315ft/sec)
Maximum range (45°): 800m (2624ft)
Maximum range (75°): 402m (1318ft)
Bomb weight: 0.85kg (1.875lb)

50-PM 39

An infantryman training with a 50-PM 39 mortar which had a maximum rate of fire of 15rpm.

50-PM 39

Calibre: 50mm (1.96in)
Barrel length: 775mm (30.5in)
Bore length: 545mm (21.46in)
Weight in action: 16.98kg (37.4lb)
Elevation: 45° to 85°
Traverse: 7°
Muzzle velocity: 96m/sec (315ft/sec)
Maximum range: 800m (2624ft)
Bomb weight: 0.85kg (1.875lb)

50-PM 40
A 50-PM 40 mortar lays down suppressive fire to cover advancing infantry. (Each 50mm HE bomb had a blast effect comparable to that of a hand grenade.)

50-PM 40
Calibre: 50mm (1.96in)
Barrel length: 630mm (24.8in)
Bore length: 533mm (21in)
Weight in action: 9.3kg (20.5lb)
Elevation (fixed): 45° and 7°
Traverse: 9° at 45° elevation, 16° at 75° elevation
Maximum range (45°): 800m (2624ft)
Maximum range (75°): 402m (1318ft)
Bomb weight: 0.85kg (1.875lb)

The Model 1940 (50-PM 40) was well suited for mass production, as its baseplate and bipod were simple steel stampings. The barrel reverted to the fixed elevation settings and gas ports as used on the Model 1938. The bipod incorporated a novel and simple method of cross levelling for laying that was so successful it was used on later and heavier mortars.

The Model 1941 (50-PM 41) marked the culmination of the Russian search for simplicity and ease of manufacture. It had a simplified sight and a barrel yoke that incorporated all the traverse and cross-levelling controls. Elevation angles remained fixed at 45 degrees and 75 degrees, but exhaust gases were vented forward through a tube under the muzzle. Ammunition remained the same as for the earlier models and continued to be propelled by a single charge with no increments.

82mm (3.2in) 82-PM 36, 82-PM 37, 82-PM 41 and 82-PM 43

The 82mm (3.2in) Model 1936 (82-PM 36) was a copy of the French Brandt

81mm (3.1in) mortar, and was virtually identical to it except for the increase in calibre. Captured examples were fielded by the Germans as the 8.2cm (3.2in) Granatwerfer 274/1(r). German 8.1cm (3.1in) mortar bombs could be fired from Russian 82mm (3.2in) mortars with some loss of accuracy.

The Model 1937 (82-PM 37) incorporated various improvements, notably the addition of recoil springs between the barrel and bipod to reduce firing stresses on the mounting and the frequency of re-laying during prolonged firing. It also introduced the circular baseplate that became characteristic of most future Russian mortars. German

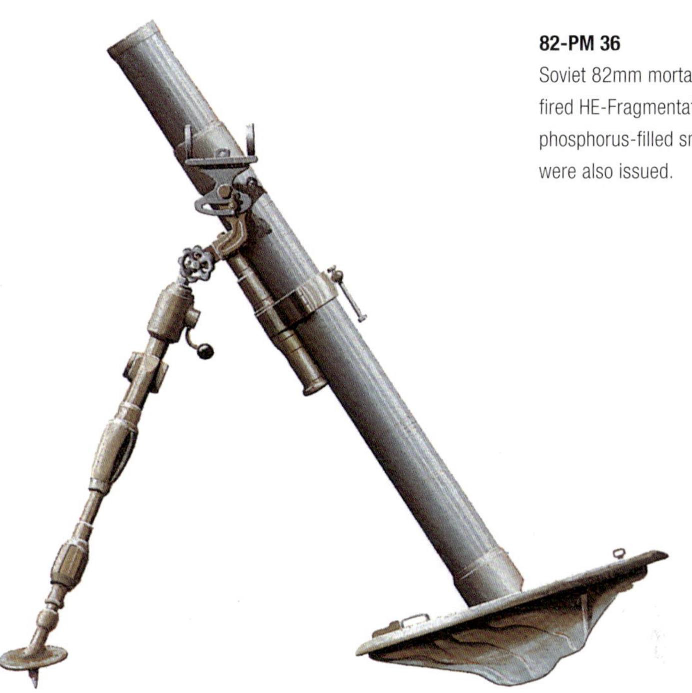

82-PM 36
Soviet 82mm mortars primarily fired HE-Fragmentation bombs, but phosphorus-filled smoke bombs were also issued.

82-PM 36

Calibre: 82mm (3.2in)
Barrel length: 1320mm (51.97in)
Bore length: 1225mm (48.23in)
Weight in action: 62kg (136.7lb)
Elevation: 45° to 85°
Traverse: 6o to 11o – variable with elevation
Maximum range: 3000m (9842ft)
Bomb weight: 3.4kg (7.5lb)

82mm (3.2in) Model 1937 mortar
Harley-Davidson 42WLA with Russian M-72 sidecar and 82mm (3.2in) Model 1937 mortar, Operation Bagration, summer 1944.

82-PM 37

Calibre: 82mm (3.2in)
Barrel length: 1320mm (51.97in)
Bore length: 1225mm (48.23in)
Weight in action: 57.34kg (126.3lb)
Elevation: 45° to 85°
Traverse: 6° to 11° – variable with elevation
Maximum range: 3100m (10,170ft)
Bomb weight: 3.4kg (7.5lb)

troops used captured examples as the 8.2cm (3.2in) Granatwerfer 274/2(r).

The Model 1941 (82-PM 41) introduced new features to improve the mortar's battlefield mobility. Stamped steel wheels could be fitted over stub axles on the bipod legs once the bipod had been secured against the baseplate. A handle attachment was then fitted over the muzzle allowing the mortar to be towed by two crewmen. This version was also used by the Germans as the 8.2cm (3.2in) Granatwerfer 274/3(r). In 1943, the idea was taken a stage further by making the wheels a permanent fixture on the bipod. In action, they were raised above the bipod feet and only came into contact with the ground when the bipod was folded back. This version was the 82mm (3.2in) Model 1943 (82-PM 43), which remained in service until well after the war.

107-PM 38 mortar battery
107-PM 38 107mm (4.2in) mortars prepare to fire in support of mountain infantry. (Each mountain artillery regiment fielded 12 of these weapons.)

107-PM 38

The 107mm (4.2in) Model 1938 Mountain Mortar (107-PM 38) was an enlarged version of the 82mm (3.2in) Model 1937 produced especially for the Red Army's Mountain Infantry Divisions. The mortar could be drop-fired or trigger-fired. The bombs were propelled by a single primary cartridge and up to four increments. Ammunition comprised HE, smoke and incendiary rounds. In keeping with its role, the Model 1938 could be broken down for pack transport across difficult terrain. Alternatively, it could be horse-drawn on a light two-wheeled carriage attached to a limber. Any that were captured by the Germans were used by them as the 10.7cm (4.2in) Gebirgsgranatwerfer 328(r).

107-PM 38
Calibre: 107mm (4.2in)
Barrel length: 1570mm (61.8in)
Bore length: 1400mm (55.12in)
Weight in action: 170.7kg (376lb)
Weight travelling: 850kg (1874lb)
Elevation: 45° to 80°
Traverse: 6°
Maximum range: 6314m (20,715ft)
Bomb weight: 8kg (17.64lb)

120-HM 38

The 120mm (4.72in) Model 1938 (120-HM 38) was another scaled-up version of the 82mm (3.2in) Model 1937. It used the same carriage as the 107mm (4.2in) Model 1938, but this was usually attached to a two-wheeled limber with an ammunition box containing 20 bombs.

The mortar's firepower and mobility impressed the Germans, who eagerly took any captured examples into service

Stalingrad

A 120-HM 38 firing in support of the defenders of Stalingrad, December 1942.

120-HM 38

120-HM 38 on tow behind a Willys MB Jeep. A few ready-use bombs would probably be carried in the towing vehicle, with the main supply in limbers towed by other jeeps.

120-HM 38

Calibre: 120mm (4.72in)
Barrel length (L/15.5): 1862mm (73.3in)
Bore length: 1536mm (60.47in)
Weight in action: 280.1kg (617lb)
Weight travelling: 477.6kg (1052lb)
Elevation: 45° to 80°
Traverse: 6°
Maximum range: 6000m (19,685ft)
Bomb weight (HE): 16kg (35.3lb)

as the 12cm (4.72in) Granatwerfer 378(r). Enthusiastic reports from units issued with these weapons prompted the Germans to manufacture a copy as the 12cm (4.72in) Granatwerfer 42.

160mm (6.3in) Model 1943

This was originally intended to be no more than an enlarged version of the 120mm (4.72in) mortar, but the design was quickly revised to incorporate breech-loading when it became obvious that no loader could drop a bomb weighing more than 40kg (88lb) down a 3m-long (10ft) barrel. Its size and range made it very much an artillery weapon, which was fitted with wheels for towing by an artillery tractor. Brigades of 32 mortars were fielded as part of the Breakthrough Artillery Divisions raised from 1942 onwards.

160mm (6.3in) Model 1943

This was the largest of all the Red Army's wartime mortars – its 41.4kg (90.1lb) bomb shown here was exceptionally powerful and almost three times the weight of that fired by the 120mm 4.72in) mortar. Below, a lend-lease US6 U3 tows a 160mm (6.3in) Model 1943 heavy mortar.

160mm (6.3in) Model 1943

Calibre: 160mm (6.3in)
Barrel length: 2896mm (114in)
Weight in action: 1080.5kg (2380lb)
Elevation (max): 50°
Traverse: 17°
Maximum range: 5150m (16,896ft)
Minimum range: 750m (2460ft)
Bomb weight (HE): 41.4kg (90.1lb)

KATYUSHA ROCKETS

By the end of the war, more than 10,000 Katyusha launchers of all types had been produced together with 12 million rockets in an estimated 200 factories.

82mm (3.2in) M-8 Rocket

The 82mm (3.2in) M-8 rocket was based on the RS-82 air-launched rocket (RS – *Reaktivnyy Snaryad*, 'rocket-powered shell'). Converting the RS-82 for ground-to-ground use primarily involved enlarging the warhead and motor, but it remained a simple, fin-stabilized, solid-fuel rocket. The type entered service in August 1941; its relatively light weight allowed large numbers to be fired from a single launcher. Medium trucks mounted a bank of rails for no less than 48 rockets, while even jeeps could be fitted with eight-round launchers.

BM-8-8 82mm (3.2in) rocket launcher on Willys MB jeep
As the Red Army's advance approached the Carpathian Mountains in 1944, the BM-8-8 was hastily developed to ensure that jeeps could give fire support in terrain that was impassable to existing Katyusha vehicles.

BM-8-48 rocket launcher on Studebaker US6 U-3
Each Studebaker US6 could fire a salvo of 48 lightweight 82mm (3.2in) M-8 rockets, giving the standard four-vehicle battery devastating short-range firepower.

82mm (3.2in) M-8 Rocket
Length: 66cm (26in)
Diameter: 82mm (3.2in)
Total weight: 8kg (17.6lb)
Propellant weight: 1.2kg (2.645lb)
HE weight: 0.5kg (1.1lb)
Maximum range: 5900m (19,356ft)

132mm (5.2in) M-13 Rocket

The M-13 was developed from the RS-132 air-launched rocket – as with the M-8, the main changes were a larger motor and warhead. (It was just entering service at the time of the German invasion and first saw action in July 1941.)

The M-13 was fired from a launcher comprising an elevating frame that carried a bank of eight parallel rails on which the rockets were mounted – eight on top of the rails and a further eight hung beneath them.

Most warheads were simple 22kg (48lb) impact-fused HE-fragmentation types, although there is a possibility that HEAT warheads may have been developed for use against tank concentrations. Some Russian reports indicate that illuminating and incendiary warheads were also used in small numbers.

Although the rockets were slow to reload and were far less accurate than conventional artillery, they had immense firepower. In 7–10 seconds, a battery of four BM-13 launchers could fire a salvo that delivered 4.42 tonnes (4.35 tons) of HE over a four-hectare impact zone. Well-trained crews could then redeploy in a matter of a few minutes to avoid counter-battery fire.

300mm (11.8in) M30/M-31/ M-13-DD Rockets

The M30 used a modified version of the M-13's rocket motor, which was fitted with a bulbous 300mm (11.8in) HE warhead containing 28.9kg (64lb) of explosive. Maximum range was only 2800m (9186ft), but this was considered

BM-13-16 132mm (5.2in) rocket launcher on Studebaker US 6x6 U3

In early 1943, the Red Army adopted the Studebaker 6x6 as the standard vehicle to mount the BM-8 and BM-13 salvo rocket launchers. Almost 105,000 Studebaker vehicles were delivered to Russia by the end of the war, many of which were adapted to give the Katyusha a high degree of cross-country mobility.

132mm (5.2in) M-13 Rocket

Length: 1.41m (55.9in)
Diameter: 132mm (5.2in)
Total weight: 42.5kg (93.7lb)
Propellant weight: 7.2kg (15.87lb)
HE weight: 4.9kg (10.8lb)
Maximum range: 8500m (27,887ft)

M-31-12 300mm (11.8in) rocket launcher on Studebaker US 6x6 U-3

Each 300mm (11.8in) rocket's warhead contained almost six times as much explosive as that of the M-13 rocket.

M-31 Rocket

Length: 1.76m (69.3in)
Diameter: 300mm (11.8in)
Total weight: 91.5kg (201.7lb)
Propellant weight: 11.2kg (24.7lb)
HE weight: 28.9kg (63.7lb)
Maximum range: 4300m (14,100ft)

acceptable in view of the warhead's devastating blast effect. The M-30 was fired directly from its packing case, four of which could be mounted on a firing frame, referred to as a Rama. In late 1942, the improved M-31 was adopted; this was very similar to its predecessor, but had a new rocket motor that gave it a maximum range of 4300m (14,100ft). (The later M-31-UK was modified to give a degree of spin-stabilization, which greatly improved accuracy.) Initially, the launcher was the same as that used by the M-30, but in March 1944, a mobile version entered service consisting of launchers for 12 M-31s on a ZiS-6 6x6 truck. Later-production batches were mounted on lend-lease Studebaker US-6 6x6 trucks.

ANTI-TANK GUNS

Although Soviet doctrine called for all artillery to be capable of acting in the anti-tank role when necessary, the Red Army fielded a number of dedicated anti-tank guns.

37mm (1.46in) anti-tank gun Model 1930 (1-K)

The 1-K was the Red Army's first anti-tank gun. It was essentially a licence-built copy of the German 3.7cm (1.46in) Pak L/45 that had entered service with the Reichsheer in 1928 and was arguably the best anti-tank gun in service at that time. The Pak L/45 was modernized in 1934 by substituting magnesium-alloy wheels and pneumatic tyres for the original spoked wooden wheels and redesignated as the 3.7cm (1.46in) Pak 35/36.

Production of the 1-K began in 1931, but all the 255 guns built in that year failed to pass quality control inspections; it was not until 1932 that the first weapons were accepted for service. A total of 509 guns were completed before production switched to the more powerful 45mm (1.77in) Model 1932 (19-K).

As the various 45mm (1.77in) anti-tank guns entered service, most 1-Ks were relegated to training units and storage depots. A few were still operational at the time of the German invasion, notably with 8th Mechanized Corps. It is probable that any serviceable weapons in storage were also rushed into active service. However, there are no confirmed reports of their combat use and most of the guns were almost certainly lost in the first few months of Operation 'Barbarossa'. The Germans assigned the type the reporting designation 3.7cm (1.46in) Pak 158(r).

45mm (1.77in) Anti-Tank Guns Model 1932 (19-K) and Model 1937 (53-K)

The 19-K was a combination of a slightly modified 1-K carriage and

45mm Anti-Tank Gun Model 1932

Although rapidly outclassed as an anti-tank gun, the 45mm (1.77in) 19-K remained effective as a light infantry gun, firing HE and canister rounds in the infantry support role.

45mm (1.77in) Anti-Tank Gun Model 1932 (19-K)

Weight (1-K carriage): 450kg (990lb)
Weight (GAZ-A wheels): 510kg (1120lb)
Length: 6.4m (21ft)
Barrel length: 2.07m (6.8ft) L/46
Shell weight: 1.43kg (3.2lb)
Elevation: –8° to +25°
Traverse: 60°
Rate of fire: 15rpm
Muzzle velocity: 760m/s (2493ft/s)
Maximum range: 4400m (14,435ft)

45mm (1.77in) Anti-Tank Gun Model 1937 (53-K)
The 45mm (1.77in) anti-tank guns were useful weapons by the standards of 1941. They were easily concealed and capable of destroying the majority of contemporary German tanks at ranges up to 500m (1640ft).

45mm (1.77in) Anti-Tank Gun Model 1937 (53-K)
Weight (travelling order): 1200kg (2645lb)
Weight (deployed): 560kg (1234lb)
Length: 6.4m (21ft)
Barrel length: 2.07m (6ft 9in) L/46
Elevation: –8° to +25°
Traverse: 60°
Rate of fire: 15–20rpm
Muzzle velocity: 760m/s (2493ft/s)
Maximum range: 4400m (14,435ft)

a new 45mm (1.77in) barrel. Initial problems with poor mobility due to the retention of spoked wooden wheels and the slow action of the manually operated breech forced a series of improvements that led to the gun being redesignated as the 53-K in 1937. The principal modifications were:

- The replacement of the manually operated breech with a semi-automatic breech.
- In 1934, the spoked wooden wheels were replaced by GAZ-A car wheels fitted with pneumatic tyres.
- 'Bulletproof' tyres filled with sponge rubber replaced pneumatic tyres in 1936.
- New sights, firing mechanism and shield mounting fittings.

A wide range of ammunition was produced for both guns, including APHE, APCR, HE and canister rounds. Both types were built in vast numbers. Totals for the 19-K may have been as high as 21,500, while more than 37,000 53-K guns had been completed when production ended in 1943.

45mm (1.77in) Anti-Tank Gun Model 1942 (M-42)

By 1942, the effectiveness of existing 45mm (1.77in) anti-tank guns was being rapidly reduced as the Germans up-armoured their tanks and assault guns. The much-delayed 57mm (2.24in) ZiS-2 anti-tank gun was acknowledged to be the best solution, but as an interim measure, the 45mm (1.77in) gun was updated by fitting a longer (L/66) barrel and being rechambered to take more powerful ammunition. The shield was also thickened to 7mm (0.27in) to give the gun crew improved protection from machine-gun fire and shell splinters.

Although the M-42 was outclassed by the Panther and Tiger, it was effective

45mm (1.77in) Anti-Tank Gun Model 1942 (M-42)
Despite having a limited anti-tank capability by the end of the war, the M-42 was easy to manhandle and was a useful close-support weapon firing HE and canister rounds.

45mm (1.77in) Anti-Tank Gun Model 1942 (M-42)
Weight (travelling order): 1250kg (2756lb)
Weight (deployed): 625kg (1378lb)
Barrel length: 3.09m (10ft) L/66
Width: 1.6m (5ft 3in)
Height: 1.2m (3ft 11in)
Elevation: –8° to +25°
Traverse: 60°
Rate of fire: 15–20rpm
Muzzle velocity: 870m/s (2854ft/s)
Maximum range: 4550m (14,927ft)

against lighter German AFVs at close range. It remained in production until mid-1945, by which time at least 10,800 had been completed.

57mm (2.24in) Anti-Tank Gun Model 1943 (ZiS-2)

The design of the ZiS-2 began in early 1940 in response to an official requirement for an anti-tank gun capable of penetrating a heavy tank with armour comparable to that of the KV-1. The requirement may have been influenced by German propaganda about their multi-turreted Neubaufahrzeug (NbFz) 'supertank', or simply assumed that the Germans would develop AFVs to match the Soviet heavy tanks that had been sent to Finland for combat trials.

It was calculated that a 57mm (2.24in) gun would meet the requirement to penetrate 90mm (3.54in) of armour, while still being relatively light and small enough to easily conceal. There was one drawback: 57mm (2.24in) was a new calibre for Soviet weaponry, so all production tooling would have to be specially designed. The gun entered production on 1 June 1941, and the few that were issued to the Red Army proved able to destroy any contemporary German AFV. However, production was halted in December 1941 after 371 had been completed. Various explanations have been given for this decision, but it seems likely that the gun was just too complex to produce in the chaotic conditions following the evacuation of war industries to the Urals. Priority was given to production of the ZiS-3 76.2mm divisional gun, which also equipped some anti-tank regiments.

The situation changed with the appearance of the Tiger I and Panther; these rendered the 45mm (1.77in) guns obsolescent and were tough targets

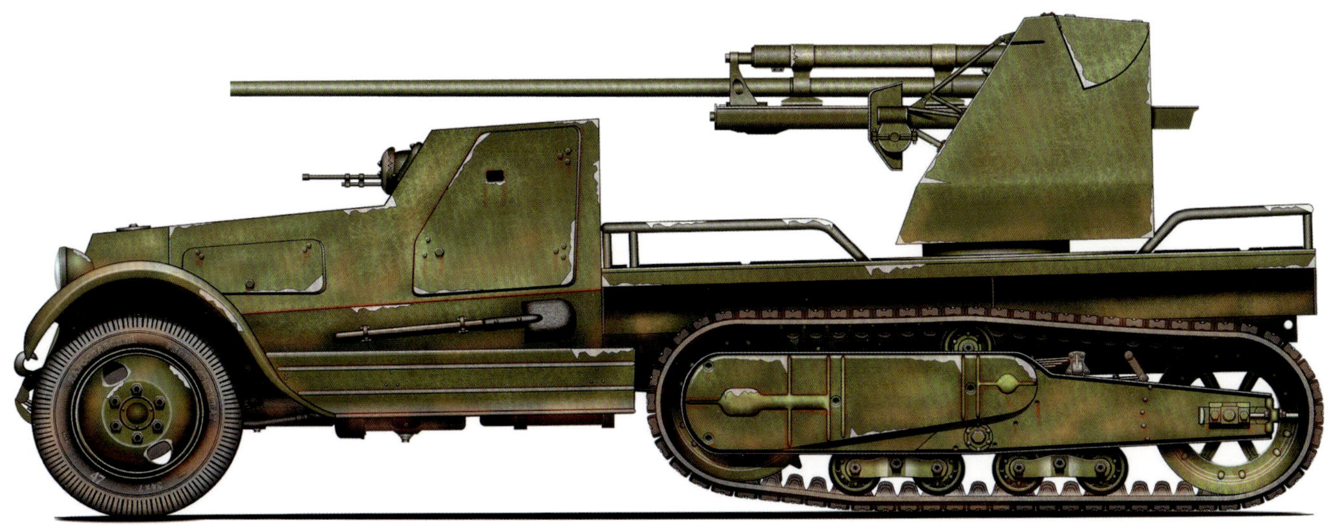

VMS-41 tank destroyer
The experimental VMS-41 tank destroyer – a ZiS-2 57mm (2.24in) gun on an armoured ZiS-22 halftrack chassis. A prototype was tested with good results in November 1941, but the project ended with the decision to terminate ZiS-2 production the following month.

57mm (2.24in) Anti-Tank Gun Model 1943 (ZiS-2)
Weight: 1250kg (2756lb)
Length: 7.03m (23ft)
Barrel length: 4.16m (13ft 8in) L/73
Width: 1.7m (5ft 7in)
Height: 1.37m (4ft 6in)
Elevation: –5° to +25°
Traverse: 56°
Rate of fire: 10rpm
Muzzle velocity: 1000m/s (3300ft/s)

for the ZiS-3. Production of the ZiS-2 – now designated the 57mm (2.24in) anti-tank gun Model 1943 – was hastily resumed, with the gun being mounted on the carriage of the ZiS-3. At least 9600 Model 1943s were completed by the time that production ended in 1945.

ANTI-AIRCRAFT GUNS

In the early stages of the war, heavy losses of AA guns combined with German air superiority led to the use of anything capable of firing skywards. (Even anti-tank rifles were reportedly used on improvised AA mounts.)

Tokarev 4M Model 1931

This was the earliest light AA weapon to be produced for the Red Army, comprising four 7.62mm (0.3in) Maxim Model 1910/30 machine guns on a heavy pedestal mount. These were manually operated, but quite successful, although rather limited by the low effective ceiling of their rifle calibre rounds. The mounting incorporated special ammunition boxes with a capacity of 500 rounds each instead of the standard 250-round belt boxes. The guns retained their original water-cooling systems, which were adapted to allow the prolonged firing likely to be required in the AA role. When the water began to boil after 500–600 rounds of rapid fire, the resulting steam escaped through valves in the cooling jackets into detachable rubber hoses that carried the steam to condensers so that

Defending Leningrad

A 4M AA mount on a Leningrad rooftop. *Luftwaffe* pilots quickly learned to respect the city's AA defences – even the veteran Stuka ace Hans Rudel wrote of the '... murderous flak. I never again experienced anything to compare with it in any theatre of war.'

GAZ-AAA with 4M AA Mount

This was one of the commonest truck-mounts for the 4M AA mount, which was also fitted to armoured trains and a variety of river craft.

Tokarev 4M Model 1931
Weight: 460kg (1014lb)
Elevation: –10° to +85°
Traverse: 360°
Action: Short recoil, toggle locked
Feed system: 4 x 500 round belts
Rate of fire: 2100rpm
Maximum ceiling: 1400m (4593ft)
Maximum range (against ground targets): 1600m (5250ft)

much of the water could be recycled. The massive weight of the Tokarev mount – 80kg (176lb) for the four guns alone, without water – meant that it was mainly restricted to use on trucks or in permanent AA emplacements to defend point targets.

The guns were aimed using simple ring AA sights that were reasonably efficient given the dispersion of rounds from four barrels and their combined rate of fire (approximately 2100rpm). The real problem with the system was that it gradually became less and less effective as the Luftwaffe deployed better-protected aircraft. Even relatively light armour gave a high degree of protection from the Maxim's rifle-calibre bullets; the heavily armoured ground attack aircraft entering service in 1942/43, such as the Hs-129, were virtually immune to these rounds.

12.7mm DShK Heavy Machine Gun

In 1925, the Red Army requested the development of a large-calibre machine gun, primarily as an anti-tank and AA weapon. By 1930, prototypes had been produced of what was basically an enlarged DP machine gun, known as the DK (Degtyarov Krupnokalibernyj – Degtyarov large calibre). This was a gas-operated, air-cooled weapon fed from top-mounted 30-round detachable drum magazines. The type went into limited production in 1933, and armed some small naval craft and river patrol boats. In service, the heavy

12.7mm DShK Heavy Machine Gun
Weight (gun only): 34kg (75lb)
Weight (including mounting): 157kg (346lb)
Length: 162.5cm (64in)
Barrel length: 107cm (42.1in)
Action: Gas-operated, flapper-locked
Feed system: 50-round belt
Rate of fire: 600rpm
Effective ceiling: 2000m (6562ft)
Maximum range: 2500m (8200ft)

ZiS-5V with DShK 12.7mm (.5in) Heavy Machine Gun
The weight of the DShK meant that dedicated AA vehicles were needed to give it reasonable battlefield mobility – by the middle of the war AA regiments fielded eight truck-mounted DShKs.

30-round drum magazine proved to be unsatisfactory as it was emptied in a few seconds' firing, while its weight made the frequent magazine changes awkward for the gun crew. It was clear that a belt-feed was needed to transform the design into a practical service weapon. By 1938, an 'add-on' belt feed unit had been developed.

This modified DK was adopted as DShK-38 (Degtyarov – Shpagin Krupnokalibernyj – Degtyarov & Shpagin large-calibre, model 1938). Although it was a satisfactory weapon with reasonable power (at least to deal with low-flying aircraft and light AFVs), it had some peculiar features. The most notable was the very heavy universal wheeled mount, which, despite its weight – 157kg (346lb) including the gun – failed to provide the necessary stability and vibration dampening for accurate long-range fire. Although this posed problems when firing against ground targets, the dispersion of fire actually helped when the DShK was employed as an AA weapon on a lighter tripod mounting.

25mm AA Gun Model 1940 (72-K)

By the early 1930s, it was becoming obvious that machine guns were likely to be ineffective against the next generation of attack aircraft. Soviet design teams came up with several weapons, the earliest being the 45mm (1.77in) K-21 of 1934, an adaptation of the Red Army's anti-tank gun. This slow-firing weapon was quickly rejected and a small batch of Bofors 25mm Model 1933 AA guns bought for trials

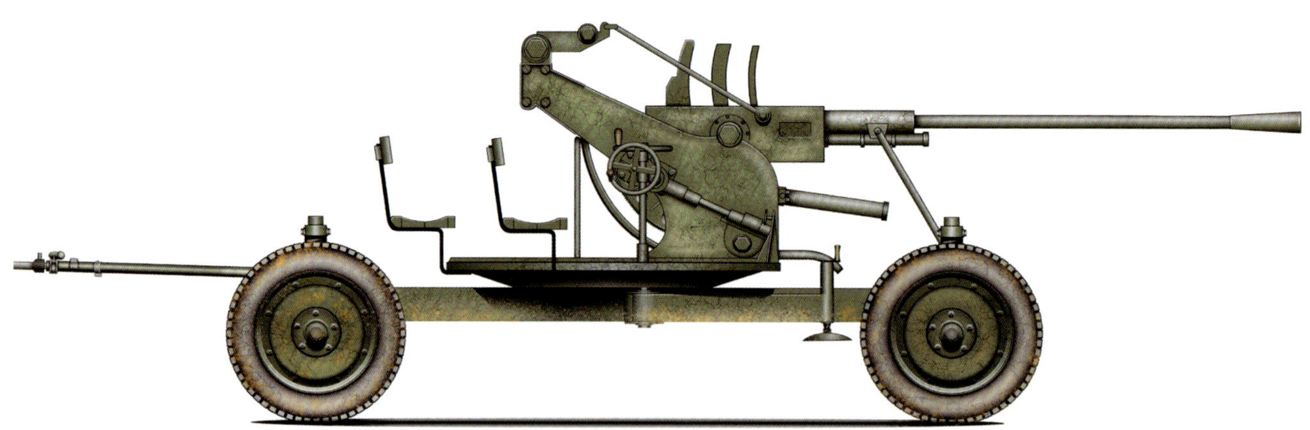

25mm AA Gun Model 1940 (72-K)
An estimated 4860 72-Ks had been completed by the time production ended in 1945.

25mm AA Gun Model 1940 (72-K)
Weight: 1210kg (2670lb)
Length: 5.3m (17ft 5in)
Barrel length: 1.915m (6ft 4in) L/76.6
Width: 1.7m (5ft 7in)
Height: 1.8m (5ft 11in)
Shell weight: 0.28kg (10oz)
Elevation: –10 to +85 °
Traverse: 360°
Feed system: Six-round clips
Rate of fire: 240rpm
Muzzle velocity: 925m/s (3035ft/s)
Maximum ceiling: 2400m (7900ft)

37mm (1.46in) AA gun Model 1939 (61-K)
Vienna 1945: a Lend-Lease Chevrolet G-7107 towing a 37mm (1.46in) 61-K 1939 AA gun. Below shows a 61-K in the firing position with stabilising jacks lowered.

37mm (1.46in) Automatic Air Defence Gun Model 1939 (61-K)
Weight: 2100kg (4600lb)
Barrel length: 2.7m (8ft 10in) L/67
Shell weight: 0.785kg (1.7lb)
Elevation: –5° to +85°
Traverse: 360°
Feed system: Five-round clips
Rate of fire: 80rpm
Muzzle velocity: 880m/s (2887ft/s)
Effective ceiling: 4000m (13,000ft)
Maximum ceiling: 5000m (16,000ft)

in 1935. These seem to have formed the basis for the design of the Model 1940, which entered service in late 1941.

37mm (1.46in) AA Gun Model 1939 (61-K)

Work on this gun began in January 1938 and the prototype underwent successful firing trials in October that year. It was mounted on a four-wheeled ZU-7 carriage and closely resembled the 40mm (1.5in) Bofors guns in general appearance. The ammunition seems to have been derived from that used by the contemporary US 37mm (1.46in) Browning AA gun and was loaded in five-round clips. The initial order for 900 guns was quickly increased. By the time Soviet production ended in 1945, almost 20,000 guns had been completed.

The type was an effective AA gun, although not the wonder weapon of Soviet propaganda, which claimed that the 61-K batteries shot down a total of 14,657 enemy aircraft, averaging 905 rounds per aircraft destroyed. As the best estimate of the total *Luftwaffe* combat losses in Russia between March 1942 and December 1944 is less than 8400 aircraft, this would seem very optimistic.

Although it was designed as an AA gun, the 61-K's potential in the anti-tank role was also appreciated, and priority was given to developing armour-piercing (AP) ammunition. Penetration at 500-m (1640-ft) range was recorded as 37mm (1.46in) of armour sloped at 60 degrees. The 61-K's high rate of fire in comparison with conventional anti-tank guns would make it a more potent tank-killer than these figures suggest. Especially at short ranges, it had a good chance of achieving multiple hits by firing short bursts at attacking AFVs.

76.2mm AA Guns Model 1931 (3-K) and Model 1938

The 3-K was the first heavy AA gun produced for the Red Army to replace the 1914-vintage 76.2mm (3in) guns inherited from the Tsar's army. It was based on the German Flak R 75mm (2.95in) AA gun, but the two-wheeled carriage with folding cruciform outriggers owed much to the carriage design of early Vickers 3-inch AA guns. A total of 3821 were completed between 1931 and 1938.

In 1938, production switched to the Model 1938. This was a similar design with a new barrel and a two-axle ZU-8 carriage. Only 960 were completed before the type was replaced in production by the 85mm (3.35in) guns.

76.2mm AA gun model 1931 (3-K)
Both the Model 1931 and Model 1938 had a potent armour-piercing performance – 78mm (3in) at 500m (1640ft) at 30 degrees.

76.2mm AA Guns Model 1931 (3-K) and Model 1938
Weight (Model 1931): 4820kg (10,630lb)
Weight (Model 1938): 4210kg (9280lb)
Weight (deployed): 3650kg (8050lb)
Barrel length: 4.1m (13ft 5in) L/55
Shell weight: 6.6kg (14.5lb)
Breech: Semi-automatic vertical sliding wedge
Recoil system: Hydro-pneumatic
Carriage: Two-wheeled carriage with collapsible cruciform outriggers
Carriage (Model 1938): Four-wheeled dual-axle trailer with twin outriggers
Elevation: –2° to +82°
Traverse: 360°
Rate of fire: 10–20rpm
Muzzle velocity: 813m/s (2667ft/s)
Maximum ceiling: 9300m (31,000ft)

85mm (3.35in) AA Gun Model 1939 (52-K)

The 52-K was essentially an enlarged and modernized version of the 76.2mm (3in) Model 1938, which proved to be so successful that the Germans regarded captured examples as prized trophies. Sufficient guns and ammunition were captured for the type to be taken into German service as the 8.5cm (3.35in) Flak M.39(r). Other captured guns were returned to German factories to be re-bored to fire standard 88mm (3.4in) ammunition. These were issued to many home defence Flak batteries as the 8.8cm (3.4in) Flak M.39(r).

85mm (3.35in) AA Gun Model 1939 (52-K)
Weight: 4500kg (9921lb)
Length: 7.05m (23ft 2in)
Barrel length: 4.7m (15ft 5in) L/55
Width: 2.15m (7ft)
Height: 2.25m (7ft 5in)
Shell weight: 9.2kg (20.3lb)
Breech: Semi-automatic vertical sliding wedge
Recoil system: Hydro-pneumatic
Carriage: Four-wheeled dual-axle trailer with twin outriggers
Elevation: –3° to +82°
Traverse: 360°
Rate of fire: 10–12rpm
Muzzle velocity: 792m/s (2598ft/s)
Effective ceiling: 10,500m (34,448ft)
Maximum ceiling: 15,650m (51,127ft)

85mm (3.35in) AA Gun Model 1939 (52-K)
The 52-K was a highly efficient heavy AA gun, with an excellent armour-piercing performance: 91mm (3.6in) at 500m (1640ft) at 30°.

76.2mm AA Gun Model 1931 battery
Significant numbers of captured guns were taken into German service under the designation 7.62cm Flak M.31(r) and used until ammunition stocks ran out. A few were re-bored to fire German 88mm ammunition and redesignated 7.62/8.8cm Flak M.31(r), but most were scrapped in 1944.

85mm AA Gun Model 1944 (KS-18)

This was virtually identical to the Model 1939, but rechambered to take a larger, more powerful cartridge that increased the gun's effective ceiling. The recoil system was also strengthened to cope with the increased loads imposed by the new cartridge.

105mm AA Gun Model 1934

Little information has come to light on this weapon, which was probably the world's most powerful AA gun of the mid-1930s. It seems likely that only small numbers were produced in Leningrad and that these were statically emplaced to protect major cities and industrial complexes.

INFANTRY GUNS

The Red Army made extensive use of infantry guns throughout the war, finding them invaluable for use against point targets requiring more accurate fire than mortars could provide.

76.2mm (3in) Regimental Gun Model 1927

This was a simple, short-barrelled infantry gun that entered service in 1928 based on the Tsarist 76.2mm (3in) Model 1913. Early-production guns had wooden spoked wheels and were towed by a four-horse team; later guns were completed with large disc wheels and solid rubber tyres to allow for towing by light artillery tractors. Almost 16,500 guns were completed

76.2mm (3in) Regimental Gun Model 1927

In 1940/41, each Soviet infantry regiment had six of these guns. They were normally deployed in the close support role, using direct fire against enemy strongpoints.

76.2mm (3in) Regimental Gun Model 1927
Weight: 780kg (1720lb)
Length: 3.5m (11ft 6in)
Barrel length: 1.25m (4ft 1in) L/16.5
Width: 1.7m (5ft 7in)
Height: 1.3m (4ft 3in)
Shell weight: 6.2kg (13.6lb)
Breech: Interrupted screw
Elevation: –6° to +25°
Traverse: 6°
Rate of fire: 10–12rpm
Muzzle velocity: 262m/s (860ft/s)
Maximum range: 4200m (13,780ft)

by the time production ended in 1943, and the type remained in service until the end of the war.

76.2mm (3in) Regimental Gun Model 1943

The limitations of the Model 1927 (primarily its weight and limited traverse) had to be accepted in the desperate conditions of 1941/42, but by 1943 manufacturing capacity was available for a modernized infantry gun. This was a combination of the barrel of the Model 1927 and the modified carriage of the 45mm (1.77in) anti-tank gun Model 1942.

The new gun was lighter and offered far greater traverse than its predecessor.

76.2mm (3in) Regimental Gun Model 1943
The issue of the BP-350M HEAT shell capable of penetrating 69mm (2.7in) of armour at 500m (1640ft) at 30 degrees gave the Model 1943 a greatly improved chance of survival against German AFVs.

76.2mm (3in) Regimental Gun Model 1943
Weight: 600kg (1322lb)
Length: 3.54m (11ft 7in)
Barrel length: 1.25m (4ft 1in) L/16.5
Width: 1.63m (5ft 4in)
Height: 1.3m (4ft 3in)
Shell weight: 6.2kg (13.7lb)
Elevation: –8° to +25°
Traverse: 60°
Rate of fire: 10–12rpm
Muzzle velocity: 262m/s (860ft/s)
Maximum range: 4200m (13,780ft)

This was especially valuable when it was forced to operate in the emergency anti-tank role using the newly issued HEAT ammunition. More than 5000 guns were completed by the time production ended in 1945.

76.2mm (3in) Divisional Guns Model 1902 and Model 1902/30

The Model 1902 was the Red Army's first field gun, with 2500 being completed by the time production ended in 1931. It remained virtually unchanged throughout its long service life, with 2066 guns still equipping Soviet units in 1941. Enormous stockpiles of ammunition for this gun led to the decision to retain the 76.2mm (3in) as the standard calibre for future field guns, in contrast to other armies that were in the throes of adopting larger calibres.

By the early 1930s, it was becoming obvious that the Model 1902 was obsolete, and attempts were made to modernize the design. The solution finally adopted was to fit a new, longer barrel and to modify the carriage to increase the maximum elevation from 17 degrees to 37 degrees.

These changes dramatically improved the gun's range. The introduction of a new 6.3kg (13.8lb) armour-piercing round in the mid-1930s gave the gun the ability to penetrate 56mm (2.2in) of armour at

500m (1640ft) at 30 degrees – a truly exceptional anti-tank capability for its time, which was further enhanced in future divisional guns.

76.2mm (3in) Divisional Gun Model 1936 (F-22)

Good as it was, the Model 1902/30 was no more than a stopgap. In the early 1930s, much research went into 'universal' divisional guns that could operate as field artillery, AA and anti-tank guns. Although it was superficially attractive, this idea was unrealistic: field guns that could also serve as AA guns had been tried during World War I, but were obsolescent in 1918, and dramatic improvements in aircraft performance had made them totally obsolete by the 1930s.

76.2mm (3in) Divisional Gun M1902/30
Weight (deployed): 1350kg (2976lb)
Weight (travelling order): 2380kg (5247lb)
Length: 4.94m (16ft)
Barrel length: 3.048m (10ft) (L/40)
Width: 1.84m (6ft)
Height 1.6m (5ft 3in)
Shell weight: 7.5kg (17lb)
Elevation: –3° to +37°
Traverse: 5°
Rate of fire: 10–12rpm
Muzzle velocity: 662m/s (2172ft/s)
Maximum range: 13,290m (43,600ft)

76.2mm (3in) Divisional Gun Model 1902/30
Although most Model 1902/30 guns retained the old-pattern wooden spoked wheels, some were refitted with rubber-tyred disc wheels to permit towing by trucks or artillery tractors.

Prototypes of the F-22 were completed in April 1935. These had muzzle brakes and were chambered for new ammunition, with a maximum range of 14,060m (46,130ft). After prolonged trials, the type was accepted for service in May 1936. Production models were chambered for standard 76.2mm (3in) ammunition, as the new round was felt to offer insufficient advantages to justify scrapping the vast numbers of existing shells. Service weapons also lacked the prototypes' muzzle brakes; it was judged that they raised too much dust on firing, which betrayed the guns' positions.

A total of 2932 guns were completed between 1936 and 1939; production was slow due to the factories' unfamiliarity with such a sophisticated weapon and the need to rectify design faults. Red Army units found that the F-22 was a mixed blessing: although its increased range was welcome, it was markedly heavier than the Model 1902/30; attempts to use it as an AA gun were quickly abandoned, as the breech mechanism repeatedly failed to operate properly at elevations higher than 60 degrees. It was also found to be impossible to track aircraft, as the carriage allowed

ZiS-3 crew

Here, the crew of a ZiS-3 take a break and have something to eat during a quiet period.

76.2mm (3in) Divisional Gun Model 1942 (ZiS-3)
Weight (deployed): 1116kg (2460lb)
Weight (travelling order): 2150kg (4730lb)
Barrel length: 3.4m (11ft 2in) L/42.6
Width: 1.6m (5ft 3in)
Height: 1.37m (4ft 6in)
Shell weight: 7.5kg (17lb)
Elevation: –5° to +37°
Traverse: 54°
Rate of fire: up to 25rpm
Muzzle velocity: 680m/s (2230ft/s)
Maximum range: 13,290m (43,600ft)

76.2mm (3in) Divisional Gun Model 1942 (ZiS-3)
The ZiS-3 was frequently used in the direct fire role. A crewman recalled that: 'Two holes were made to the left and right of a gun's wheels – one for the gunner, the other for the loader. ZIS-3 guns didn't require simultaneous presence of the entire crew near the gun… it was usually enough for only one person to be present. The gunner, after firing, could hide himself in his hole while the loader would drive the next shell into the barrel. Now the gunner could take his place, aim, and fire, and the loader would be taking cover at that time. Even after a direct hit into the gun at least one of the two had a chance to survive. The other crew members were spread out in similar holes…. Practical experience… as far back as the Battle of the Kursk Salient, allowed [the guns crews] to minimize casualties.'

only 60 degrees traverse. Armour-piercing performance was better than that of earlier guns, and the greatly improved traverse was welcome in the anti-tank role, but the crew were hindered by the awkward positioning of sights and elevation controls on different sides of the barrel.

76.2mm (3in) Divisional Gun Model 1939 (F-22 USV)

The flaws of the F-22 became apparent as soon as it entered service; in March 1937, an official requirement was issued for a replacement. The new gun was to fire existing 76.2mm (3in) ammunition, have a maximum elevation of 45 degrees, and its weight in action was not to exceed 1500kg (3300lb). The USV outperformed all its competitors and entered production in 1939. At least 9800 guns were completed by the time production ended in 1942.

76.2mm (3in) Divisional Gun Model 1942 (ZiS-3)

Design of the ZiS-3 began in late 1940. It was essentially a combination of the F-22 USV's barrel and the carriage of the 57mm (2.24in) ZiS-2 anti-tank gun. A muzzle brake was fitted to prevent the recoil damaging the relatively lightweight carriage.

Despite a lack of official support, the designer, Vasiliy Grabin, took the enormous risk of authorizing production on his own authority and persuaded the Red Army to accept guns for unofficial combat trials.

Enthusiastic reports on these guns prompted an official demonstration attended by Stalin. He was deeply impressed by the ZiS-3, describing it as '…a masterpiece of artillery systems design.'

With his support, production began in early 1942 with the highest priority;

more than 103,000 were completed by the end of the war.

100mm (3.94in) Field Gun Model 1944 (BS-3)

The BS-3 was based on the 100mm (3.94in) B-34 naval AA gun and entered service in 1944. Despite its excellent armour-piercing capability, it was not officially listed as an anti-tank gun, but was initially issued to corps artillery brigades as a field gun. However, by December 1944, its value in the anti-tank role was appreciated, and orders were given for the re-equipment of one regiment in each of 12 anti-tank artillery brigades with 100mm (3.94in) guns (16 per regiment) by 15 January 1945.

When the 9th Guards Army was formed in early 1945, it received an additional anti-tank brigade incorporating a BS-3 regiment, together with three new artillery brigades (61st, 62nd and 63rd Guards Artillery Brigades), each including a regiment of 100mm (3.94in) guns. A total of 268 guns were completed by the end of the war. Production continued until 1951, by which time almost 600 had been built.

107mm (4.2in) Corps Gun Model 1910/30

This gun was the outcome of a series of design studies to modernize the 107mm (4.2in) Model 1910 guns that had been inherited from the Tsar's army. The Model 1910/30 entered production in 1931 and incorporated several modifications, including:

- Lengthening the barrel by 10 calibres and fitting a muzzle brake.
- Rechambering to take separate-loading ammunition.
- Improvements to the recuperator, cradle and elevation mechanism.

100mm (3.94in) Field Gun Model 1944 (BS-3)
The excellent anti-tank performance of the BS-3 came at a price – the considerable bulk and weight of both the gun and its ammunition.

100mm (3.94in) Field Gun Model 1944 (BS-3)
Weight: 3650kg (8047lb)
Length: 9.37m (30ft 9in)
Barrel length: 5.34m (17ft 6in) L/53.5
Width: 2.15m (7ft 1in)
Height: 1.5m (4ft 11in)
Shell weight: 15.88kg (35lb)
Elevation: –5° to +45°
Traverse: 58°
Rate of fire: 8–10rpm
Muzzle velocity: 900m/s (2953ft/s)
Maximum range: 20,000m (65,600ft)

107mm (4.2in) Corps Gun Model 1910/30
The Model 1910/30 fired a wide variety of ammunition, including HE, shrapnel, incendiary, smoke and APCBC rounds. However, its mobility was limited by its wooden spoked wheels, which restricted its towing speed to about 6km/h (4mph).

107mm (4.2in) Corps Gun Model 1910/30
Weight (deployed): 2535kg (5589lb)
Weight (travelling order): 3000kg (6614lb)
Length: 7.53m (24ft 8in)
Barrel length: 3.9m (12ft 10in) L/36.6
Width: 2.06m (6ft 9in)
Height: 1.74m (5ft 9in)
Shell weight: 17.18kg (37.8lb)
Elevation: –5° to +37°
Traverse: 6°
Rate of fire: 5–6rpm
Muzzle velocity: 670m/s (2953ft/s)
Maximum range: 16,130m (52,900ft)

Most guns remained horse-drawn throughout their long service lives. More than 800 (conversions and new builds) were completed by the time production ended in 1935. Several hundred seem to have survived until 1943, and a few remained in service until 1945.

107mm (4.2in) Divisional Gun M1940 (M-60)

Development of the M-60 began in 1938, with the intention of producing a more powerful gun than the 76.2mm (3in) weapons that had been the mainstay of Russian field artillery since 1902. Initial studies concentrated on 95mm (3.7in) designs, but a 107mm (4.2in) gun was finally selected. This was largely because weapons of this calibre were already in service and it would be easier to make use of existing production tooling rather than start from scratch with a new 95mm (3.7in) gun.

A further reason was Marshal Kulik's obsession with the idea that the Germans were producing super-heavy tanks that could only be countered by a weapon as powerful as a high-velocity 107mm (4.2in) gun.

The M-60 was accepted for service in October 1940. A total of 139 were completed before production was halted shortly after the German invasion. This was due to several factors, including:

- Massive losses of equipment in the first months of Operation 'Barbarossa' meant that there was a dire shortage of artillery tractors capable of towing the relatively heavy M-60.
- There was no immediate requirement for an anti-tank gun as large and heavy as the 107mm (4.2in).
- The gun was complex to produce and demanded considerable maintenance. Given the imminent mass evacuation of war industries to unprepared sites in the Urals, it was unrealistic to attempt to resume production in such primitive conditions.

Most M-60s seem to have been lost in the defeats of 1941/42, although a few survivors were still in action at Kursk in 1943. Six were reportedly still in service with Soviet forces at the recapture of Sevastopol in 1944.

107mm (4.2in) Divisional Gun M1940 (M-60)

The M-60 was a powerful weapon, but impractical for service with the Red Army in the chaotic conditions of 1941/42.

107mm (4.2in) Divisional Gun M1940 (M-60)

Weight (deployed): 4000kg (8818lb)
Weight (travelling order): 4300kg (9480lb)
Length: 8.09m (26ft 7in)
Barrel length: 4.47m (14ft 8in) L/41.8
Width: 2.2m (7ft 3in)
Height: 1.92m (6ft 4in)
Shell weight: 17.4kg (38.4lb)
Elevation: –4.5° to +45°
Traverse: 60°
Rate of fire: 6–7rpm
Muzzle velocity: 670m/s (2953ft/s)
Maximum range: 16,130m (52,900ft)

122mm Howitzer Model 1909/37

The Model 1909/37 was a modernized version of the Krupp-designed Model 1909 that had served with the Tsar's army. Large numbers of these howitzers survived to be taken over by the Red Army. They remained unaltered until 1937, when their increasing obsolescence prompted a modernization programme. More than 900 were rechambered to accept a larger propellant charge, had their carriages strengthened and were fitted with new sights. About 800 of these Model 1909/37 howitzers remained in service in June 1941. Many were lost in the defeats of 1941/42, and most of the survivors were withdrawn from service by 1943.

Kalinin Front
A sentry stands guard over a battery of 122mm (4.8in) M-30 howitzers during the winter of 1941/42.

122mm (4.8in) Howitzer Model 1910/30

The Model 1910/30 was a modernized version of the Schneider-designed Model 1910, which had served with the Imperial Russian Army. From 1930, surviving howitzers were rebuilt with enlarged chambers to accept larger propellant charges, together with strengthened carriages and elevating mechanisms. Recoil systems were also upgraded and new sights fitted. Besides converting surviving Model 1910 howitzers, a large number of new weapons were built. The type remained in production until 1941, by which time 5900 had been completed.

122mm (4.8in) Howitzer Model 1910/30
Weight (deployed): 1466kg (3232lb)
Weight (travelling order): 2510kg (5534lb)
Length: N/k
Barrel length: 1.53m (5ft) L/12.6
Width: N/k
Height: 1.84m (6ft)
Shell weight: 21.76kg (48lb)
Elevation: –3° to +45°
Traverse: 4°
Rate of fire: 2rpm
Muzzle velocity: 364m/s (1194ft/s)
Maximum range: 8910m (29,230ft)

122mm (4.8in) Howitzer Model 1938 (M-30)

By the late 1930s, it was becoming clear that the Model 1909/37 and the Model 1910/30 howitzers were in need of replacement by an entirely new design: both types were not only out-ranged by foreign equivalents, but also had poor elevation and traverse. Various 122mm (4.8in) howitzers underwent prolonged service trials in 1938/39, leading to the acceptance of the M-30 in 1940.

The design was so successful that production continued until 1960, by which time more than 19,000 had been completed.

East Prussia, Spring 1945
A dug-in M-30 firing in support of 3rd Belorussian Front's advance on Königsberg.

122mm Howitzer Model 1938 (M-30)
Although it was primarily an indirect fire weapon, the M-30 did have a significant anti-tank capability after the introduction of the BP-460A HEAT shell in mid-1943, which could penetrate 100–160mm (3.94–6.3in) of armour at 90 degrees.

122mm (4.8in) Howitzer Model 1938 (M-30)
Weight (deployed): 2450kg (5401lb)
Weight (travelling order): 3100kg (6834lb)
Length: 5.9m (19ft 4in) (with limber)
Barrel length: 2.67m (8ft 9in) L/21.9
Width: 1.98m (6ft 6in)
Height: 1.82m (6ft)
Shell weight: 21.76kg (48lb)
Elevation: –3° to +63.5°
Traverse: 49°
Rate of fire: 5–6rpm
Muzzle velocity: 458m/s (1503ft/s)
Maximum range: 11,800m (38,700ft)

Towed artillery
A camouflaged 122mm Gun Model 1931/37 towed by a Stalinez ChTZ S-65 artillery tractor.

122mm (4.72in) Gun Model 1931 (A-19) and Model 1931/37 (A-19M)

Design studies for new long-range artillery for the Red Army began in 1927, but the first prototypes were only completed in 1931. After initial trials, these were returned to the factory for extensive modifications; it was not until 1935 that the gun was finally accepted for service. Between 450 and 500 were completed by 1939, when production switched to the Model 1931/37.

Once in service, the Model 1931 began to show problems – the

122mm (4.8in) Gun Model 1931 (A-19)
The A-19 saw action with the Red Army throughout the war: 387 were in service in June 1941, of which 289 remained in May 1945.

122mm (4.8in) Gun Model 1931 (A-19)
Weight (deployed): 7100kg (15,653lb)
Weight (travelling order): 7800kg (17,196lb)
Length: 8.9m (29ft 2in)
Barrel length: 5.48m (20ft) L/45
Width: 2.345m (7ft 8in)
Height: 1.99m (6ft 6in)
Shell weight: 25kg (48lb)
Elevation: –2° to +45°
Traverse: 56°
Rate of fire: 3–4rpm
Muzzle velocity: 800m/s (2640ft/s)
Maximum range: 20,400m (66,930ft)

elevation mechanism was slow and unreliable, while its solid-tyred wheels restricted towing speeds. Production was also hindered by the complex carriage design. The 152mm (5.98in) gun-howitzer M1937 had a more modern carriage; the solution adopted was to convert this to take the barrel of the A-19.

The new gun passed its service trials in 1938 and entered service as the Model 1931/37. As many as 1300 may have been in service at the time of the German invasion; almost 2500 had been completed by the time production ended in 1946.

152mm (5.98in) Howitzer Model 1909/30

The Schneider-designed 152mm (5.98in) Model 1909 howitzer had equipped the Tsar's army during World War I, and remained in service with the Red Army throughout the 1920s. A modernization programme began in 1931; work was initially limited to rechambering to take an increased propellant charge.

Most howitzers retained their original wooden spoked wheels, but from 1937 some were fitted with metal wheels with solid rubber tyres to allow higher towing speeds.

152mm (5.98in) Howitzer Model 1909/30

This is a late-production Model 1909/30 fitted with rubber-tyred disc wheels for towing by trucks or artillery tractors.

152mm (5.98in) Howitzer Model 1909/30

Weight (deployed): 2810kg (6195lb)
Weight (travelling order): 3270kg (7209lb)
Length: 5.84m (19ft 2in)
Barrel length: 1.9m (6ft 3in) L/13.1
Width: 1.89m (6ft 2in)
Height: 1.92m (6ft 4in)
Shell weight: 40kg (88lb)
Elevation: 0° to +41°
Traverse: 2°50'
Rate of fire: 2rpm
Muzzle velocity: 344m/s (1129ft/s)
Maximum range: 8850m (29,035ft)

152mm (5.98in) Howitzer Model 1938 (M-10)

The M-10 used separate-loading ammunition, with eight different charges. One of the more unusual projectiles was the G-530 HEAC anti-concrete shell, which could penetrate more than 1m (3.3ft) of reinforced concrete at a range of 1000m (3280ft).

152mm (5.98in) Howitzer Model 1938 (M-10)
Weight (deployed): 4150kg (9049lb)
Weight (travelling order): 4550kg (10,031lb)
Length: 6.39m (20ft 11in)
Barrel length: 3.7m (12ft 2in) (L/25)
Width: 1.9m (6ft 2in)
Height: 2.09m (6ft 10in)
Shell weight: 40kg (88lb)
Elevation: –1° to +65°
Traverse: 50°
Rate of fire: 3–4rpm
Muzzle velocity: 508m/s (1667ft/s)
Maximum range: 12,400m (40,680ft)

As many as 2600 converted and new-build Model 1909/30s may have been completed by the time that production ended in 1941; the type was the most numerous 152mm (5.98in) howitzer in Soviet service in June 1941. Although the M1909/30 began to be replaced by the new 152mm (5.98in) D-1 howitzer from 1943, it was still in service at the end of the war.

152mm (5.98in) Howitzer Model 1938 (M-10)

By the late 1930s, it was clear that the 152mm (5.98in) howitzers currently in service were at best obsolescent. Design studies for a replacement began in 1937 and prototypes were trialled in the following year. These trials revealed so many structural defects that the design had to be extensively modified and strengthened. The new version, which was adopted in September 1939 as the 152mm (5.98in) Howitzer Model 1938, also incorporated a lengthened barrel.

About 1500 M-10s were completed between 1939 and 1941, when production ended: the type was too complex to produce in the primitive factories set up following the evacuation of Soviet war industries to the Urals.

152mm (5.98in) Howitzer Model 1943 (D-1)
The D-1 was a highly successful design; more than 2800 were completed between 1943 and 1949.

152mm (5.98in) Howitzer M1943 (D-1)
Weight (deployed): 3640kg (8025lb)
Weight (travelling order): 3600kg (7937lb)
Length: 6.7m (22ft)
Barrel length: 3.117m (10ft 3in) L/24.6
Width: 1.8m (5ft 11in)
Height: 1.8m (5ft 11in)
Shell weight: 40kg (88lb)
Elevation: –3° to +63.5°
Traverse: 35°
Rate of fire: 3–4rpm
Muzzle velocity: 508m/s (1667ft/s)
Maximum range: 12,400m (40,690ft)

152mm (5.98in) Howitzer Model 1943 (D-1)

Design studies for a mobile 152mm (5.98in) howitzer based on the carriage of the 122mm (4.8in) M-30 and the barrel of the 152mm (5.98in) M-10 began in 1942. The only significant modification was the addition of a muzzle brake to allow the relatively light carriage to absorb the recoil without damage. Trials were carried out in May 1943 and the type was approved for service in August of that year. Production was able to get under way exceptionally quickly using existing stocks of components for the M-30 and M-10.

The new howitzer was far more mobile than its predecessors, with maximum towing speeds of 40km/h (25mph) on paved roads, 30km/h (19mph) on cobbled/corduroy roads and 10km/h (6mph) off-road. Although it was out-ranged by similar enemy weapons such as the 15cm (5.9in) sFH 18, it was almost 1.8 tonnes (2 tons) lighter, which greatly improved its mobility in the appalling terrain of the Eastern Front.

152mm (5.98in) Gun Model 1910/30

At the end of the Russian Civil War, the Red Army inherited about 25 Schneider-designed 152mm (5.98in) Model 1910 guns. These remained in service throughout the 1920s. The surviving guns were updated from 1930, becoming the Model 1910/30. The most important modifications were:

- Rechambering to accept a larger propellant charge.
- Fitting a large, multi-baffle muzzle brake.
- Lengthening the trail to improve stability when firing at low elevations.

The modernization was considered a success. After the few surviving Model 1910 guns had been converted, production of new-build weapons was authorized and continued until 1935, by which time 152 had been completed. Most of these were still in service at the time of the German invasion, but few seem to have survived beyond 1942.

152mm (5.98in) Gun Model 1910/34

The Model 1910/34 was a further attempt to modernize the Model 1910/30, using the modern split-trail carriage of the 122mm (4.8in) gun Model 1931.

The barrel of the Model 1910/30 was unchanged, but the new carriage dramatically improved mobility, as the

152mm (5.98in) Gun Model 1910/34
A 152mm (5.98in) Gun Model 1910/34 being loaded. A shell's fuse is set and a loader stands by ready to ram the shell into the breech, whilst another cartridge is brought up to be added to those already laid out beside the gun.

152mm (5.98in) Gun Model 1910/34
Weight (deployed): 7100kg (15653lb)
Weight (travelling order): 7820kg (17,240lb) (with limber)
Length: 8.1m (26ft 7in)
Barrel length: 4.3m (14ft 1in) L/29 (without muzzle brake)
Width: 2.34m (7ft 8in)
Height: 1.99m (6ft 6in)
Shell weight: 43.6kg (96lb)
Elevation: –4° to +45°
Traverse: 56°
Rate of fire: 3–4rpm
Muzzle velocity: 650m/s (2133ft/s)
Maximum range: 17,265m (56,640ft)

Limbering up

The crew of a 152mm (5.98in) Model 1937 prepare to move out. The barrel has been pulled back to the travelling position and the gun is mounted on its two-wheeled limber, ready to be hitched to an artillery tractor.

barrel no longer had to be removed for transport. A total of 275 guns were completed between 1934 and 1937, when production was halted in favour of the ML-20.

152mm (5.98in) Gun-Howitzer Model 1937 (ML-20)

This was the final modernization of the Model 1910/30. The barrel was again virtually unchanged, but the new carriage offered greater elevation and traverse. The ML-20 was in production between 1937 and 1947, by which time 6800 had been completed.

The type was one of the most successful Soviet artillery pieces of the war. It out-ranged its main German opponents, such as the 15cm (5.9in) sFH 18, which often allowed it to bring down counter-battery fire without risk of retaliation.

152mm (5.98in) Gun Model 1935 (Br-2)

The first project to develop a long-range 152mm (5.98in) gun began in 1929

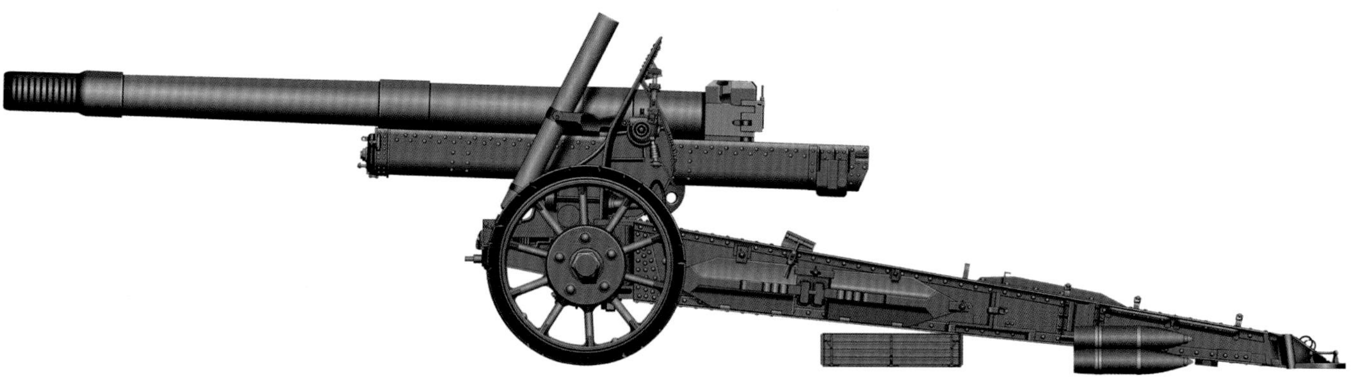

152mm (5.98in) Gun-Howitzer Model 1937 (ML-20)

This is an early-production ML-20 fitted with the solid-tyred spoked wheels of the Model 1910/34.

152mm (5.98in) Gun-Howitzer Model 1937 (ML-20)

Weight (deployed): 7270kg (16,027lb)
Weight (travelling order): 7930kg (17,482lb)
Length: 8.18m (26ft 10in) (with limber; barrel retracted for travel)
Barrel length: 4.3m (14ft 1in) L/29 (without muzzle brake)
Width: 2.35m (7ft 9in)
Height: 2.27m (7ft 5in)
Shell weight: 43.6kg (96lb)
Elevation: –2° to +65°
Traverse: 58°
Rate of fire: 3–4rpm
Muzzle velocity: 650m/s (2133ft/s)
Maximum range: 17,265m (56,640ft)

and resulted in the B-10, intended to be mounted on an unusual tracked carriage. Prototype guns were ready in 1932, but prolonged trials revealed major problems including slow elevation, a poor rate of fire and unacceptably short barrel life.

Various attempts to resolve these problems were unsuccessful before the project was superseded by an official requirement for a trio of heavy artillery pieces – a 152mm (5.98in) gun, plus 203mm (8in) and 280mm (11in)

152mm (5.98in) Gun Model 1935 (Br-2)
Weight (deployed): 18,200kg (40,100lb)
Weight (travelling order): 19,500kg (43,000lb)
Length: 11.44m (37ft 6in)
Barrel length: 7.17m (23ft 6in) L/47.2
Width: 2.49m (8ft 2in)
Height: 3.2m (10ft 6in)
Shell weight: 49kg (108lb)
Elevation: 0° to +60°
Traverse: 8°
Rate of fire: 1 round every 2–3 minutes
Muzzle velocity: 880m/s (2887ft/s)
Maximum range: 27,000m (88,580ft)

152mm (5.98in) Gun Model 1935 (Br-2)
The Br-2 served throughout the war, notably at Kursk in 1943. Br-2s were frequently used in the direct-fire role against German strongpoints in Berlin, as shown above.

howitzers – all of which would use the same tracked carriage.

The Br-2, which was adopted to meet this requirement, had a barrel closely based on that of the B-10, mounted on the tracked carriage of the 203mm (8in) B-4 howitzer. The gun was accepted for service in 1936; an estimated 37 were completed by the time production ended in 1940.

Despite the gun's prolonged development, it still had problems with rapid barrel wear that were never fully solved. Poor mobility was also an issue: the complete gun could be towed for short distances by a Voroshilovets heavy artillery tractor at speeds of up to 8km/h (5mph), but for longer moves, the barrel had to be removed from the carriage and loaded onto a special transporter. Reassembling the gun was a slow business – a minimum of 45 minutes was needed to bring it into action after a long-distance move.

Attempts were made to design a more modern wheeled carriage to permit high-speed towing, but these were unsuccessful until 1955, when the gun was mounted on a new multi-wheeled carriage that allowed long-distance moves without removing the barrel. The updated gun was designated Br-2M and remained in service until the 1970s.

203mm (8in) Howitzer Model 1931 (B-4)

This was another member of the 'family' of weapons sharing a common tracked carriage that was developed in the 1930s. The B-4 was accepted for

203mm Howitzer Model 1931 (B-4)
In the final days of the war, B-4s were frequently used in the direct-fire role against German strongpoints in Berlin, becoming known as 'Stalin's sledgehammer'.

203mm (8in) Howitzer Model 1931 (B-4)
Weight (deployed): 17,700kg (39,022lb)
Weight (travelling order): 19,000kg (41,888lb)
Length: 11.15m (36ft 7in)
Barrel length: 5.087m (16ft 8in) L/25
Width: 2.7m (8ft 10in)
Height: 2.5m (8ft 2in)
Shell weight: 100kg (220lb)
Elevation: 0° to +60°
Traverse: 8°
Rate of fire: 1 round every 2–3 minutes
Muzzle velocity: 607m/s (1990ft/s)
Maximum range: 18,000m (59,055ft)

service in 1934 and probably remained in production until 1944/45, by which time an estimated 870 had been completed. In common with the Br-2, the complete gun could be towed for short distances by a Voroshilovets heavy artillery tractor at speeds of up to 8km/h (5mph); for longer moves, the barrel had to be removed from the carriage and loaded onto a special transporter.

The B-4 remained in service after the war. It was modernized in the mid-1950s with a new four-wheeled carriage that allowed high-speed towing over long distances without removing the barrel. These updated howitzers remained in service until at least the 1970s.

280mm (11in) Howitzer Model 1939 (Br-5)

This was the final member of the 'family' of weapons sharing a common tracked carriage that were developed in the 1930s. Little data is available on this howitzer, but it seems likely that a total of 45 were completed in 1939/40 and that all served throughout the war.

Heavy metal
A battery of 203mm (8in) B-4 howitzers in action. A significant number were captured and taken into German service as the 20.3cm H 503/1(r), seeing action in France and Italy as well on the Eastern Front.

Chapter 3

Infantry Equipment

Soviet infantry training was always basic. In theory, the average conscript could expect to spend three months in a training regiment before being posted to an operational unit. However, even before the war, the expansion of the Red Army (from 885,000 men in 1934 to 1,300,000 in 1939) placed an intolerable strain on the training organization. In some cases, training centres had no barrack blocks, and their primitive kitchens caused repeated cases of food poisoning. In one case, a consignment of rotten fish put 350 conscripts in hospital.

If living conditions were bad, the training itself was crippled by shortages of equipment and the seemingly endless hours reserved for political indoctrination. A depressingly high percentage of conscripts failed to reach basic marksmanship standards. This was scarcely surprising, as many fired no more than five rounds throughout their training and high rates of drunkenness contributed to frequent shooting accidents.

During the war years, the situation was not helped by an official daily ration of 100ml (3.5oz) of vodka; as late as 1944/45, troops were taking wholly unnecessary casualties after drinking themselves insensible. During the siege of Budapest, the German and Hungarian defenders would frequently

Opposite:
House clearing training
Infantry armed with PPD-40 submachine guns and RDG-33 grenades learn the basics of house clearing. Soviet infantry training was basic and brutal – live ammunition was used and fatalities were regarded as proof that the training was realistic.

On the march

Red Army infantry move up to the front line armed with a typical mixture of weapons including PPSh-41 submachine guns, an SVT-40 self-loading rifle and a DP light machine gun.

withdraw from a building, leaving plenty of alcohol lying around for the Russians to find when they followed up. Very few Red Army conscripts could resist such bait and a counterattack next morning was usually a walkover against badly hungover opponents.

When the Red Army went into action in the Winter War against Finland, failings in infantry training were ruthlessly exposed. Soviet infantry and motor rifle units suffered particularly badly. Many were conscripts from Ukraine who lacked even basic cold-weather clothing, and were not acclimatized to the extreme conditions of a Finnish winter. To add to their misery, the ramshackle supply system quickly broke down, and men went without hot food for days at a time. Unsurprisingly, many Red Army casualties (possibly as many as 60,000) were due to hypothermia and disease. The small, but highly motivated Finnish army also inflicted massive casualties, totalling almost 85,000 dead and over 186,000 wounded, while losing no more than 26,000 dead and 44,000 wounded. Many of the Red Army's combat casualties were due to the Communist Party dogma that had largely replaced tactical training since the purges – some senior officers even banned any use of camouflage, as it was 'a sign of cowardice'.

Although the Winter War provided the necessary shock to begin the process of rebuilding an effective Red Army, so much damage had been done by the purges that the work was still far from complete at the time of the German invasion. Although all arms of service had severe problems, the infantry were arguably in the worst position. The Soviet system of conscription did nothing to help matters: the most intelligent and best-educated conscripts tended to be assigned to the NKVD's internal security forces or technical arms of service such as the engineers, leaving the infantry with a high proportion of illiterate or semi-literate peasants and unskilled workers.

The vast majority of infantry and motor rifle formations that were caught up in the early German offensives were woefully ill trained and often did not know how to work effectively with tanks and artillery. Their experienced opponents generally had little difficulty in pinning them down with well-directed artillery and mortar fire, so the unsupported Soviet armour was frequently massacred by anti-tank guns and panzers.

For much of the war, a chronic shortage of trucks forced motor rifle units to deploy most of their men as tank riders (tankodesantniki). Initially, there was little or no special provision for carrying infantry on the tanks. At best, rope 'grab lines' might be lashed to the hull and turret. This added to the already considerable risks run by the riflemen crowded onto the tanks' decks. The official carrying capacity of each class of tank was:

- Heavy tanks: 10–12 men
- Medium tanks: 8–10 men
- Light tanks: 5–6 men

In practice, tanks frequently went into action seriously overloaded: a T-34 might well have up to 15 infantrymen clinging to its hull and turret.

Later-production examples of most Soviet tanks and assault guns were fitted with handrails to make life slightly less hazardous for their passengers, and occasionally logs would be lashed along the sides and rear of tanks' hulls to provide makeshift platforms. Bitterly won experience gradually led to greater

Attack!

An infantry squad launch an attack, equipped with Mosin-Nagant carbines and PPSh-41 submachine guns.

professionalism, but infantry tactics tended to remain crude and costly until the end of the war.

By 1944, despite the Red Army's increasing success, it was facing significant manpower shortages – there was simply no way that its 500-plus divisions could be maintained at full strength. The tank and mechanized formations tended to receive enough replacement personnel to keep at something approaching their authorized strengths, but rifle divisions fared less well.

Although the official strength of a rifle division had steadily dropped from 14,483 in April 1941 to 9380 in July 1943, even this was almost impossible to meet. 'Bayonet' strengths – the numbers of front-line infantry – were even worse. As early as September 1943, 81st Guards Rifle Division was reduced to 3188 men with a bayonet strength of only 539. At the end of 1943, the Germans began to notice that an increasing percentage of prisoners were either under 18 or in their 50s – the Soviet authorities had made desperate attempts to find more manpower. As the Red Army advanced, virtually all men under 60 in the newly 'liberated' territories were forced to join its ranks. Front commanders were being authorized to issue emergency tables of organization and equipment (TO&Es) for under-strength formations. Although there was a fair degree of variation between Fronts, it was not unusual to find provisions for rifle division strengths ranging from 8000 to as low as 4400.

As the war went on, it was increasingly common for penal units to supplement weak rifle divisions. Although evidence is sketchy, it seems likely that penal units

Awaiting the panzers

A PTRS-41 anti-tank rifle in a dangerously exposed position at Kursk. An anti-tank rifle needed good cover and camouflage in order to survive long enough to open fire at its effective range.

(one battalion per army) had existed in the Red Army since the Winter War. Stalin's Order No. 227 of July 1942 greatly increased the number of these units, and they were far more extensively used for the remainder of the war. The first of the new penal battalions was sent to the Stalingrad Front on 22 August 1942, shortly before Germans reached the Volga. After three days of combat, there were only 300 survivors of the unit's 929 prisoners (all former officers).

Manpower shortages

The composition of Soviet penal units was standardized by Zhukov's order of 26 November 1942, 'The Status of Penal Units of the Army'. Penal battalions, or *shtrafbats*, each had an official strength of 360, while penal companies were to have 100 to 150 men per unit who were issued only with arms and ammunition immediately before going into action. (Each penal unit also had a small, heavily armed guard detachment.) It has been estimated that at least 500,000 military personnel and prisoners from the Gulag were sentenced to service in penal battalions during the war.

The number of such units grew rapidly: 2nd Guards Army had seven battalions, while there were ultimately no less than 1049 penal companies in the Red Army as a whole.

Offenders were sentenced to between one month and three months' service in infantry penal battalions and companies. The maximum term was usually applied to those qualifying for the death penalty, the standard punishment for Order No. 227. Convicts sentenced to infantry penal units were eligible for early release and transfer to a Red Army line unit if they sustained a combat wound (the crime was considered to be 'cleansed in blood') or if they had shown outstanding heroism. They could theoretically receive military decorations and were officially fully rehabilitated at the end of their sentences, although those suspected of political disloyalty remained marked men.

Understandably, penal battalion service was viewed by many Soviet prisoners as tantamount to a death sentence. Penal units were forced into attacks by the guns of the guard detachments, who were sometimes reinforced by additional 'blocking units'. The official view was that, as the men were unreliable, they were highly expendable and should be used to reduce losses in regular units by a variety of means, including:

- spearheading attacks on enemy defences.
- their use as 'tramplers' – units that advanced across minefields ahead of the main assault to detonate mines.
- decoy assaults to draw enemy fire – these were most effective in winter operations as penal units were not issued with snow camouflage suits.

Initially, the guard detachments and blocking units were drawn from the most reliable regular army personnel, but following a number of incidents in which such units were not sufficiently ruthless in gunning down retreating troops, they were replaced by NKVD or SMERSH personnel (SMERSH – Smert shpionam, 'Death to spies' – the military counter-intelligence branch of the NKVD, which was formed in April 1943).

By May 1943, each Russian Front commander had 10 to 15 penal battalions at his disposal. It became standard practice for any Soviet offensive to be preceded by the advance of several such battalions, which were usually wiped out.

In contrast to the acute manpower shortages of 1944/45, there was a large enough surplus of infantry weapons to allow production to be cut back in 1944. Output of rifles and carbines dropped from 3,850,000 in 1943 to 2,060,000 in the following year.

REVOLVERS AND PISTOLS

Although not major front-line weapons, durable revolvers and pistols proved invaluable to special forces and partisans.

Nagant Model 1895 Revolver

The Nagant Model 1895 had been the standard service revolver of the Imperial Russian Army and remained in production until 1945. It had an unusual mechanism that, as the hammer was cocked, first turned the cylinder and then moved it forward, closing the gap between the cylinder and the barrel. As the cylinder moved forward, the mouth of the elongated cartridge case was pushed into a conical section at the rear of the barrel and completed the gas seal; this increased the muzzle velocity by 15 to 45m/s (50 to 150ft/s.)

The revolver was primarily carried by Army and NKVD officers, but small numbers were fitted with silencers for use by the *razvedchiki* (scouts) of regimental reconnaissance platoons. Total production of all versions may have reached 2,000,000.

Tokarev TT-33 Pistol

The first Tokarev automatic pistol to enter service with the Red Army was the TT-30, several thousand of which were issued for troop trials in the early 1930s. These led to requests for a number of modifications that were incorporated into the new TT-33 pistol.

Roughly 600,000 TT-33s were produced before the opening of Operation 'Barbarossa'. The type remained in production until 1952,

Nagant Model 1895 Revolver
The Nagant's long service life was largely due to its extreme sturdiness and resistance to abuse. As one former Imperial Russian army officer supposedly remarked: '...if anything went wrong with the Model 1895, you could fix it with a hammer.'

Nagant Model 1895 Revolver
Calibre: 7.62mm (0.3in)
Length: 235mm (10.5in)
Length of barrel: 114mm (4.5in)
Weight: 0.8kg (1.8lb)
Feed system: 7-round cylinder
Muzzle velocity: 272m/sec (750ft/sec)
Effective range: 22m (25 yards)

Tokarev TT-33 Pistol
Calibre: 7.62mm (0.3in)
Length: 194mm (7.6in)
Length of barrel: 116mm (4.6in)
Weight: 0.854kg (1.88lb)
Feed system: 8-round detachable box magazine
Muzzle velocity: 420m/sec (1378ft/sec)
Effective range: 22m (25 yards)

Tokarev TT-33 Pistol
The Germans captured a significant number of TT-33s and used them under the designation Pistole 615(r), firing German 7.63mm Mauser ammunition, which was similar to the Tokarev's 7.62mm round.

by which time 1,700,000 had been completed.

SUBMACHINE GUNS

Marshal Kulik's opposition to submachine guns delayed their adoption by the Red Army until the effectiveness of Finnish Suomi KP/-31 submachine guns in the Winter War forced him to back down.

PPD-40

The initial production model ofVasily Degtyaryov's PPD (Pistolet-Pulemyot Degtyaryova), designated PPD-34, entered service with Soviet forces in 1935. It was only issued in small numbers (mainly to the NKVD) before production switched to the modified PPD-34/38 and its derivative, the PPD-40.

A total of approximately 90,000 weapons (mainly PPD-40s) were completed before the type was replaced by the PPSh-41.

PPD-40
The PPD-40 was a conventional submachine gun of its period, well-made, but difficult to maintain in the field and unsuited to mass production.

PPD-40
Calibre: 7.62mm (0.3in)
Length: 788mm (31.02in)
Length of barrel: 273mm (10.75in)
Weight: 3.2kg (7.05lb)
Feed system: 71-round detachable drum magazine
Muzzle velocity: 489m/sec (1604ft/sec)
Rate of fire: 1000rpm
Effective range: 160m (175 yards)

PPSh-41

Although the PPD-40 was an effective submachine gun, it was not well suited to wartime mass production. The PPSh-41 was carefully designed by Georgi Shpagin to make the greatest possible use of metal stampings to ease production, while its chrome-lined barrel reduced the essential maintenance required in the front line.

Early-production models were fitted with the 71-round drum magazines of the PPD-40, but later examples used a simpler and more reliable 35-round box magazine.

Most were selective-fire weapons, with the settings for single shot or full automatic being made by a small lever just ahead of the trigger. The type proved to be highly effective even in the most severe combat conditions. Soviet factories completed approximately 6,000,000 before production ended in 1945.

PPSh-41

The PPSh-41 had a simple but reliable firing mechanism (above). The type was also prized for its reliability, even in sub-zero temperatures (top).

PPSh-41

Calibre: 7.62mm (0.3in)

Length: 843mm (33.2in)

Length of barrel: 269mm (10.6in)

Weight: 3.63kg (8lb)

Feed system: 71-round detachable drum magazine, or 35-round detachable box magazine

Muzzle velocity: 488m/sec (1601ft/sec)

Rate of fire: 900rpm

Effective range: 200m (219 yards)

PPS-43
Calibre: 7.62mm (0.3in)
Length: 820mm (32.25in)
Length of barrel: 254mm (10in)
Weight: 3.39kg (7.5lb)
Feed system: 35-round detachable box magazine
Muzzle velocity: 488m/sec (1601ft/sec)
Rate of fire: 700rpm
Effective range: 200m (219 yards)

PPS-43
The weapon's design reduced the number of machined components to a bare minimum, drastically cutting production time in comparison with the PPSh-41 and saving over 50 percent in raw steel usage (above). The model was popular with frontline troops (below) as its magazine was much easier to load and less prone to jamming than that of the PPSh-41.

PPS-42 and PPS-43

In 1942, an official requirement was issued for a submachine gun firing the same ammunition as the PPSh-41, but with a lower rate of fire and cheaper and easier to produce. The resulting PPS-42 was certainly a simple design, with most components being sheet-steel stampings, which cut production time and reduced the requirement for skilled labour. It was fitted with a simple folding stock and was only capable of fully automatic fire fed by a 35-round box magazine. More than 46,000 were completed before production switched to the improved PPS-43. This was a very similar weapon, but had a different design of folding stock and safety catch.

Under normal circumstances, the PPS-43 would probably have been adopted as the Red Army's standard submachine gun. However, a massive investment had already been made for PPSh-41 production, which was running at over 1,000,000 a year, that it would have been uneconomical to completely switch production to the PPS. By end of the war, at least 2,000,000 PPS-43s had been made, but in view of the Red Army's massive reserve stocks of submachine guns, production ceased in 1946.

Red Army sniper
A Soviet sniper armed with a Moisin-Nagant Model 1891/30 rifle fitted with a 3.5 magnification PU telescopic sight. Rifles were checked for accuracy and quality – the best were approved for conversion to sniper rifles by fitting telescopic sights and a modified bolt.

RIFLES AND CARBINES

Despite the massive disruption caused by the evacuation of arms factories to the Urals, production of rifles and carbines was maintained throughout the crisis of 1941/42, although such weapons lacked the fine finish of pre-war examples.

Mosin-Nagant Model 1891/30 Rifle

Mosin-Nagant bolt-action rifles entered service with the Imperial Russian Army in 1891. They were not finally superseded until the 1960s, when the last models were replaced by the Dragunov sniper rifle. The Model 1891/30 was the standard Soviet infantry weapon at the time of the German invasion, and was little more than a slightly shorter version of the original 1891 design with modernized sights.

Although it was long and rather clumsy, especially when fitted with the standard 432mm (17in) spike bayonet, it remained in service throughout the war. An estimated 13,000,000 had been completed by the time production ended in 1945.

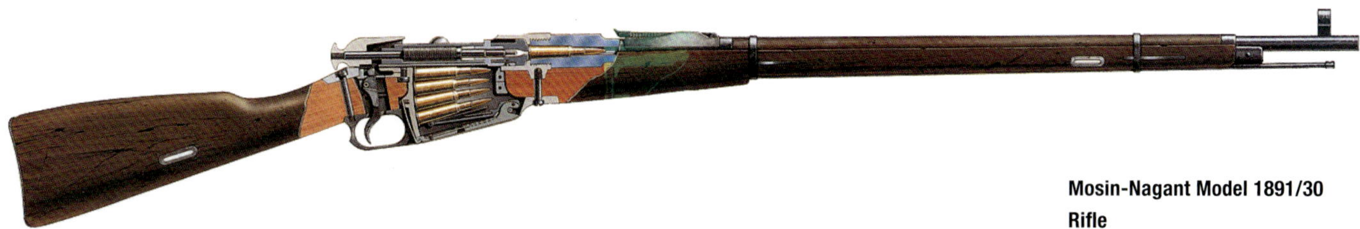

Mosin-Nagant Model 1891/30 Rifle

This was a sturdy, if rather heavy weapon. Its worst feature was an awkward safety mechanism which was operated by rotating a knob at the rear of the bolt. This was prone to freezing solid and troops were taught to urinate on it as an emergency thaw-out technique.

Mosin-Nagant Model 1891/30 Rifle
Calibre: 7.62mm (0.3in)
Length: 1.234m (48.6in)
Length of barrel: 730mm (28.7in)
Weight: 3.8kg (8.4lb)
Feed system: 5-round fixed box magazine
Muzzle velocity: 1100m/sec (3609ft/sec)
Effective range: 400m (437 yards)

Mosin-Nagant Model 1944 Carbine

Although the Model 1944 only saw service at the end of the war, it was a popular weapon as it was far easier to handle than the long Model 1891/30 rifle.

Mosin-Nagant Model 1944 Carbine
Calibre: 7.62mm (0.3in)
Length: 1.03m (40.4in)
Length of barrel: 520mm (20.5in)
Weight: 4.03kg (8.9lb)
Feed system: 5-round fixed box magazine
Muzzle velocity: 800m/sec (2625ft/sec)
Effective range: 300m (328 yards)

Mosin-Nagant Model 1938 and Model 1944 Carbines

By the late 1930s, it was obvious that the M91/30 rifle was too large and awkward to be an effective weapon for engineers, gun crews and the host of other 'non-infantry' troops of the Red Army. A carbine version of the basic Model 1891/30, the Model 1938, was developed to meet this requirement and its handiness led to it being widely issued as an infantry weapon during the war. The Model 1944 was basically a Model 1938 adapted to take a folding spike bayonet. Production began in 1943 and continued until 1948, by which time almost 4,000,000 had been completed.

SVT-40 Self-Loading Rifle

Russian interest in self-loading rifles dated back to the Fedorov Avtomat of 1915. Research in the 1930s led to the development of Fedor Tokarev's SVT-38, which was withdrawn from service after it showed numerous faults in action during the Winter War against Finland in 1939/40. An improved version of the basic design, the SVT-40, entered production in July 1940, and it was

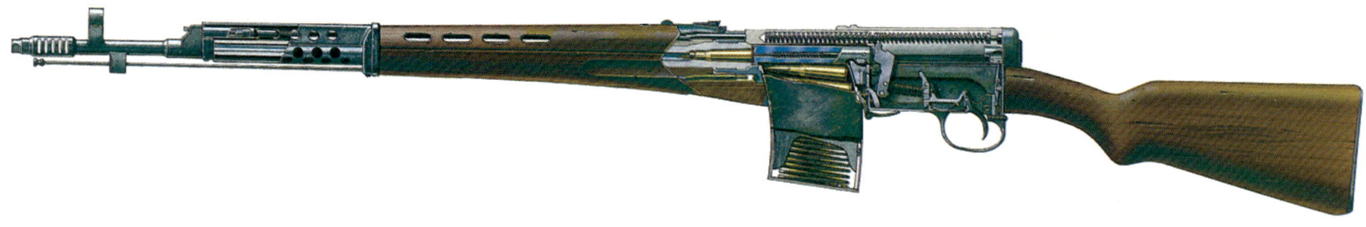

SVT-40

One unusual variant of the SVT was the AVT-40, a selective fire weapon intended for use as a light machine gun. It entered service in mid-1942, but was found to be virtually uncontrollable when set to fully automatic fire, which frequently caused jams and breakages. The problem was so severe that the use of the AVT's automatic fire mode was banned and production ended in the summer of 1943.

SVT-40 Self-Loading Rifle
Calibre: 7.62mm (0.3in)
Length: 1.26m (49.6in)
Length of barrel: 625mm (24.6in)
Weight: 3.85kg (8.5lb)
Feed system: 10-round detachable box magazine
Muzzle velocity: 840m/sec (2756ft/sec)
Effective range: 500m (547 yards)

intended that the type would largely replace the Mosin-Nagant 91/30 in front-line infantry units.

In the aftermath of the German invasion, it was found that the type was too complex for rapid mass production; this complexity also made it difficult for hastily trained conscripts to use the weapon effectively. As a result, production was tapered off in favour of Mosin-Nagant rifles and PPSh submachine guns.

MACHINE GUNS

The Red Army's wartime machine guns were reliable, but very heavy – as late as 1943 even the new Goryunov SG-43 was issued with a wheeled mount complete with an armoured shield.

DP Light Machine Gun

The DP was another of Vasily Degtyaryov's designs that was adopted as the Red Army's standard light machine gun in 1928. Although it was

DP Light Machine Gun

With only six working parts, the DP could tolerate considerable dirt and carbon fouling – so much so that Russian troops joked that the weapon fired best after it had been buried in sand.

DP Light Machine Gun
Calibre: 7.62mm (0.3in)
Length: 1.27m (50in)
Length of barrel: 604mm (23.8in)
Weight: 9.2kg (20.11lb)
Feed system: 47-round detachable pan magazine
Muzzle velocity: 840m/sec (2755ft/sec)
Rate of fire: 500–600rpm
Effective range: 800m (875 yards)

Maxim Model 1910/30 Medium Machine Gun
A Maxim in action during the Winter War against Finland – the gun lacks the large water filler port and cap added to most Maxims in 1940/41.

Maxim Model 1910/30 Medium Machine Gun
Calibre: 7.62mm (0.3in)
Length: 1.07m (42in)
Length of barrel: 720mm (28.3in)
Weight: 63kg (138.9lb)
Feed system: 250-round belt
Muzzle velocity: 862.6m/sec (2830ft/sec)
Rate of fire: 520–580rpm
Effective range: 1000m (1094 yards)

an effective weapon, it suffered from a poorly designed bipod and rather fragile 47-round 'pan' magazines that were awkward to load. The DP, together with the modernized DPM and RP-46, remained in service with the Red Army until the 1960s. Production figures for all variants probably totalled 795,000.

Maxim Model 1910/30 Medium Machine Gun

The Maxim Model 1910/30 that equipped the Red Army throughout the war was essentially the same machine gun that had entered service with the Imperial Russian Army in 1910. The type was modernized in 1930 with the introduction of new ammunition – a heavier, streamlined bullet that increased the gun's theoretical maximum range to almost 5000m (16,400ft). Apart from this, the only other significant modification was to replace the original small filler port for the water jacket with a much larger one, covered by a hinged cap. This allowed water to be poured in far more easily, while in winter, snow or ice could be crammed into the water jacket.

By the middle of the war, it was clear that the Maxim was at best obsolescent. One report from 1st Ukrainian Front noted that: '…the Maxim 7.62mm machine gun is quite satisfactory in regard to its reliability and stability. It is durable, can deliver sustained fire and it is trusted by the soldiers. However, its weight renders it totally ineffectual; it reduces manoeuvrability, forcing the crews to lag behind their units in the advance and sometimes leaves attacks without fire support. Combat experience with heavy machine guns shows that all those weighing more than 40kg (88lb) are a burden in an offensive and do not meet battlefield mobility requirements'.

Although the Maxim was replaced by the Goryunov SG-43 in Soviet service after 1945, many were supplied to China and saw action in the Korean War.

Goryunov SG-43 Medium Machine Gun

By 1939/40, it was recognized that Maxim was overdue for replacement

Goryunov SG-43 Medium Machine Gun

The Goryunov's original wheeled mount was very heavy and later production guns were issued with a lighter tripod mount. (These guns also had longitudinally fluted barrels, which saved weight and improved air cooling.)

Goryunov SG-43 Medium Machine Gun

Calibre: 7.62mm (0.3in)
Length: 1.15m (45.3in)
Length of barrel: 720mm (28.3in)
Weight: 41kg (90.4lb)
Feed system: 250-round belt
Muzzle velocity: 862.6m/sec (2830ft/sec)
Rate of fire: 500–700rpm
Effective range: 1100m (1200 yards)

DShK Heavy Machine Gun
Calibre: 12.7mm (0.5in)
Length: 1.625m (64in)
Length of barrel: 1.07m (42.1in)
Weight: 157kg (346.13lb)
Feed system: 50-round belt
Muzzle velocity: 850m/sec (2788ft/sec)
Rate of fire: 600rpm
Effective range: 2000m (2187 yards)

DShK Heavy Machine Gun
Weighing in at 157kg (346lb) on its wheeled mount, the DShK could only be manhandled for very short moves, but it had a useful performance against light AFVs, being capable of penetrating 15mm (0.59in) armour at 500m (1640ft).

by a lighter, more modern machine gun. The designer, Peter Maximovitch Goryunov, was already working on a new tank-mounted machine gun; this was reworked as a medium machine gun, retaining its belt-fed, air-cooled design.

A two-wheeled carriage, similar to that of the Maxim, was used. Early examples even had a small shield, which added significantly to the all-up weight. Reliability was good, partly due to the heavy barrel with its chrome-plated bore, and the type was accepted for service in 1943 as the SG-43.

Although it was intended to replace the obsolescent Maxim, production could not keep up with the Army's demand, and both types remained in service for the duration of the war.

DShK Heavy Machine Gun

The DShK (Degtyaryova-Shpagina Krupnokaliberny, 'Degtyaryov-Shpagin Large-Calibre') entered service with the Red Army in 1938 as an infantry heavy support weapon, incorporating features designed by both Vasily Degtyaryov and Georgi Shpagin. The type was also fitted to many AFVs and saw widespread use in the AA role.

PTRD-41 Anti-Tank Rifle
The PTRD had an immense muzzle blast which often betrayed it's firing position. It also tended to jam during cartridge ejection – crews sometimes tried to cure this by dipping rounds in oil before loading, but oiled ammunition acted as a magnet for dirt, which could itself cause jams.

ANTI-TANK RIFLES

Although out-classed by later German AFVs, the 14.5mm (0.57in) round fired by PTRD and PTRS anti-tank rifles was very powerful and was adopted for the post-war KPV heavy machine gun.

PTRD-41

The Red Army was one of the last major armies to be issued with anti-tank rifles. A design by Rukavishnikov was issued for troop trials in 1939, but this proved to be too complex and unreliable. Marshal Kulik, the head of

PTRD-41
Calibre: 14.5mm (0.57in)
Length: 2.02m (79.5in)
Length of barrel: 1.35m (53in)
Weight: 17.3kg (38.14lb)
Feed system: Bolt-action, single-shot
Muzzle velocity: 1012m/sec (3320ft/sec)
Effective range: 400m (1312ft)
Armour penetration: 25mm (0.98in) at 500m (547 yds)

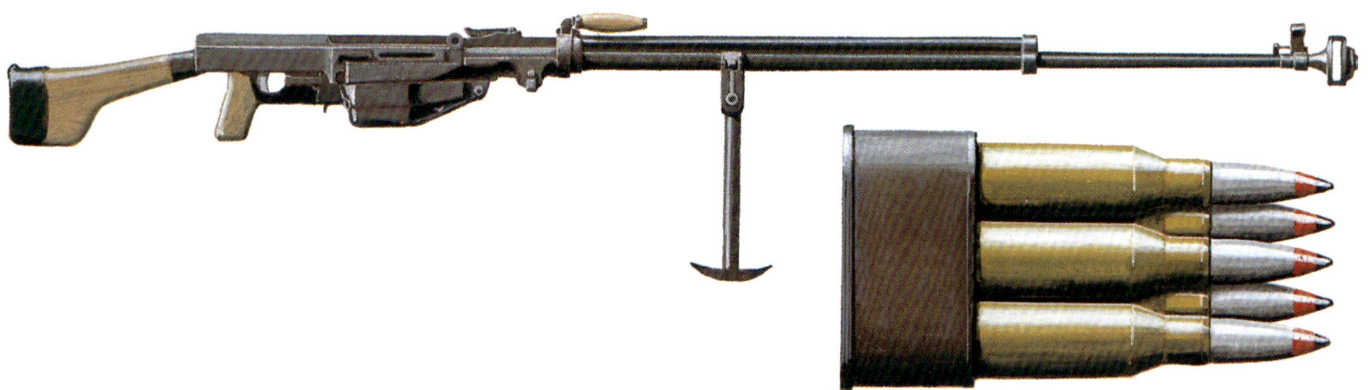

PTRS-41 Anti-Tank Rifle
The PTRS was even heavier than the PTRD and less reliable as the considerable fouling produced by the 14.5mm (0.57in) ammunition tended to jam its gas-operated mechanism.

PTRS-41
Calibre: 14.5mm (0.57in)
Length: 2.108m (83in)
Length of barrel: 1.219m (48in)
Weight: 20.9kg (46lb)
Feed system: 5-round box magazine
Muzzle velocity: 1012m/sec (3320ft/sec)
Effective range: 400m (1312ft)
Armour penetration: 25mm (0.98in) at 500m (547 yds)

the Red Army's Artillery Directorate, was opposed to the whole concept of infantry anti-tank weapons, and Vasily Degtyaryov's simple, single-shot PTRD-41 had to be rushed into service as an emergency measure in July 1941, just after the German invasion. Although it was a fairly effective close-range weapon against the lighter German AVFs of 1941/42, its usefulness rapidly declined as newer and better-protected panzers were encountered.

Attempts were made to maintain its effectiveness by training crews to fire at tank vision ports at long range rather than attempting to penetrate the vehicles' armour. The idea proved to be impractical: although the PTRD-41's maximum range was about 1000m (3280ft), the standard iron sights were ineffective against such small targets beyond 300m (984ft). Although the muzzle brake was effective, its blast created a very visible cloud of dust or snow on firing, which frequently gave away firing positions. Despite these limitations, about 5000 were completed by the time production ceased in 1945.

PTRS-41

The PTRS-41 entered service within a few months of the PTRD-41. Its designer, Sergei Simonov, had chosen a semi-automatic configuration for the weapon as it was believed that the improved rate of fire would make it a more effective tank-killer than the PTRD-41. In practice, it was found to be very heavy and increasingly ineffective against tanks. Nonetheless, like the PTRD-41, it was kept in service until the end of the war,

Private, Anti-Tank Battalion
This gunner in standard summer uniform is armed with a PTRD anti-tank rifle. This view emphasises the sheer bulk of the weapon, which made it an awkward load when its two-man crew had to move to a new firing position.

primarily for use against light AFVs such as armoured cars and APCs.

FLAMETHROWERS

The Red Army pioneered the use of thickened flame fuel which dramatically improved the maximum range of their flamethrowers.

ROKS-2 & ROKS-3 Flamethrowers

These were the principal Soviet wartime infantry flamethrowers: the ROKS-2 was an elaborate design dating from 1935 with the fuel cylinders disguised to resemble a standard infantry backpack and a flame projector in the shape of a normal rifle. The practical value of this disguise was questionable; wartime production shifted to the ROKS-3 with conventional fuel cylinders and a simplified flame gun.

GRENADES

Soviet infantry relied heavily on grenades throughout the war, referring to them as their 'pocket artillery'.

ROKS-3

The ROKS-2 flamethrower was a wartime expedient version of the ROKS-2. It was designed for mass production, and performance was improved with the introduction of thicker fuel.

ROKS-2 & ROKS-3 Flamethrowers

Weight: 22.7kg (50lb)
Fuel capacity: 9 litres (2 gallons)
Range: 35–45m (38–49 yards)
Duration of fire: 6–8 seconds

Molotov cocktails

The Molotov cocktail was one of the most widely used weapons of World War II. (Left to right: An improvised Russian example made from a vodka bottle, an 'official' Red Army version, British, Japanese and Finnish variants.)

Below: *Narodnoe Opolcheniye* (People's Militia) training with Molotov cocktails, winter 1941/42.

Molotov Cocktails

The idea of converting domestic glass bottles into incendiary grenades seems to have originated during the Spanish Civil War. These weapons were later used very effectively by Finnish forces against Red Army tanks during the Winter War of 1939/40. At the time, Molotov was Stalin's foreign minister, and the Finns jokingly referred to the grenades as 'Molotov cocktails'.

The name was quickly adopted in the West, but was regarded as subversive in the paranoid world of Stalin's Russia. As a result, when the Red Army adopted the weapons in the chaotic aftermath of the German invasion, they were officially termed *butylkas goryuche smes'yu* ('bottles with flammable mixture'). Initially, these were 'homemade' by units from petrol-filled vodka bottles with oily rags tied around the necks that were lit immediately before throwing. Later, factory-produced 'incendiary liquid kits' were issued. These were no more than elastic bands and two glass tubes filled with sulphuric acid for attachment to petrol-filled bottles – the acid ignited the petrol when the bottle shattered on impact with its target. Despite the obvious risks to the user, these incendiaries remained in front-line use throughout the war.

F1

The F1 fragmentation grenade, generally known as the *limonka* (lemon), was a pre-war design derived from the French F1 grenade. It remained in service (and production) well after 1945.

RDG-33

The RDG-33 fragmentation grenade was another 1930s' design that proved to be too complex for wartime mass production. It was gradually superseded by the much simpler RG42.

RG-42

The RG-42 was a very simple cylindrical fragmentation grenade that was far easier to mass-produce than pre-war designs.

RPG-40

The RPG-40 (Ruchnaya Protivotankovaya Granata – handheld anti-tank grenade) was the first purpose-designed Soviet anti-tank grenade. Although it entered service in 1940, it was a crude weapon that was little different from the earliest anti-tank grenades that were undergoing trials at the end of World War I. In common with these, it relied purely on the blast effect of its large explosive charge, which could penetrate 20mm (0.79in) of armour.

RPG-43

The RPG-43 was the first Soviet-designed HEAT anti-tank grenade that began entering service in 1943. This was

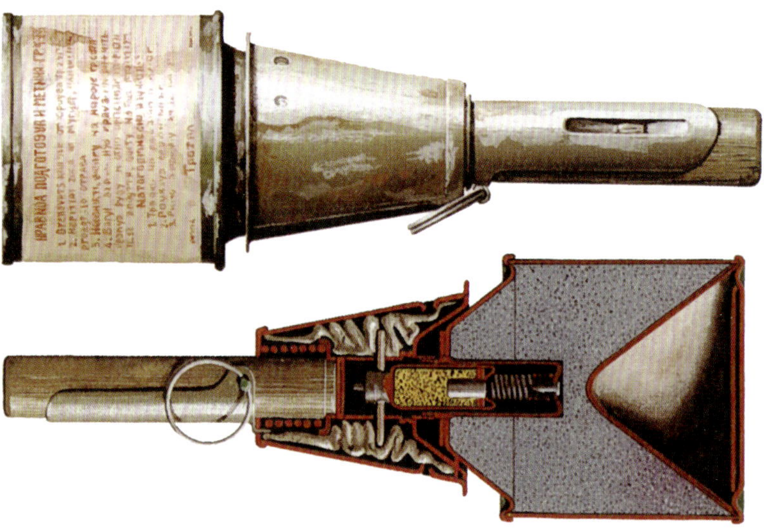

RPG-43

The RPG-43 resembled an oversized stick grenade with a 95mm HEAT warhead. When thrown, a cylindrical metal cone was released from the rear of the grenade and held by fabric strips to stabilize flight and increase accuracy.

RPG-43
Length: N/k
Diameter: 95mm (3.74in)
Weight: 1.247kg (2.75lb)
Explosive: 612g (1.35lb) TNT
Fuse: Impact
Throwing range: 18.28m (20 yards)
Armour penetration: 75mm (2.95in)

a far more sophisticated weapon than the RPG-40 with a greatly improved armour-piercing performance.

MINES

The Red Army used enormous numbers of mines – at Kursk Soviet troops laid 503,663 anti-tank mines and 439,348 anti-personnel mines.

Anti-Personnel Mines: PMD Series

These were all simple wooden-cased mines with few metal components, and were very difficult targets for wartime mine detectors. The PMD-6, which entered service in 1939, was very crude with poor safety measures and proved to be almost as dangerous to the Red Army as to the enemy.

The later developments of the type were less hazardous to their users, but as late as 1943, Red Army combat engineers preferred to use stocks of captured German mines whenever possible. The entire PMD series were blast mines that had a common design of an explosive-filled wooden box with a hinged lid. A slot in the lid pressed down against a retaining pin, which held back the striker. When sufficient pressure was applied to the box lid, the retaining pin was released, allowing the striker to hit the detonator.

Grenades
A defensive position well-supplied with grenades – three RDG-33s in the foreground with two RPG-40s behind them.

Anti-Personnel Mines Compared					
Type	PMD-6	PMD-6M	PMD-7	PMD-7ts	PMD-57
Total weight	400g (0.88lb)	400g (0.88lb)	400g (0.88lb)	400g (0.88lb)	N/k
Weight of explosives	200g (0.44lb)	200g (0.44lb)	75g (0.165lb) or 200g (0.44lb)	50g (0.11lb) or 75g (0.165lb)	400g (0.88lb)
Length	198mm (7.8in)	190mm (7.48in)	152mm (6in)	152mm (6in)	200mm (7.87in)
Width	85mm (3.46in)	89mm (3.5in)	76mm (3in)	76mm (3in)	100mm (3.94in)
Height	65mm (2.56in)	65mm (2.56in)	51mm (2in)	51mm (2in)	80mm (3.15in)
Operating pressure	1kg (2.2lb) to 10kg (22lb)	6kg (13.22lb)	1kg (2.2lb) to 9kg (19.84lb)	1kg (2.2lb) to 9kg (19.84lb)	19kg (41.89lb)

Mine clearing
A Waffen-SS combat engineer cautiously lifts a Russian wooden-cased PMD anti-personnel mine.

All PMD mines were prone to failure, as their wooden cases deteriorated quickly. Some variants used 50mm (1.96in) mortar bombs instead of the normal blocks of explosives.

DOG MINES

The Red Army formed anti-tank dog units as early as 1935. Each dog carried 10–12kg (22–26lb) of explosives in two canvas pouches, detonated by pressure on an upright wooden lever. The idea was that the dogs would be trained to destroy enemy tanks by diving under them; this would push the lever back, triggering the explosives.

Dogs were trained by being fed under tanks and were gradually acclimatized to the noise and smells of revving engines and gunfire. Peacetime exercises seemed to indicate that the theory was sound, but almost everything went wrong when the first units saw combat in 1941.

The first problem was that the dogs associated food with the smells of the Russian tanks used in their training, and

Anti-Tank Mines

TMD-B

This was another wooden-cased mine that was hard to detect, but prone to rot if buried in wet ground. Rotting cases could cause the type to detonate under pressure of as little as 3kg (6.6lb) instead of the designed 200–300kg (440–661lb).

TMD-40 AND TM-35

The TMD-40 was a lighter wooden-cased mine, with similar advantages and drawbacks to those experienced with the TMD-B.

The TM-35 was a conventional metal-cased mine, which was far more durable than its wooden equivalents.

TMD-B

Weight: 9–10kg (19.8–22lb)
Explosive content: 5–7kg (11–15.4lb) TNT or picric acid
Length: 320mm (12.6in)
Width: 290mm (11.42in)
Height: 160mm (6.3in)
Operating pressure: 200–300kg (440–661lb)

TMD-40

Weight: 5kg (11lb)
Explosive content: 3.6kg (8lb) TNT
Length: 600mm (23.6in)
Width: N/k
Height: 100mm (3.94in)
Operating pressure: 250kg (551lb)

TM-35

Weight: 4.75kg (10.47lb)
Explosive content: 2.8kg (6.17lb) TNT
Length: 220mm (8.66in)
Width: 216mm (8.5in)
Height: 59mm (2.32in)
Operating pressure: 250kg (551lb) (estimated)

made straight for any Soviet AFVs in the area as soon as they were released. Secondly, many dogs understandably panicked in the noise and chaos of the battlefield and ran back to Russian lines in search of their handlers, often killing them as they jumped into their trenches. Soviet propaganda claimed that anti-tank dogs destroyed a total of 300 German AFVs, but the actual number seems to be no more than 30. The whole concept was abandoned after 1942.

Anti-tank dogs
A detachment of dogs on their way to the front – the whole concept sickened many dog trainers, some of whom went so far as to openly criticize the programme, complaining that, not content with the human sacrifice of the war, the Red Army was now slaughtering dogs. Many of these outspoken critics ended up in penal battalions.

CHAPTER 4

Soviet Aircraft

The pre-war Red Air Force was subjected to considerable interference from Stalin. His interest had the malign effect of ensuring that all reports on it were wildly optimistic. This 'spin' became outright faking where statistics were concerned, with false figures being routinely submitted for everything from aircraft production to aircrew training.

The endemic faking of data throughout the Stalin era means that statistics relating to the Red Air Force are even more uncertain than those for the Red Army, but it had at least 10,000 front-line aircraft at the time of the German invasion, of which roughly half were serviceable.

Luftwaffe attacks on the first day of Operation 'Barbarossa' destroyed roughly 800 of these on the ground, while German fighters shot down a further 400 in the same period. At this time, equipment varied wildly, ranging from the modern to the antique. Early examples of the ultra-modern Pe-2 bomber were in service alongside more than a thousand antiquated I-15bis fighter biplanes dating from the mid-1930s.

STRUCTURE

The wartime Red Air Force comprised the following elements:

Opposite:
Bombing up
A mixture of FAB-100 and FAB 250 bombs being unpacked from their crates in readiness for loading onto Pe-2 light bombers at a forward airstrip.

Shturmovik
An early production single-seat Shturmovik in snow camouflage, winter 1941/42.

VVS – *Voenno-Vozdushnye Sily Krasnoi Armii* (Military Air Forces of the Red Army)

The term VVS is sometimes loosely used to refer to the entire Red Air Force, but more correctly covers tactical air force units and formations that were grouped into air armies in 1942.

The VVS was always the largest component of the Red Air Force. It expanded throughout the war – notably in December 1944, when ADD, the strategic bomber force, was demoted to become the 18th Air Army.

ADD – *Aviatsiia Dalnego Deistviya* (Long Range Aviation)

This was formed in March 1942 with long-range, but largely obsolete, aircraft. Although nominally a strategic bombing force, it rarely operated in this role, as it tended to have its units assigned piecemeal to various air armies in need of reinforcements. An estimated 43 per cent of all ADD sorties were flown in close support of ground forces, with the balance split between interdiction raids on Axis supply lines and air transport duties, plus no more than a token number of attacks on Berlin and the Ploesti oil refineries.

As noted above, in December 1944, the ADD was absorbed into the VVS as the 18th Air Army. This was probably a tacit recognition that the increasing ability of the RAF and USAAF to strike at targets in Eastern Europe had left the ADD without any real role.

PVO Strany – *Protivovozdushinaia Oborona Strany* (Air Defence of the Interior)

This was an air defence command controlling interceptor fighters, AA units and the civilian home defence organization. Although its main role was to protect major cities and industrial complexes, its interceptors and AA units were often redeployed to reinforce the VVS.

VVS VMF – *Vozduzhnye Vooruzhennye Sily Voenno-Morskovo Flota* (Naval Aviation)

Naval Aviation's primary roles were to provide maritime reconnaissance and anti-submarine patrols, besides giving air cover for naval operations. In June 1941, it had 1445 combat aircraft based around the Black Sea and the Baltic. The majority of these (roughly 55 per cent) were interceptors, 25 per cent reconnaissance aircraft, 14 per cent bombers and 6 per cent torpedo bombers. Almost the entire inventory was obsolete or obsolescent; unsurprisingly, Naval Aviation took heavy losses in the early stages of the war. By late 1943, it had been rebuilt to a strength of more than 1000 aircraft, including 123 torpedo bombers and almost 200 Shturmoviks. The latter had proved to be effective in attacking torpedo boats and small escort vessels.

GVF – *Grazhdanskii Vozdushnyi Flot* (Civil Air Fleet)

The civil air fleet was mobilized immediately after the German invasion and reorganized into air transport units tasked with various duties including: 'Airlift of ammunition, weapons and POL for ground and VVS forces, maintenance of communications between the staffs of the ground forces and air armies, dropping or landing airborne forces, evacuation of the wounded… assistance to partisans… reconnaissance and occasional bombing.'

GVF units flew 1,595,943 sorties during the war, carrying more than 1,500,000 personnel, of whom at least 100,000 were dropped or landed behind enemy lines. Over 123,958 tonnes (122,000 tons) of cargo were carried, including 25,400 tonnes (25,000 tons) of ammunition

Polikarpov I-16s

A flight of I-16s in the first months of the war. The vulnerable tight 'vic' formation is typical of this period – lacking radios, pilots had to watch for their flight leader's hand signals, and such close formations made it easier for them to keep him in sight.

and 78,235 tonnes (77,000 tons) of weapons and rations.

Soviet military doctrine emphasized the need for combined arms operations involving full coordination of air and ground forces. The 1939 Field Service Regulations stressed that aviation should '…act in close operational-tactical contact with ground forces', besides carrying out attacks on deep objectives and air superiority missions. However, the Winter War showed major failings, including poor navigation, an almost total lack of experience of operating at night or in bad weather, and indifferent air gunnery. The VVS had overwhelming numerical superiority and initially deployed at least 800 fighters and bombers in the Leningrad Military District against the 120 aircraft of the Finnish Air Force. Despite feeding in reinforcements throughout the war, the Russians lost 579 aircraft against only 62 Finnish.

No real improvements had been made by the time of the German invasion, when the majority of newly qualified Soviet pilots could do little more than take off and land. When combined with manufacturing faults in many of the new aircraft entering service in 1940/41, the results were devastating. Alarming numbers of early-production MiG-3s had faulty gun synchronization gear and shot their propellers off, while the wooden LaGG-3 had so many defects that it was dubbed *Lakirovanny Garantirovanny Grab*

Flight of Yak-9s
Yak-9D long-range fighters of a Guards unit over the Crimea, 1944. The issue of radios allowed the adoption of loose formations such as this in which each pilot could concentrate on searching for the enemy instead of constantly watching his leader.

('varnished guaranteed coffin') by its hapless pilots.

AIR DEFENCE

Soviet air defence was equally primitive at the beginning of the war. So many fighters had been lost in the first weeks of Operation 'Barbarossa' that a motley collection of obsolete and obsolescent types such as the I-16 had to be kept in service to provide some semblance of air cover for the hard-pressed Red Army. Soviet radar development had been badly disrupted by Stalin's purges, and there was nothing comparable to the sophisticated British and German radar systems. Although a number of lend-lease British and US radars were received from 1942 onwards to supplement a handful of Soviet sets, there were never enough to provide coverage for anything more than a few high-value targets well behind the front line. This forced Russian fighters to fly standing patrols little different from those of World War I – a highly inefficient form of air cover. German air superiority in 1941/42 was so complete that the *Luftwaffe* came to regard the Eastern Front as an operational training area for its fighter aircrew; several German aces (such as Erich Hartmann, with 352 victories) shot down phenomenal numbers of VVS aircraft.

In April 1942, Stavka appointed General Novikov as Commander of the VVS and Deputy Commissar for Aviation. He immediately set about rejuvenating the Red Air Force by combining Front and Army air units into combined air armies. These large formations maximized the effective use of frontal aviation and allowed concentrations of air power in support of ground operations. Each air army was allocated to support a Front. Close cooperation was ensured by placing the air army's deputy commander and his staff with the Front HQ. The Front and air army commanders jointly worked out operational plans, with the Front commander determining the priority of missions.

The first air armies were formed in May 1942. Others followed in June, July, August and November, by which time 13 separate air armies had been formed. Each air army consisted of two fighter divisions (each with four regiments) and two mixed air divisions (each formed from two fighter and two ground attack regiments). Additional units were added – generally a bomber regiment, a reconnaissance regiment, a night bomber regiment and a training regiment. A gradual process of standardization ensured that each regiment was equipped with a single type of aircraft to eliminate the logistical problems inherent in trying to maintain a variety of aircraft types. The strength of each air regiment was increased from two squadrons to three, giving a total of 32 aircraft per regiment. The centralization of air regiments also simplified operational planning, logistics, training, maintenance and command.

Although the *Luftwaffe* never lost its qualitative and technological advantages, and continued to run up an impressive tally of victories, it was a wasting asset, unable to win the war of attrition to which it had been committed. In contrast, the Red Air Force could

Red Air Force Strengths and Losses					
	1941	**1942**	**1943**	**1944**	**1945**
Total strength	29,900	33,000	55,000	68,100	58,300
Combat losses	10,300	7800	11,200	9700	4100
Non-combat losses	7600	4300	11,300	15,100	6900

absorb its tremendous losses, thanks to high rates of production of proven aircraft types, backed up by large-scale lend-lease deliveries. By 1945, it had an estimated 16,000 aircraft in front-line service, backed up by substantial reserves. In comparison, the *Luftwaffe* had roughly 2000 machines, most of which were non-operational due to crippling fuel shortages.

FIGHTER AIRCRAFT

Polikarpov I-15 and I-153

The prototype I-15 first flew in October 1933 and entered service in 1934. It was a typical biplane fighter of its era, unusual only in the design of its upper gull wing. This feature was unpopular with many pilots, who felt that it dangerously restricted their field of view, but 674 were completed before

Polikarpov I-15

An I-15 of the VVS in the mid-1930s. The upper gull wing restricted the pilot's field of view and small windows were fitted below the windscreen in an attempt to give a degree of forward and downward vision. These were generally felt to be inadequate and the I-15bis adopted a conventional upper wing.

I-15
Type: Single-seat fighter
Length: 6.10m (20ft)
Wingspan: 9.75m (32ft)
Height: 2.2m (7ft 3in)
Wing area: 23.55m² (236ft²)
Empty weight: 1012kg (2231lb)
Loaded weight: 1415kg (3120lb)
Maximum take-off weight: N/k
Powerplant: 1 × M-22 radial engine, 353kW (473hp)
Maximum speed: 350km/h (220mph)
Range: 500km (310 miles)
Service ceiling: 7250m (23,800ft)
Rate of climb: 7.6m/s (1490ft/min)
Wing loading: 65kg/m² (13lb/ft²)
Armament: 4 × 7.62mm (0.3in) PV-1 machine guns, plus up to 100kg (220lb) of bombs or 6 × RS-82 rockets

Polikarpov I-153
A Polikarpov I-153 on patrol over Sebastapol, 1942. By this stage in the war the biplane was outdated and unable to match German fighters of the era.

I-153
Type: Single-seat fighter
Length: 6.17m (20ft 3in)
Wingspan: 10m (32ft 9in)
Height: 2.8m (9ft 2in)
Wing area: 22.14m² (238.3ft²)
Empty weight: 1452kg (3201lb)
Loaded weight: 1960kg (4221lb)
Maximum take-off weight: 2110kg (6652lb)
Powerplant: 1 × Shvetsov M-62 radial engine, 597kW (800hp)
Maximum speed: 444km/h (280mph) at 4600m (15,100ft)
Range: 470km (292 miles)
Service ceiling: 10,700m (35,000ft)
Rate of climb: 15m/s (2985ft/min)
Armament: 4 × 7.62mm (0.3in) ShKAS machine guns, plus up to 100kg (220lb) of bombs or 6 × RS-82 rockets

production switched to the I-15bis. This had a longer-span, conventional upper wing. It remained in production until 1940, by which time at least 2400 had been made.

Almost 350 I-15s saw service with the Chinese Nationalists against the Japanese during the 1930s; a further 116 equipped Republican fighter squadrons (alongside at least 230 licence-built by CASA near Madrid) during the Spanish Civil War. More than 1000 I-15bis still equipped VVS units at the time of the German invasion, when it operated primarily in the ground attack role. By late 1942, all surviving aircraft were relegated to second-line duties.

The I-153 was a rarity – a biplane fighter with a retractable undercarriage. The type was essentially a development of the I-15/I-15bis and entered service in 1939. Production ran from 1939 until 1941, by which time more than 3400 had been completed.

Polikarpov I-16

The little I-16 was arguably the world's most advanced fighter when the first examples were delivered to the VVS in 1934/35. At that time, biplane fighters such as the He-51 and the Gloster Gauntlet still equipped *Luftwaffe* and RAF fighter squadrons. For all their high speed and manoeuvrability, early examples of the I-16 had significant problems, including a forward-sliding cockpit canopy that restricted the pilot's visibility and that tended to jam shut during forced landings.

The retractable undercarriage was operated by a hand crank that gradually stiffened up as the wheels were raised; it wasn't uncommon for the mechanism to jam halfway through the process. Pilots were issued with wire-cutters to sever the undercarriage cables in an emergency. That dropped the wheels, but there was no guarantee that they would safely lock in the 'down' position.

The cockpit canopy problem was relatively easy to solve – later variants of the I-16 were completed with open cockpits and just a small curved windscreen. However, it seems that the issues with the undercarriage were never fully resolved throughout the aircraft's service life.

A total of 276 I-16s equipped Republican squadrons during the Spanish Civil War. They quickly demonstrated their superiority over the Condor Legion's He-51s and most other Nationalist fighters until the arrival of the first Bf 109s in 1937 redressed the balance. The I-16 also played a prominent role in combat against the Japanese at Khalkhin Gol in 1939, where it suffered heavy losses.

Polikarpov I-16, Type 24

The I-16 of Lev Shestakov, commander of the 69th Fighter Regiment, Odessa, 1941. Shestakov was a veteran of the Spanish Civil War and was credited with 26 victories when he was killed in action in 1944.

I-16 Type 24
Type: Single-seat fighter
Length: 6.13m (20ft 1in)
Wingspan: 9m (29ft 6in)
Height: 3.25m (10ft 8in)
Wing area: 14.5m^2 (156.1ft^2)
Empty weight: 1490kg (3285lb)
Loaded weight: 1941kg (4279lb)
Maximum take-off weight: 2095kg (4619lb)
Powerplant: 1 × Shvetsov M-63 radial engine, 820kW (1100hp)
Maximum speed: 525km/h (326mph) at 3000m (9845ft)
Range (with drop tanks): 700km (435 miles)
Service ceiling: 9700m (31,825ft)
Rate of climb: 14.7m/s (2900ft/min)
Wing loading: 134kg/m^2 (27lb/ft^2)
Armament: 2 × 7.62mm (0.3in) ShKAS machine guns, 2 × 20mm (0.79in) ShVAK cannon, plus 6 × RS-82 rockets or up to 500kg (1102lb) of bombs

Take-off
An I-16 taxis out in the summer of 1941. The fins of three RS-82 rockets are just visible under the starboard wing.

At least 110 were shot down, many in combat with the highly manoeuvrable Nakajima Ki-27 fighter.

Unsurprisingly, a report issued in the same year concluded that the I-16 had reached the limit of its development potential. By 1941, it was gradually being replaced by the LaGG-3, MiG-3 and Yak-1 fighters. However, large numbers were still in service in June 1941, when it represented about 40 per cent of the total Russian fighter force and 38 per cent of the 4226 fighters based in the western military districts facing the German invasion.

In common with all other types of Soviet aircraft, vast numbers of I-16s were lost on the ground in the first weeks of the war. Thereafter, it just about held its own, suffering a similar rate of losses to the modern VVS fighters.

When flown by experienced pilots, the later variants of the I-16 could barely hold their own against the Bf 109E, but were definitely outclassed by the Bf 109F, which was rapidly replacing the earlier version in 1941. Soviet pilots were not only hard-pressed by the Bf 109s, but also had severe problems in successfully intercepting the more modern German bombers. The I-16 was slower than the Ju 88, while the well-armoured He 111 could often survive a surprising number of hits; Russian pilots had to be constantly on the alert for attacks from escorting fighters.

The I-16 was quickly phased out of front-line service as later types became available. Production ended in 1941, after which losses could only be replaced until stocks ran out. By the end of 1941, the number of I-16s with fighter units had fallen from just over 1600 at the time of the German invasion to only 240. By 1 July 1943, only 42 were still in use. The type remained on the strength of units in Siberia until the end of the war.

Mikoyan-Gurevich MiG-1 and MiG-3

The MiG-1 was designed to meet a 1939 requirement for a high-altitude fighter. The prototype first flew on 5 April 1940 and was swiftly ordered into production. The first batch of production aircraft was delivered for operational trials in December 1940. These trials revealed a number of serious defects, including dangerously limited visibility when taxiing, poor-quality Plexiglas in the canopy that obscured the pilot's view, heavy controls, poor longitudinal stability, difficulty in opening the canopy and a '...dangerous propensity to flick from a simple stall into a spin from which it was almost impossible to recover'.

Some modifications were hastily introduced to rectify the worst problems, notably fitting a sliding cockpit canopy that could be jettisoned in an emergency instead of the original side-opening type, but the aircraft was largely unchanged when issues to fighter units began early in 1941. A total of about 60 were operational at the time of the German invasion, but most were destroyed or captured within a matter of weeks.

The MiG-1's problems were so acute that remedial work resulted in what was virtually a new aircraft, designated MiG-3. Deliveries began in the spring of 1941. Most pilots found it hard to adapt to such a demanding aircraft after the relatively docile Polikarpov fighters that had been in service for so long. Although the worst of the MiG-1's faults had been eliminated, there were still more than enough to cause a string of often-fatal crashes. The oxygen supply was often unreliable, and the stall and

MiG-3

A late production MiG-3 flown by A. V. Shlopov in the defence of Moscow during the winter of 1941/42. It is fitted with two additional 12.7mm (0.5in) UB machine guns in underwing pods.

MiG-3
Length: 8.25m (27ft 1in)
Wingspan: 10.2m (33ft 5in)
Height: 3.3m (10ft 10in)
Wing area: 17.44m² (188ft²)
Empty weight: 2699kg (5965lb)
Loaded weight: 3355kg (7415lb)
Maximum take-off weight: 3318kg (7317lb)
Powerplant: 1 × Mikulin AM-35A liquid-cooled V12 engine, 1007kW (1350hp)
Maximum speed: 640km/h (398mph)
Range: 820km (510 miles)
Service ceiling: 12,000m (39,370ft)
Rate of climb: 20m/s (3970ft/min)
Wing loading: 155kg/m² (39.3lb/ft²)
Armament: 1 × 12.7mm (0.5in) Berezin UB machine gun and 2 x 7.62mm (0.3in) ShKAS machine guns, plus 6 × RS-82 rockets or 2 × 100kg (220lb) bombs; later models could mount additional 2 x 12.7mm (0.5in) UB machine guns in underwing pods

12th Guards Fighter Regiment, PVO Strany

The MiG-3s of 12th Guards Fighter Regiment lined up for inspection at Klin, near Moscow, in early 1942. More than 3000 MiG-3s were completed before production ended in December 1941.

spin characteristics remained dangerous, especially to inexperienced pilots. This was demonstrated on 10 April 1941, when three pilots of the 31st Fighter Regiment were forced to bail out after their aircraft entered irrecoverable spins as they attempted to intercept a German JU 86P high-altitude reconnaissance aircraft at 9000m (30,000ft) over Kaunas, Lithuania. However, skilled pilots could get the best out of their aircraft in these circumstances – the 4th Fighter Regiment claimed the destruction of three Ju 86Ps in the months before the German invasion.

By 1 June 1941, 1029 MiG-3s were on strength, but over half were non-operational as there were only 494 trained pilots. However, even the best pilots were handicapped by the fact that most air-to-air engagements on the Eastern Front took place at low level, where the MiG-3 was completely outclassed by the Bf 109. The massive losses of Soviet ground-attack aircraft in 1941 forced it into that role as well, for which it was totally unsuited. Pilot Alexander Shvarev recalled that: 'The MiG was perfect at altitudes of 4,000 metres and above. But at lower altitudes it was, as they say, "a cow". That was the first weakness. The second was its armament – weapons failures dogged this aircraft. The third weakness was its inaccurate gunsight – that's why we closed in as much as we could and fired at point blank range.'

Production of the MiG-3 ended in December 1941 after more than 3000 had been completed. The total unsuitability of the type for front-line service led to the transfer of virtually all the surviving aircraft from the VVS to the home defence PVO Strany, where they were flown at medium and high altitudes at which their limitations were less apparent.

Lavochkin-Gorbunov-Gudkov LaGG-3

The LaGG-3 was developed from the LaGG-1 that had been designed in 1938 as a lightweight fighter of largely laminated wood construction. The first prototype flew on 30 March 1940, and was assessed to be a promising design. An initial 100 aircraft were ordered for service evaluation, but proved to be badly underpowered and poorly constructed. Reports from trials units were so damning that plans for mass-production were cancelled. The design was drastically revised to become the LaGG-3, which entered service January 1941.

Initially, the LaGG-3 was as unpopular as the short-lived LaGG-1 – the new fighter was still underpowered and poorly built. Operational units listed dozens of mechanical problems, including defective hydraulic systems, broken connecting rods, oil leaks and overheating engines.

Other faults included tail wheels that broke on landing and such ill-fitting cockpit canopies that pilots often flew with them open or removed them altogether. Disillusioned pilots dubbed the type 'The Mortician's Friend'. As

LaGG-3

Yuri Schchipov's LaGG-3 with his distinctive personal emblem of a lion's head in a red heart and his eight victory markings. Schchipov flew with the Black Sea Fleet's 9th Fighter Regiment in the defence of Sevastopol in 1942 and was the unit's second highest scoring pilot.

LaGG-3

Type: Single-seat fighter
Length: 8.81m (28ft 11in)
Wingspan: 9.8m (32ft 2in)
Height: 2.54m (8ft 4in)
Wing area: 17.4m^2 (188ft^2)
Empty weight: 2205kg (4851lb)
Loaded weight: 2620kg (5764lb)
Maximum take-off weight: 3190kg (7018lb)
Powerplant: 1 × Klimov M-105PF liquid-cooled V-12, 924kW (1260hp)
Maximum speed: 575km/h (357mph)
Range: 1000km (621 miles)
Service ceiling: 9700m (31,825ft)
Rate of climb: 14.9m/s (2926ft/min)
Wing loading: 150kg/m^2 (31lb/ft^2)
Armament: 2 × 12.7mm (0.5in) Berezin UB machine guns, 1 × 20mm (0.79in) ShVAK cannon, plus 6 × RS-82 or RS-132 rockets

La-5FN, 240th Fighter Regiment, April 1944

This La-5FN was flown by Ivan Kozhedub – by the end of April 1944 he was credited with 37 victories and was well on his way to becoming the top-scoring Allied fighter pilot of the war.

La-5FN
Type: Single-seat fighter
Length: 8.67m (28ft 5in)
Wingspan: 9.8m (32ft 2in)
Height: 2.54m (8ft 4in)
Wing area: 17.5m² (188ft²)
Empty weight: 2605kg (5743lb)
Loaded weight: 3265kg (7198lb)
Maximum take-off weight: 3402kg (7500lb)
Powerplant: 1 × Shvetsov ASh-82FN radial engine, 1385kW (1850hp)
Maximum speed: 648km/h (403mph)
Range: 765km (475 miles)
Service ceiling: 11,000m (36,089ft)
Rate of climb: 16.7m/s (3280ft/min)
Wing loading: 187kg/m² (38lb/ft²)
Armament: 2 × 20mm (0.79in) ShVAK cannon with 200 rounds per gun, plus 2 × bombs of up to 100kg (220lb) each

early as February 1941, the deluge of complaints led to an order for 2228 modifications to the design.

Although these changes eliminated some of the problems, more than enough remained – one of the worst being that the type was chronically underpowered and soldiered on with the same inadequate engine throughout its service life. Unsurprisingly, it was thoroughly outclassed by the Bf 109 in 1941/42 and was phased out in favour of the far superior La-5 from mid-1942, although as many as 6500 may have been completed.

Lavochkin La-5

The La-5FN was derived from the unsuccessful LaGG-1 and LaGG-3 fighters, which had experienced constant problems with their underpowered in-line engines. During the winter of 1941/42, Lavochkin unofficially redesigned the LaGG-3 to accept the more powerful Shvetsov ASh-82 radial engine, which transformed the type's performance. The new aircraft impressed test pilots, and it was rapidly ordered into production as the La-5. Initial production was speeded by the conversion of stocks of incomplete LaGG-3 airframes.

Although the La-5 was still inferior to the newest German fighters at high altitudes, its low-level performance was outstanding. Pilots also appreciated its armament of two 20mm (0.79in) cannon, which provided a welcome increase in firepower compared to earlier Soviet fighters.

La-7

Ivan Kozhedub's La-7 which he flew from late 1944 until the end of the war. He thought very highly of the type – the first Soviet fighter which was fast enough at low altitudes to catch Focke-Wulf Fw 190 fighter-bombers.

La-7
Type: Single-seat fighter
Length: 8.6m (28ft 3in)
Wingspan: 9.8m (32ft 2in)
Height: 2.54m (8ft 4in)
Wing area: 17.59m^2 (189.3ft^2)
Empty weight: N/k
Loaded weight: 3315kg (7308lb)
Maximum take-off weight: N/k
Powerplant: 1 × Shvetsov ASh-82FN radial engine, 1385kW (1850hp)
Maximum speed: 661km/h (411mph)
Range: 665km (413 miles)
Service ceiling: 10,450m (34,280ft)
Rate of climb: 15.72m/s (3095ft/min)
Wing loading: N/k
Armament: 2 x 20mm (0.79in) ShVAK cannon with 200 rounds per gun, plus 2 × bombs of up to 100kg (220lb) each; later-production batches were armed with 3 x 20mm (0.79in) Berezin B-20 cannon with 100 rounds per gun

Lavochkin La-7

The La-7 was the final development of the La-5, incorporating more light alloy components to reduce weight. It was always intended to fit three of the new B-20 20mm (0.79in) cannon, but production delays forced the completion of early La-7s with twin ShVAK cannon, which were becoming ineffective against increasingly well-armoured *Luftwaffe* aircraft.

The new fighter became operational in October 1944 after completing a month of combat trials. It was generally well liked for its good performance, although there were frequent engine problems. Roughly 2000 aircraft were delivered by the end of the war. Production continued until 1946, by which time more than 5700 had been completed. The British test pilot Eric 'Winkle' Brown flew an La-7 at the former *Luftwaffe* experimental centre at Tarnewitz on the Baltic coast just after the German surrender in May 1945. He assessed the handling and performance as '...quite superb', but felt that the armament and sights were '...below par', while the aircraft's '... wooden construction would have withstood little combat punishment' and the instrumentation was '... appallingly basic'.

Yakovlev Yak-1 and Yak-7

The Yak-1 was ordered into production on 19 February 1940, but the original design required almost 15,000 modifications before the type began to enter service in quantity in late 1941.

Yak-1

The markings indicate this is a late production Yak-1 of the Polish 1st 'Warszawa' Fighter Regiment operating in Warsaw area, 1944.

Early-production Yak-1

Type: Single-seat fighter

Length: 8.5m (27ft 11in)

Wingspan: 10m (32ft 10in)

Height: 2.64m (8ft 6in)

Wing area: 17.2m² (185.1ft²)

Empty weight: 2394kg (5267lb)

Loaded weight: 2883kg (6343lb)

Maximum take-off weight: N/k

Powerplant: 1 × M-105PA V-12 liquid-cooled piston engine, 780kW (1050hp)

Maximum speed: 563km/h (350mph)

Range: 700km (435 miles)

Service ceiling: 10,000m (32,808ft)

Rate of climb: 12m/s (2400ft/min)

Wing loading: 171kg/m² (377lb/ft²)

Armament: 1 × 20mm (0.79in) ShVAK cannon, 2 × 7.62mm (0.3in) ShKAS machine guns

Yak-1, 31st Guards Fighter Regiment

A late production Yak-1 flown by Major B.N.Yeremin during the winter of 1942/43. The inscription reads: 'To the pilot of the Stalingrad Front Guards Major comrade Yeremin. From the collective farmworkers of the Collective Farm 'Stakhanov' comrade F.P.Golovatov'.

The first production batches were still plagued with faults, including severe engine vibration. This was sufficient to fracture fuel and oil lines, causing a number of fires, until the problem was finally cured by a redesigned engine mounting. This was just one of a further 5000 modifications made in 1942 that finally turned the Yak-1 into an effective and reliable fighter.

The Yak-1 had a distinct edge over the Bf 109E encountered in 1941, but was inferior to the later Bf 109F and Bf 109G – its main opponents – in rate of climb at all altitudes. Although it took an experienced pilot to get good results from its light armament, a number of aircraft were modified by removing the 7.62mm (0.3in) ShKAS machine guns, leaving only the single ShVAK cannon.

Rearming
A female armourer cocking the 12.7mm (.5in) UBS machine gun of a Yak-9D.

These lighter aircraft were popular with expert pilots, for whom the reduction in armament was acceptable and combat experience showed a much-improved kill-to-loss ratio. Production of the Yak-1 ended in July 1944, with around 8700 built.

The Yak-7 started life as a two-seat trainer version of the Yak-1, but it was soon adapted as a single-seat fighter that proved to be superior to the Yak-1.

Yakovlev Yak-9

The Yak-9, which entered service in late 1942, was essentially a lighter version of the Yak-7 with the same armament. It was the first major variant to have a lowered rear fuselage and an all-round vision canopy. Visibility was further improved by replacing the conventional steel armour behind the pilot's head with a thick panel of toughened glass. This offered almost the same protection without restricting rearward vision.

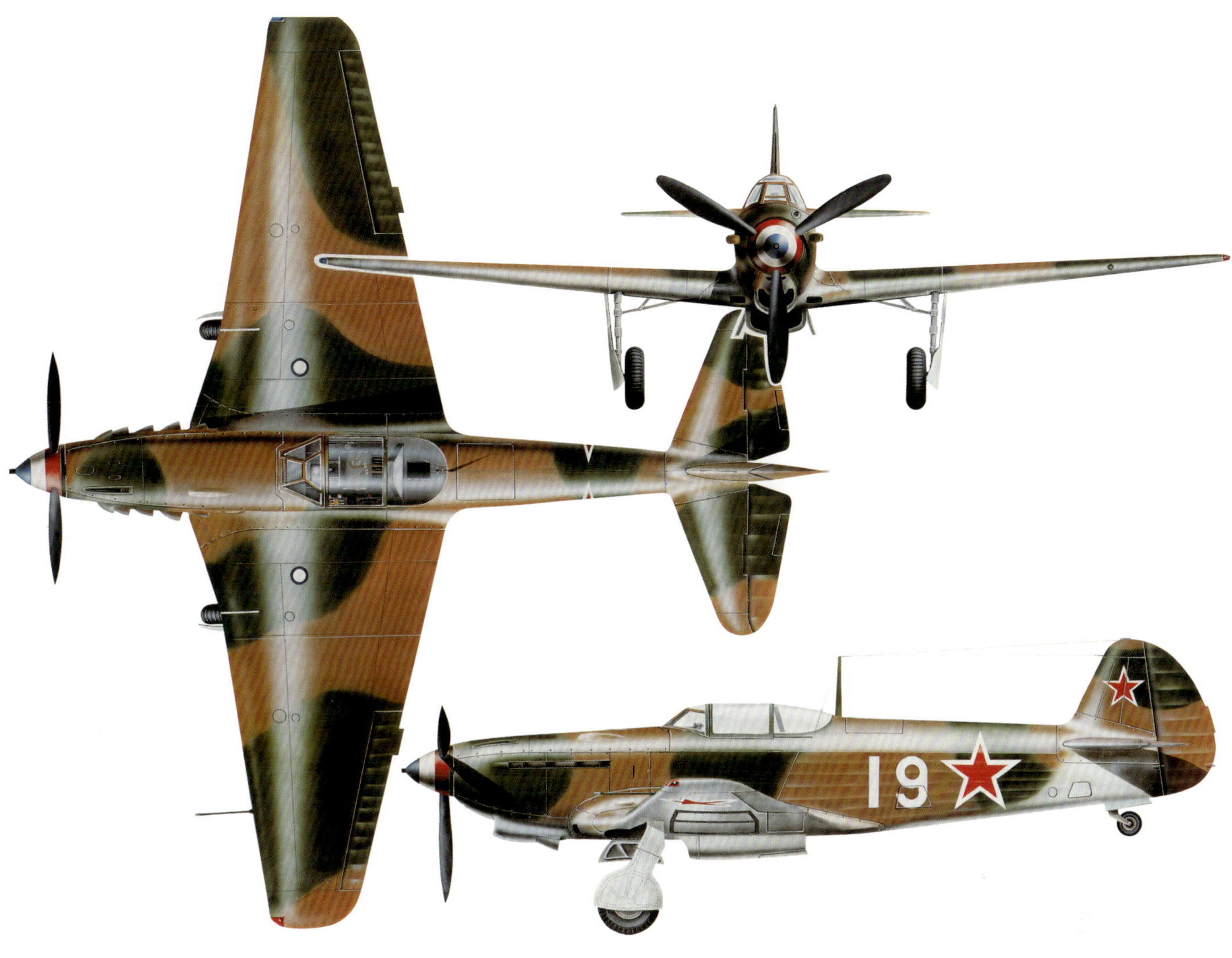

Yak-9

A Yak-9 of the Régiment de Chasse Normandie-Niemen. The Regiment was a Free French fighter unit which operated on the Eastern Front from March 1943 until the end of the war. It claimed 273 enemy aircraft shot down, 37 probables, for the loss of 87 aircraft and 52 pilots.

Yak-9D

Type: Single-seat long-range fighter
Length: 8.55m (28ft)
Wingspan: 9.74m (31ft 11in)
Height: 3m (9ft 10in)
Wing area: 17.2m² (185.1ft²)
Empty weight: 2350kg (5170lb)
Loaded weight: 3117kg (6858lb)
Maximum take-off weight: N/k
Powerplant: 1 × Klimov M-105 PF V-12 liquid-cooled piston engine, 880kW (1180hp)
Maximum speed: 597km/h (371mph)
Range: 1360km (845 miles)
Service ceiling: 9100m (30,000ft)
Rate of climb: 13.7m/s (2690ft/min)
Wing loading: 181kg/m² (37lb/ft²)
Armament: 1 × 20mm (0.79in) ShVAK cannon with 120 rounds and 1 × 12.7mm (0.5in) UBS machine gun with 200 rounds

Production continued until 1948, by which time at least 16,700 had been completed. Variants incorporated two different wings, five engines, six fuel tank layouts and seven types of armament configurations.

Operating mainly at low level, the Yak-9 was faster and more

Yak-3s in flight

Pairs of Yak-3 fighters pass over central Moscow sometime late during the war.

Yak-3

Type: Single-seat fighter
Length: 8.5m (27ft 10in)
Wingspan: 9.2m (30ft 2in)
Height: 2.39m (7ft 11in)
Wing area: 14.85m^2 (159.8ft^2)
Empty weight: 2105kg (4640lb)
Loaded weight: 2692kg (5864lb)
Maximum take-off weight: N/k
Powerplant: 1 × Klimov VK-105PF-2 V-12 liquid-cooled piston engine, 970kW (1300hp)
Maximum speed: 655km/h (407mph)
Range: 650km (405 miles)
Service ceiling: 10,700m (35,000ft)
Rate of climb: 18.5m/s (3645ft/min)
Wing loading: 181kg/m^2 (37lb/ft^2)
Armament: 1 × 20 mm (0.79in) ShVAK cannon with 120 rounds and 1 × 12.7mm (0.5in) UBS machine gun with 200 rounds

manoeuvrable than its main opponent, the Bf 109, but was less well armed. Soviet pilots considered the Yak-9 to be a match for the Bf 109G and Fw 190A-3/A-4.

Yakovlev Yak-3

With little prospect of significantly more powerful engines becoming available for future versions of the Yak-1/Yak-7/Yak-9 series, the Yakovlev design bureau looked at drastic weight-saving measures to improve performance. The resulting Yak-3, which began to equip VVS fighter units in mid-1944, was certainly not problem-free – there were a number of cases of its plywood skinning coming unstuck when the aircraft pulled out of a high-speed dive. In addition, the type suffered from short range and poor engine reliability. Despite these drawbacks, the Yak-3 was a superb low-altitude fighter, proving to be so effective that the *Luftwaffe* issued an order to '...avoid combat below five

Su-2
Type: Two-seat close-support aircraft
Length: 10.46m (34ft 4in)
Wingspan: 14.3m (46ft 11in)
Height: 3.75m (12ft 3in)
Wing area: 29m² (312ft²)
Empty weight: 3220kg (7100lb)
Loaded weight: 4700kg (10,360lb)
Maximum take-off weight: N/k
Powerplant: 1 × Shvetsov M-82 radial engine, 1044kW (1400hp)
Maximum speed: 485km/h (300mph)
Range: 1100km (685 miles)
Service ceiling: 8400m (27,560ft)
Rate of climb: N/k
Wing loading: N/k
Armament: 6 × 7.62mm (0.3in) ShKAS machine guns (4 in the wings, 1 in a manually operated dorsal turret, 1 in ventral hatch); plus up to 600kg (1320lb) of bombs in the internal bomb bay and underwing hardpoints, or 10 × RS-82 rockets or 8 × RS-132 rockets

Sukhoi Su-2
Approximately 900 Su-2s had been completed when production ceased in 1942, but the type was obsolescent by 1941 and at least 220 were lost in combat before the survivors were relegated to training duties.

thousand metres with Yakovlev fighters lacking an oil cooler intake beneath the nose.'

BOMBER AIRCRAFT

Sukhoi Su-2

The Su-2 originated with a 1936 requirement for a close-support and reconnaissance aircraft. The type seems to have become operational in late 1939, and went through a succession of updates, primarily to try to improve survivability by fitting more powerful engines. The 820kW (1100hp) Tumansky M-88 radial of initial production batches was ultimately replaced by the 1134kW (1520hp) Shvetsov M-82, but even this could not significantly reduce the appalling loss rate experienced in 1941/42. The Su-2 proved to be highly vulnerable to German fighters, largely due to its weak defensive armament and poor manoeuvrability. Nonetheless, it was kept in production until about mid-1942, when it was replaced by the Il-2 'Shturmovik'.

Iluyshin Il-2M3 'Shturmovik'

Iluyshin's design team began working on studies for an armoured ground-attack aircraft in 1938. Uniquely for an aircraft of its era, the 700kg (1540lb) armoured shell protecting the crew, engine, cooling system and fuel tanks was designed as an integral part of the airframe, which saved a significant amount of weight. Even so, the Mikulin AM-35 1022kW (1370hp) engine left the two-seat prototype markedly underpowered. The aircraft was radically redesigned as single-seater with a 1254kW (1680hp) Mikulin AM-38 engine, a development of the AM-35 designed to deliver maximum power at low altitude.

This single-seater was accepted for service as the Il-2 and began to equip VVS units in May 1941. Almost 250 had been completed by the time of the German invasion, and the type proved to be very effective in the ground attack role. However, the armour that gave a high degree of protection from light AA fire limited the aircraft's manoeuvrability and made it vulnerable to German fighters.

In common with the rest of the Soviet aircraft industry, the factories producing the Il-2 had to be hastily evacuated and re-established east of the Urals as the German armies overran much of European Russia in 1941. Despite the type's high loss rate, it was already highly valued. When Stalin saw an unusually honest report on the slow rate of Il-2 production at the new sites, he sent a furious telegram to the factory:

You have let down our country and our Red Army. You have the nerve not to manufacture Il-2s until now. Our Red Army now needs Il-2 aircraft like the

Il-2M3 'Shturmovik'

The *Shturmovik*'s effectiveness steadily improved as crews learned to exploit its strengths. Early low-level direct attacks were soon abandoned in favour of approaching the target from one side before turning to attack from a shallow 30° dive.

Il-2

Type: Two-seat close-support aircraft
Length: 11.6m (38ft 1in)
Wingspan: 14.6m (47ft 11in)
Height: 4.2m (13ft 9in)
Wing area: 38.5m² (414ft²)
Empty weight: 4360kg (9612lb)
Loaded weight: 6160kg (13,580lb)
Maximum take-off weight: 6380kg (14,065lb)
Powerplant: 1 × Mikulin AM-38F liquid-cooled V-12, 1285kW (1720hp)
Maximum speed: 414km/h (257mph)
Range: 720km (450 miles)
Service ceiling: 5500m (18,045ft)
Rate of climb: 10.4m/s (2050ft/min)
Wing loading: 160kg/m² (31.3lb/ft²)
Armament: 2 × 23mm (0.9in) VYa-23 cannon, with 150 rounds per gun, 2 × 7.62mm (0.3in) ShKAS machine guns, with 750 rounds per gun, plus 1 × manually aimed 12.7mm (0.5in) Berezin UBT machine gun in rear cockpit with 300 rounds; up to 600kg (1320lb) of bombs and/or 8 × RS-82 rockets or 4 × RS-132 rockets

air it breathes, like the bread it eats. Shenkman produces one Il-2 a day and Tretyakov builds one or two MiG-3s daily. It is a mockery of our country and the Red Army. I ask you not to try the government's patience, and demand that you manufacture more Il-2s. This is my final warning.
– Stalin

Within weeks of the outbreak of war, some Shturmovik units began to convert their aircraft to two-seaters by cutting a hole in the fuselage immediately behind the cockpit to serve as an improvised rear gunner's position. A variety of machine guns were fitted, with the 12.7mm (0.5in) UBT machine gun used whenever possible, as its firepower was significantly greater than that of rifle-calibre weapons. Although the rear gunner had no armour protection and only a limited field of fire, these two-seaters suffered markedly fewer losses from German fighters, and a redesigned two-seater entered production in September 1942. This offered an improved field of fire for the rear gunner, but his position was still virtually unprotected.

The Il-2 remained in production until 1945, by which time at least 36,000 had been completed. Given their role, losses were unsurprisingly high – an estimated 10,700 between 1941 and 1945.

Il-2M3 'Shturmoviks'
After experiencing the unnerving sight of their fire bouncing off the Shturmoviks' armour, *Luftwaffe* fighter pilots learned to make attacks from below and behind, targeting the vulnerable oil cooler and poorly-protected rear gunner.

Polikarpov U-2/Po-2

The Polikarpov U-2, or Po-2, was a reliable, uncomplicated and forgiving aircraft, powered by a 74kW (99hp)

Shvetsov air-cooled radial engine, that had first flown in January 1928. It was designed as a basic trainer and agricultural aircraft – its low cost and easy maintenance ensured a production run of at least 20,000, and manufacture continued into the 1950s.

The massive losses of Soviet aircraft in the opening stages of Operation 'Barbarossa' prompted the type's use as an improvised light bomber in 1941, initially in the defence of Odessa. It was soon discovered that the aircraft was particularly well suited to making night attacks, and a purpose-built bomber version was produced under the designation U-2VS (*voyskovaya seriya* – military series). This variant equipped a number of night harassment units throughout the war and proved to be so effective that *Luftwaffe* commissioned urgent studies to find an aircraft suitable for conversion as a night fighter.

Conventional types of aircraft already deployed in this role, such as the Bf 110 and Ju 88, could not be used, as their stalling speeds were higher than the Russian biplanes'

Polikarpov U-2/Po-2

The U-2 entered service in 1929 as the Red Air Force's standard primary trainer, but proved to be invaluable as a night harassment aircraft. It equipped numerous units, including the 588th Night Bomber Regiment, a unit with all-female aircrew and ground staff that became famous for its daring low-altitude night raids on German rear-areas.

Po-2

Type: Two-seat night harassment aircraft
Length: 8.17m (26ft 10in)
Wingspan: 11.40m (37ft 5in)
Height: 3.1m (10ft 2in)
Wing area: 33.2m² (357ft²)
Empty weight: 770kg (1698lb)
Loaded weight: 1030kg (2271lb)
Maximum take-off weight: 1350kg (2976lb)
Powerplant: 1 × Shvetsov M-11D 5-cylinder radial engine, 93kW (125hp)
Maximum speed: 152km/h (94mph)
Range: 630km (391 miles)
Service ceiling: 3000m (9843ft)
Rate of climb: 2.78m/s (546ft/min)
Wing loading: 41kg/m² (8.35lb/ft²)
Armament: 1 x manually aimed 7.62mm (0.3in) ShKAS machine gun in the rear cockpit plus up to 6 x 50kg (110lb) bombs

Tupolev TB-3
A TB-3 unloads its cargo of paratroopers in what appears to be a training exercise somewhere in the Soviet Union.

TB-3-4M-17F, 1934 Model
Type: Six-seat heavy bomber/transporter
Length: 24.4m (80ft 1in)
Wingspan: 41.8m (137ft 2in)
Height: 8.5m (27ft 11in)
Wing area: 234.5m² (2,524ft²)
Empty weight: 11,200kg (24,690lb)
Loaded weight: 17,200kg (37,920lb)
Maximum take-off weight: 19,300kg (42,550lb)
Powerplant: 4 × Mikulin M-17F V12 engines, 525kW (705hp) each
Maximum speed: 212km/h (129mph) at 3,000m (9,800ft)
Range: 2000km (1,240 miles)
Service ceiling: 4800m (15,750ft)
Rate of climb: 1.25m/s (246ft/min)
Wing loading: 73kg/m² (15lb/ft²)
Armament: Up to 8 x 7.62mm (0.3in) DA machine guns, plus up to 2000kg (4400lb) of bombs

maximum speed. Eventually, about 30 Fw 189 tactical reconnaissance aircraft were fitted with cannon and radar and provided a degree of protection from the U-2 raids.

Tupolev TB-3

The TB-3 originated with a 1929 requirement for a heavy bomber. Tupolev's design bureau developed an all-steel, corrugated skinned monoplane with four engines that was essentially an enlarged version of his earlier TB-1 bomber. The prototype TB-3 first flew on 22 December 1930, and the type was approved for mass production on 20 February 1931. As the aircraft entered service, it became clear that most examples were at least 10 per cent overweight – the extra 1100kg (2425lb) or so had a dire effect on the already barely adequate performance figures. The problem was traced to crude manufacturing methods and poor quality control that allowed the use of overweight components such as wing and fuselage panels. A crash programme of weight-saving measures was implemented, but even so, weights of individual production aircraft could vary by several hundred kilos.

When it became operational in 1932, the TB-3 was arguably the world's most advanced heavy bomber, capable of carrying 2200kg (4850lb) of bombs and a defensive armament of up to eight machine guns. Improved versions remained in production until 1937, by which time more than 800 had been completed.

The type was scheduled to be phased out of front-line service from 1939, but saw action against the Japanese at Khalkin Gol and against the Finns during the Winter War. More than 500 were still operational at the time of the German invasion; they suffered horrendous losses when used in daylight raids during the opening stages of Operation 'Barbarossa'. The survivors were hastily redeployed as night bombers, and continued to be used in this role until at least 1943. Thereafter, dwindling numbers remained in service as transport aircraft until the end of the war.

The TB-3 was also used for one of the most unusual projects of the period – the Zveno project – in which it acted as the mothership for up to five fighters. Several versions were produced, but the only one to be used in action was the SPB (*Sostavnoi Pikiruyuschiy Bombardirovschi*k – Combined Dive Bomber). This carried a Polikarpov I-16 under each wing, each armed with a pair of 250kg (550lb) FAB-250 bombs. In July 1941, two SPBs took off from Eupatoria in the Crimea to attack the Constan a oil depot in Romania. They launched their I-16s 40km (25 miles) from the target that was successfully attacked before the fighters returned to base under their own power.

Over the next few months, the type was used in further raids on the Romanian targets, including the King Carol I Bridge over the Danube that carried the Ploiesti-Constanta oil pipeline. The Zveno project was terminated in 1942 after perhaps 30 missions, due to German air superiority and the increasing vulnerability of TB-3s and I-16s.

Petlyakov Pe-8

In 1934, an official requirement was issued for a heavy bomber to replace the TB-3, and the prototype of what was to become the Pe-8 first flew in December 1936. However, the arrest of Petlyakov and much of his design team during the Great Purge of 1937 disrupted the development programme, and the second prototype did not make its first flight until 26 July 1938.

Stalin's micro-management of this prestige project did not help matters. Although factories were ordered to begin tooling up as early as 1936, production did not begin until 1939. Even then, the type was plagued by a

Pe-8
Few wartime bombers had heavier defensive armament than the Pe-8, although it was limited by the Soviet inability to produce reliable power-operated turrets. The traverse and elevation rates of its manually-operated turrets were too slow to be really effective.

Pe-8/AM-35A
Type: Nine-seat heavy bomber
Length: 23.2m (76ft)
Wingspan: 39.13m (128ft 4in)
Height: 6.2m (20ft 4in)
Wing area: 188.66m² (2030.7ft²)
Empty weight: 18,571kg (40,941lb)
Loaded weight: 27,000kg (59,400lb)
Maximum take-off weight: 35,000kg (77,000lb)
Powerplant: 4 × Mikulin AM-35A liquid-cooled V12 engines, 999kW (1340hp) each
Maximum speed: 443km/h (275mph)
Range: 3700km (2299 miles)
Service ceiling: 9300m (30,504ft)
Rate of climb: 5.9m/s (1154ft/min)
Wing loading: 143kg/m² (29lb/ft²)
Armament: 2 x 20mm (0.79 in) ShVAK cannon (dorsal and tail turrets), 2 x 12.7mm (0.5in) UBT machine guns (engine nacelles) and 2 x 7.62mm (0.3in) ShKAS machine guns (nose turret); up to 5000kg (11,000lb) of bombs, including the 5000kg (11,000lb) FAB 5000 bomb

dire shortage of suitable engines, and no more than 93 were completed before production ended in 1944.

The Pe-8 was the sole modern Soviet heavy bomber to see action during the war, making night attacks on targets such as Berlin, Königsberg and Danzig as well as battlefield interdiction raids in support of the Red Army. A significant number of aircraft were shot down by *Luftwaffe* night fighters and flak, but production just about kept pace with losses, and as many as 32 may still have been in service at the end of the war.

Tupolev SB-2

The SB-2 was developed in response to a 1933 requirement for a high-speed bomber, and the type began entering service in 1936. At that time, the SB-2 was one of the world's most advanced medium bombers, able to out-pace contemporary fighters. A total of 93 aircraft were sent to equip Republican bomber squadrons in the Spanish Civil War, and proved to be virtually immune to interception by the Nationalist's Heinkel He 51 and Fiat CR 32 biplane fighters. This immunity ended with the appearance of Nationalist Messerschmitt Bf 109s in 1937, after which SB-2 losses increased dramatically; only 19 survived to be incorporated in the Nationalist air force at the end of the war. At least 220 aircraft were also in service with the Chinese Nationalists between 1937 and 1941 and saw extensive combat against the Japanese.

Tupolev SB 2M-103

This late production aircraft incorporates the improved defensive armament layout fitted from 1940 onwards – modified nose and ventral gun positions with improved fields of fire and a new dorsal turret.

SB 2M-103

Type: Three-seat medium bomber
Length: 12.57m (41ft 3in)
Wingspan: 20.33m (66ft 8in)
Height: 3.6m (11ft 10in)
Wing area: 56.7m² (610.3ft²)
Empty weight: 4768kg (10,512lb)
Loaded weight: 6308kg (14,065lb)
Maximum take-off weight: 7880kg (17,370lb)
Powerplant: 2 × Klimov M-103 liquid-cooled V12 engine, 716kW (960hp) each
Maximum speed: 450km/h (280mph) at 4100m (13,450ft)
Range: 2300km (1429 miles)
Service ceiling: 9300m (30,510ft)
Rate of climb: N/k
Wing loading: N/k
Armament: 4 × 7.62mm (0.3in) ShKAS machine guns (two in nose, one in dorsal and one in ventral position); 6 × 100kg (220lb) or six 50kg (110lb) bombs in bomb-bay, 2 × 250kg (550lb) bombs on wing racks

SB 2M-103

Summer 1941 – armourers 'bombing up' a late production SB with streamlined engine nacelles.

By 1939, the SB-2 was obsolescent – the type suffered heavy losses to the agile Japanese Nakajima Ki-27 fighters during the fighting at Khalkhin Gol. The Winter War against Finland emphasized the SB-2's growing vulnerability, with the loss of at least 100 to Finnish fighters and AA fire.

At the time of the German invasion, the SB-2 was theoretically being phased out of service in favour of the Pe-2, but in practice it still represented 94 per cent of the Soviet operational bomber force, with anything up to 2000 machines based in the Western Military Districts. Many of these were destroyed on the ground in the initial *Luftwaffe* raids; the survivors were thrown into unescorted daylight raids, only to be decimated by flak and fighters. After a few days, the remaining SB-2s were restricted to night bombing. By early 1942, all had been relegated to transport duties.

Ilyushin DB-3 and Il-4

The DB-3 was a long-range bomber that first flew in 1935 and began entering service in 1937. At the time of its service debut, it was markedly superior to the contemporary Heinkel He 111B. However, despite being fitted with a succession of uprated engines from 1938 onwards, the DB-3 was obsolescent by the time production ended in 1939, after more than 1500 had been completed.

A torpedo bomber derivative, the DB-3T, was introduced in 1937 (the 'T' standing for torpedonosyets – 'torpedo'). It was a simple conversion of the standard DB-3 bomber, fitted with centreline shackles for a single Type 45-36 torpedo. Alternatively, the DB-3T could carry airdropped mines or standard bombs. VVS VMF (Naval Aviation) was impressed with the aircraft, which was its first properly designed torpedo bomber and allowed the formation of a new 'Torpedo Aviation' arm.

The Il-4 started life as an updated version of the DB-3, designated DB-3F (Forsirovanniye – 'boosted'), which entered service in 1939. The most obvious feature of the new variant was a lengthened and streamlined nose that gave more room for the navigator/bomb aimer and significantly reduced drag.

Ilyushin Il-4
Type: Four-seat medium bomber
Length: 14.76m (48ft 5in)
Wingspan: 21.44m (70ft 4in)
Height: 4.2m (13ft 9in)
Wing Area: 66.7m² (718ft²)
Empty weight: 5,800kg (12,787lb)
Loaded weight: 10,000kg (22,046lb)
Maximum take-off weight: 12,120kg (26,720lb)
Powerplant: 2 × Tumansky M-88B radial engines, 820kW (1100hp) each
Maximum speed: 410km/h (255mph) at 6,500m (21,325ft)
Range: 2600km (1616 miles) with 1000kg (2200lb) bombs
Service ceiling: 8,700m (28,500ft)
Armament: 2 × 7.62mm (0.3in) ShKAS machine guns (1 in nose, 1 in ventral hatch); 1 × 12.7mm (0.5in) UBT machine gun in dorsal turret; 2 × BETAB-750DS 305mm (12in) rockets or 1 × 940kg (2,100lb) Type 45-36AN torpedo or up to 2700kg (6000lb) of bombs or mines

Ilyushin Il-4
The Il-4 took part in most of the strategic bombing raids carried out by the Red Air Force and remained in production until 1944, when just over 5200 had been built.

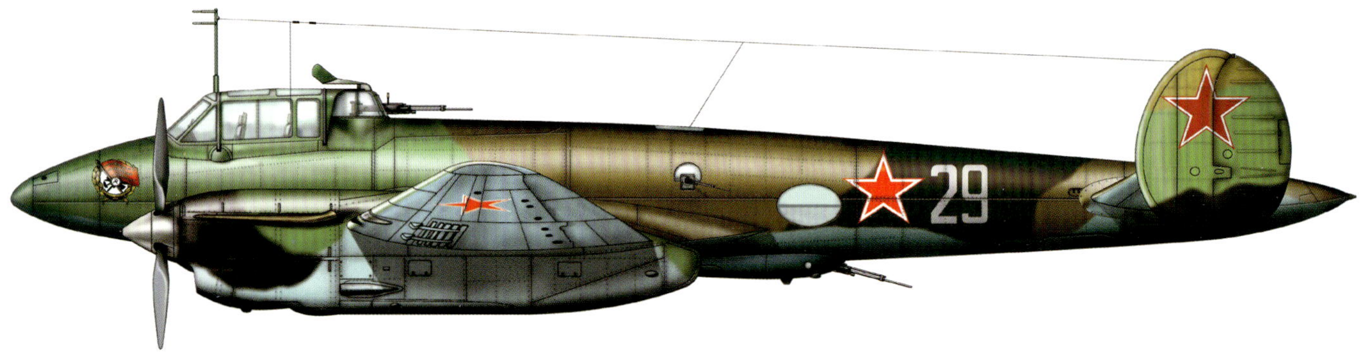

Petlyakov Pe-2

The Pe-2 began to enter service in mid-1941 and quickly proved to be an exceptionally capable high-performance light bomber that was sometimes referred to as the 'Russian Mosquito'. Total production of all variants exceeded 11,000 aircraft.

Early-production Pe-2
Type: Three-seat light bomber
Length: 12.66m (41ft 6in)
Wingspan: 17.16m (56ft 3in)
Height: 3.5m (11ft 6in)
Wing area: 40.5m² (436ft²)
Empty weight: 5875kg (12,952lb)
Loaded weight: 7563kg (16,639lb)
Maximum take-off weight: 8495kg (18,728lb)
Powerplant: 2 × Klimov M-105PF liquid-cooled V-12, 903kW (1210hp) each
Maximum speed: 580km/h (360mph)
Range: 1160km (721 miles)
Service ceiling: 8800m (28,870ft)
Rate of climb: 7.2m/s (1410ft/min)
Wing loading: 186kg/m² (38lb/ft²)
Armament: 2 × 7.62mm (0.3in) fixed forward-firing ShKAS machine guns, one replaced by a 12.7mm (0.5in) UB machine gun in later versions, plus 1 × 7.62mm (0.3in) ShKAS in dorsal and ventral positions. From mid-1942, defensive armament included 1 x UB machine gun in a manually operated dorsal turret, 1 x ventral UB machine gun and 1 x ShKAS that could be fired from port, starboard or dorsal hatch mountings. Up to 1600kg (3520lb) of bombs.

Other changes were introduced, including the replacement of the dorsal 7.62mm (0.3in) ShKAS machine gun by a 12.7mm (0.5in) UBT machine gun and limited armour protection for the gunners' positions. A torpedo bomber version, the Il-4T, was also produced; this operated in the anti-shipping role, with BETAB-750DS 305mm (12in) rockets and torpedoes.

DB-3s and Il-4s made several long-range night bombing raids against Berlin in 1941. In contrast to these purely propaganda missions, the vast majority of attacks were short-range battlefield interdiction raids in which the Il-4s often carried an extra 1000kg (2204lb) of bombs under their wings, in addition to their internal load of 2500kg (5512lb).

Petlyakov Pe-2

The Petlyakov Pe-2 Peshka dive-bomber was designed by a team headed by Vladimir Petlyakov in a 'sharashka' – one of the secret research and development centres of the Soviet Gulag labour camp system. It was originally intended to be a high-altitude two-seat long-range fighter capable of escorting bombers such as the Pe-8 on deep penetration raids.

The prototype made its first flight in December 1939 and was approved for service. However, just as production was about to begin, it was hastily redesigned as a three-seat dive-bomber following the success of the *Luftwaffe*'s dive-bombers in the Battle of France.

The Pe-2 required careful handling, but its high speed gave it a considerable degree of protection from the German fighters of 1941. As the *Luftwaffe* introduced more potent interceptors, losses rose, largely due to the type's limited defensive armament of two fixed forward-firing 7.62mm (0.3in) ShKAS machine guns, plus another in the dorsal position and a fourth firing through a ventral hatch. Various attempts were made to improve this – reportedly including experimental fittings of twin launch rails for RS-82 rockets in dorsal and ventral positions. More practical measures included replacing three of the ShKAS with 12.7mm (0.5in) UBT machine guns and fitting more powerful engines in later-production aircraft.

Initially, aircraft had internal stowage for six 100kg (220lb) FAB-100 bombs: four in the fuselage bomb bay and one in a bomb cell in each engine nacelle, behind the wheel wells. The need to increase this bomb load was quickly recognized, and four external hardpoints were added to carry up to four 250kg (550lb) FAB-250 bombs. In the first months of the war, the type's

Petlyakov Pe-2s
March 1944 – a formation of Pe-2s over Estonia heading for Narva. The old city was virtually flattened in a series of VVS raids.

Bomb loading

VVS armourers prepare captured German SC-250 bombs for loading onto a Pe-2.

dive-bombing capability was not fully exploited, as crews had never been trained in the technique.

However, tactics were gradually devised at unit level, primarily by Colonel Ivan Polbin, the commander of the 150th Bomber Regiment. By early 1942, he had perfected the 'Vertushka' (Dipping wheel) attack, in which the Pe-2s approached the target in a 'Vee

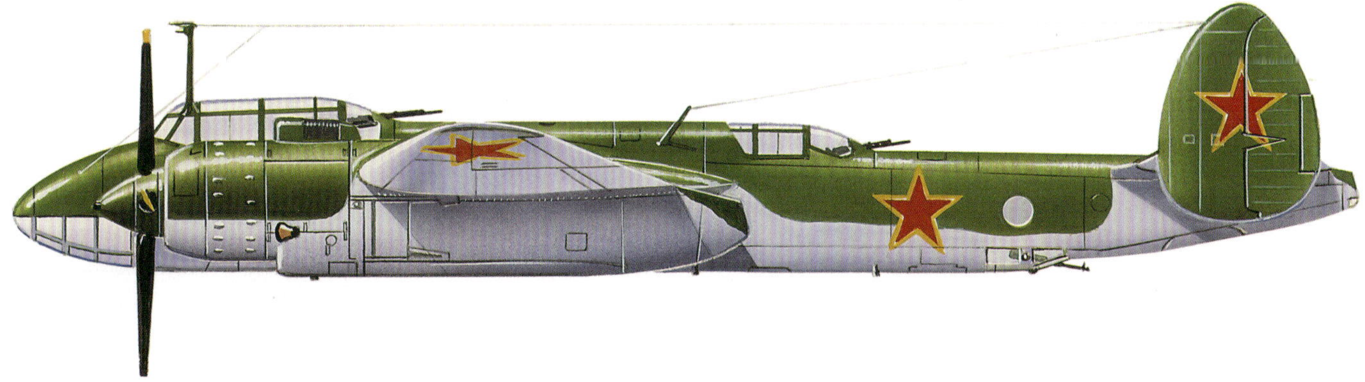

Tu-2
Two experimental ground-attack versions were tested in 1944 under the designation Tu-2Sh: one with a 76.2mm (3in) centreline gun and another with a battery of 88 PPSh-41 submachine guns in the bomb bay, fixed to fire forwards and downwards at a 30° angle. (Neither went into production.)

Tu-2 (1943 production onwards)
Type: Four-seat light bomber
Length: 13.8m (45ft 3in)
Wingspan: 18.86m (61ft 10in)
Height: 4.13m (13ft 7in)
Wing area: 48.8m² (525ft²)
Empty weight: 7,601kg (16,757lb)
Loaded weight: 10,538kg (23,232lb)
Maximum take-off weight: 11,768kg (25,944lb)
Powerplant: 2 × Shvetsov ASh-82 radials, 1380kW (1850hp) each
Maximum speed: 550km/h (342mph)
Range: 2020km (1260 miles)
Service ceiling: 9000m (29,528ft)
Rate of climb: 8.2m/s (1610ft/min)
Wing loading: 220kg/m² (45lb/ft²)
Armament: 2 x fixed forward-firing 20mm (0.79in) ShVAK cannon, one in each wing root, with 200 rounds per gun plus 3 x 12.7mm (0.5in) UBT machine guns (2 x dorsal and 1 x ventral) with 250 rounds per gun. Up to 1000kg (2200lb) of bombs internally and racks for a further 2000kg (4400lb) under the wings inboard of the engines

of Vees' formation before moving into line astern with about 610m (2000ft) between each aircraft. They would then circle the target before making individual attacks from 70-degree dives, which would be maintained until all bombs had been dropped.

Tupolev Tu-2

The Tu-2 was another design that originated in a 'sharashka' in response to a 1938 requirement for a fast bomber. The prototype first flew on 29 January 1941 and showed a spectacular turn of speed – 635km/h (395mph). Problems with the Mikulin AM-37 engines that powered the prototypes forced the adoption of less powerful ASh-82FN radial engines, although performance was only marginally reduced.

Series production began in February 1942, but was suspended to allow resources to be concentrated on urgently needed fighters and Pe-2s after only a small number of aircraft had been completed. Production of the type was reinstated in April 1943, largely due to pressure from front-line units for bombers with greater range and bomb load than the Pe-2. More than 1100 Tu-2s were delivered by the end of the war. Production continued until 1948, by which time at least another 1400 had been completed.

SOVIET AIRCRAFT WEAPONS

MACHINE GUNS

PV-1 machine gun

This was a lightened, air-cooled derivative of the Maxim Model 1910 with an improved rate of fire that entered service in 1928 and armed the majority of Soviet aircraft of the interwar period.

ShKAS machine gun

The ShKAS began entering service in 1933 and rapidly proved to be far superior to the PV-1. It was produced in fixed forward-firing and flexible versions, with average ammunition loads of 750 rounds per gun for the fixed models and 1000 to 1500 for the flexible. The gun's light weight and high rate of fire (1880rpm on early-production models, increased to 2000rpm from 1937 onwards) made it one of the best rifle-calibre aircraft weapons of the war.

However, it did have its faults. One armourer recalled that it: '... had a high rate of fire, but it also had 48 ways of jamming. Some of them could be fixed immediately; some could not. And 1800 rounds a minute was an insanely high rate of fire. If you pulled the trigger for too long, the ShKAS would fire all its ammo in one go and that would be it!'

Berezin UB heavy machine gun

The UB entered service in 1941 and succeeded in eliminating the problems experienced with the BS heavy machine gun of 1939. The UB was produced in three versions: the wing-mounted UBK, the synchronized UBS (primarily fitted above the engines of fighters such as the Yak-1) and the turret-mounted UBT. Unlike the precision-made ShKAS, the UB was designed for rapid mass-production and to be replaced rather than repaired if it developed a major fault.

CANNON

ShVAK cannon

This was a compact, lightweight cannon that armed the majority of Soviet wartime fighters. Although it had a good rate of fire, its performance was degraded by light shells with small bursting charges.

Volkov-Yartsev VYa-23 cannon

The Vya-23 was developed in 1940/41, primarily as an airborne anti-tank weapon. It was significantly more powerful than the ShVAK, and its ammunition weighed more than twice as much as the ShVAK's 20mm (0.79in) rounds. Although it could penetrate up to 25mm (0.98in) of armour at 400m (1312ft), the appearance of better-protected German AFVs in 1942/43 meant that it was soon outclassed in the anti-tank role. However, it remained effective as an air-to-air and ground attack weapon thanks to its high velocity and very good HE ammunition.

Nudelman-Suranov NS-37 and NS-45 cannon

The NS-37 was developed in 1941/42 and accepted for service following combat trials in 1943. Although it was an excellent anti-tank gun, capable of penetrating 48mm (1.88in) of armour at 500m (1640ft), it was also effective in the air-to-air role, as a single hit was enough to destroy an aircraft. However, the recoil made accurate aiming difficult, especially at the relatively low speeds necessary to acquire AFV targets.

The NS-37 was installed in about 3500 Il-2 Sturmoviks, which carried two (with 40 rounds per gun) in large underwing gondolas. Smaller numbers of LaGG-3 and Yak-9 fighters were also armed with the weapon (and 30 rounds of ammunition) firing through the hollow propeller shaft.

The NS-45 was an enlarged version of the NS-37 that was fitted with a muzzle brake to reduce its fierce recoil. It was the main armament of the Yak-9K, which primarily operated as a 'bomber destroyer'. However, only 50 or so of these aircraft were issued to VVS units, as the engine-mounted cannon's recoil frequently caused mechanical damage. A pair were also fitted beneath the wings of an Il-2 Sturmovik for trials in the anti-tank role, but proved to be too inaccurate, and the recoil was well in excess of what the airframe could safely absorb.

ROCKETS

RS-82 and RS-132 Rockets

Development of these fin-stabilized rockets began in the early 1930s; the RS-82 officially entered service in 1937, followed by the RS-132 in 1938. It seems that the RS-82 was primarily intended for use as an air-to-air weapon. Polikarpov I-16 fighters claimed 19 victories with the rockets against Japanese aircraft in August 1939, during the Battle of Khalkhin Gol. In all probability, these claims are greatly exaggerated: the RS-82's impact-fused warhead was quite capable of destroying any contemporary aircraft, but the rocket's speed was too low for a salvo of six – the I-16's maximum load – to stand much chance of hitting an aerial target.

Various Soviet fighters carried the RS-82 in the first months of the war. Their use in the air-to-air role seems to have been abandoned by 1942, although Il-2 Sturmoviks quite frequently carried up to eight as ground-attack weapons.

The RS-132 was never intended as anything other than an air-to-ground weapon and reportedly equipped a small number of Tupolev SB bombers for combat trials during the Winter War against Finland. However, the primary user seems to have been the Il-2 Sturmovik, which could carry up to four as an alternative to the RS-82.

BETAB-750DS Rockets

From 1938, a family of anti-shipping rockets were developed for the VVS VMF (Naval Aviation). These included the BETAB-170DS, which seems to have remained in service until the 1970s, and the huge BETAB-750DS, which was carried by Il-4T torpedo bombers from 1942 onwards.

450mm (17.7in) Type 45-36AN torpedo

This was based on an Italian 450mm (17.7in) torpedo design that was purchased in 1932. Initial production batches (Type 45-36N) were surface-launched weapons intended to arm older Soviet destroyers, but the type was later modified for aircraft use. The torpedo was strengthened to take the impact of water entry, and the selective speed setting of the Type 45-36N was deleted.

BOMBS

The Russian term for a general-purpose bomb is *fugasnaya aviatsionnaya bomba* (FAB), followed by the bomb's nominal weight in kilogrammes. During the 1930s, the FAB-25, FAB-50, FAB-100, FAB-250 and FAB-500 became standard weapons of the Red Air Force. In 1941, these were supplemented by the FAB-1000, with the FAB-2000 and FAB-5000 following in 1943. The latter two were rarities, as they were too large for any Soviet bomber other than the Pe-8, only 93 of which were produced.

In addition to these 'standard' bombs, the little PTAB – *Protivo Tankovaja Avia Bomba* (Anti-Tank Aviation Bomb) was produced on a vast scale (over 9,000,000) between 1943 and 1945. Its light weight meant that large numbers could be carried by most VVS aircraft such as the Il-2 Sturmovik, which could carry up to 192 internally. When dropped from a typical height of 70m (230ft), this load would form a beaten zone of 15 x 70m (49 x 230ft).

Chapter 5

Lend-Lease Weapons

In early December 1941, reconnaissance units of the German 7th Infantry Division reached the town of Khimki, no more than 18km (11 miles) from the Moscow Kremlin. At that point there were just 670 Soviet tanks available to defend Moscow, 465 of which were obsolescent light tanks.

British tanks (mainly Matildas and Valentines) were crucial at this time when about 90 were already in action. These tanks probably comprised 30-40 per cent of the Red Army's heavy and medium tank strength defending Moscow at the beginning of December 1941, and deliveries were rapidly increasing. By the end of 1941 Britain had delivered 466 tanks.

By 1943, units solely equipped with lend-lease vehicles accounted for as much as 17 per cent of the total Red Army tank force. Large-scale deliveries of the M4A2 Sherman in 1944/45 led to entire tank and mechanized corps being equipped with the type, including 1st Guards Mechanized Corps.

By the end of the war, the total of lend-lease AFVs supplied to the Red Army equalled approximately 16 per cent of Soviet wartime tank production and 12 per cent of self-propelled gun production.

Lend-lease aircraft supplied by Britain and the USA played a key role in

Opposite:

Ford GPA, ¼-ton, 4x4, Amphibian

A column of Ford GPA 'amphibious jeeps' in Germany, 1945. The Red Army received 3,500 of these vehicles which proved to be invaluable in crossing the numerous rivers encountered during the campaigns of 1944/45.

M4A2

An M4A2 in action – the tank has the all-metal T49 tracks, which were far more efficient in the conditions of the Eastern Front than those with rubber track pads.

maintaining the strength of the Red Air Force despite its horrendous accident rate and the equally appalling losses inflicted by the *Luftwaffe*.

Lend-lease aircraft represented 18 per cent of all aircraft flown by the Red Air Force, 20 per cent of all bombers, at least 16 per cent of all fighters and 29 per cent of all naval aircraft. In some commands, the proportion of lend-lease aircraft was even higher – of the 9888 fighters delivered to PVO Strany fighter units in 1941–45, 6953 (more than 70 per cent) were British or American.

BRITISH AND CANADIAN LEND-LEASE AFVS

A steady stream of British-made tanks arrived via the Arctic Convoys and the Persian Corridor during the spring and summer of 1942. Canada eventually produced 1420 Valentines, almost exclusively for the Soviet Union. By July 1942, the Red Army had 13,500 tanks in service, of which more than 16 per cent were lend-lease vehicles. At that time, more than half of these AFVs were British.

Official Soviet sources heavily criticized the quality of lend-lease tanks, often comparing them unfavourably to the T-34 and KV-1. Although this was undoubtedly true of many types such as the Valentine and Matilda, they were all that British and Canadian factories could supply in 1941/42 and were far superior to the T-60 and T-70 that were in volume production at the time.

Infantry Tank Mark II Matilda II

Matilda II infantry tanks were some of the first lend-lease AFVs to be sent to the Red Army; 1084 were shipped, of which 918 survived the hazards of the Arctic Convoys. British instructors were sent with the first shipments and were surprised to find that Soviet crews were reluctant to use the radios, preferring to rely on signal flags. More surprisingly, they preferred to use the back-up manual turret traverse rather than the primary hydraulic-powered system.

Although the Red Army had mixed feelings about the Matildas, their thick armour, comparable to that of the KV-1, was greatly appreciated – one Soviet crewman claimed that his tank had survived 87 hits. In contrast, mobility and firepower were more problematic; the Matilda had never been intended to operate in the depths of a Russian winter and it could be immobilized by packed snow that rapidly built up between the tracks and the armoured side skirts. The tracks themselves were less than ideal for Russian conditions, as the relatively smooth track plates gave little traction on snow or ice. In this case, Soviet units were able to solve the problem by simply welding short lengths of steel bar to each track plate.

The firepower issue was never fully resolved – the Matilda's 2-pounder (40mm) gun was considered equivalent to the 45mm (1.77in) gun of the T-26 and BT tanks, but was unpopular as it lacked an HE round to deal with

Infantry Tank Mark II Matilda II
Crew: 4
Weight: 26.92 tonnes (26.5 tons)
Length: 5.61m (18ft 5in)
Width: 2.59m (8ft 6in)
Height: 2.52m (8ft 3in)
Engine: 2 x 64.8kW (95hp) Leyland 6-cylinder diesel
Speed: 26km/h (16mph)
Range: 258km (160 miles)
Armour: 78mm/20mm (3.07in/0.79in)
Armament: 1 x 40mm (1.57in) 2pdr Ordnance Quick-Firing (OQF) gun (Mk IV CS – 1 x 76.2mm/3in Ordnance QF howitzer), plus 1 x coaxial 7.92mm (0.31in) Besa MG
Radio: Wireless Set No. 11

Matilda II
Here is a Mk II Matilda II of 38th Tank Brigade at Kharkov, May 1942.

Valentine Mark IV

Valentine IV of 36th Tank Brigade, Kharkov, May 1942. This vehicle has a Bren machine gun fitted with the rarely used 100-round drum magazine on the collapsible Lakeman AA mount.

Infantry Tank Mark III Valentine Mark IV

Crew: 3
Weight: 17.27 tonnes (17 tons)
Length: 5.89m (19ft 4in)
Width: 2.64m (8ft 8in)
Height: 2.29m (7ft 6in)
Engine: 97.73kW (131hp) GMC 6004 diesel
Speed: 24km/h (14.9mph)
Range: 145km (90 miles)
Armour: 60mm/7mm (2.36in/0.28in)
Armament: 1 x 40mm (1.57in) 2pdr Ordnance Quick-Firing (OQF) gun, plus 1 x coaxial 7.92mm (0.31in) Besa MG
Radio: Wireless Set No. 11

Valentine Mark IX

The later Valentines armed with 6-pounder (57mm) guns such as this Mark IX were particularly popular with the Red Army and remained in service throughout the war.

Infantry Tank Mark III Valentine Mark IX

Crew: 3
Weight: 18.6 tonnes (18.3 tons)
Length: 6.32m (20ft 9in)
Width: 2.64m (8ft 8in)
Height: 2.29m (7ft 6in)
Engine: 157kW (210hp) GMC 6004 diesel
Speed: 24km/h (14.9mph)
Range: 225km (140 miles)
Armour: 65mm/7mm (2.55in/0.28in)
Armament: 1 x 57mm (2.24in) 6pdr Ordnance Quick-Firing (OQF) gun
Radio: Wireless Set No. 11

German anti-tank guns. A partial solution was found by sending Matilda Mk IV Close Support (CS) tanks armed with the 76.2mm (3in) howitzer, which fired effective HE and smoke shells.

By 1943, most surviving Matildas had been withdrawn from front-line units, but a few may have seen action against Japanese forces in the invasion of Manchuria in August 1945.

Infantry Tank Mark III Valentine

Valentines were the commonest British-designed tanks in service with the Red Army. The first examples were sent to Russia in 1941 and were highly valued for their low silhouette, reliability and good battlefield mobility. Most Marks of Valentine were supplied, totalling almost 2400 British-built tanks and 1388 Canadian vehicles. In 1943, the Russians turned down a British offer to send new Cromwell tanks, requesting more Valentines. It had been intended to phase out Valentine production during 1943, but the type continued to be manufactured well into 1944 solely to meet Soviet requirements.

Valentine Mark IX

The later Valentines armed with 6-pounder (57mm) guns such as this Mark IX were particularly popular with the Red Army and remained in service throughout the war.

Churchill Marks I & II

The first production model, the Churchill Mark I, was armed with a 40mm (2-pounder) gun and coaxial Besa machine gun in a small cast turret, supplemented by a 76.2mm (3in) howitzer in a limited traverse mounting alongside the driver. This was a somewhat archaic armament fit; it was soon revised by fitting a second Besa in place of the howitzer in what became the Mark II.

All these early vehicles that entered British service in the summer of 1941 suffered from their rushed development – there were severe problems with the engine, transmission, tracks and steering. One of the few good points was the armour protection of up to 102mm (4in) – far better than that of any other contemporary British tank.

Despite these problems, 45 Mark IIs (26 of which arrived safely) were

Churchill Mark II
The Red Army tank crews assigned to Churchill-equipped units had to learn to follow a demanding maintenance schedule, including the daily greasing of each tank's 22 bogies.

shipped to Russia in late 1941 on the Arctic Convoys. Understandably, the Red Army was not impressed with these slow, unreliable tanks, but they had to be used operationally given enormous losses of Soviet AFVs in the opening stages of Operation 'Barbarossa'.

Churchill Mark III

Although British and Soviet tank crews struggled to cope with the mechanical problems of the early Churchills, considerable effort was put into designing a new turret to mount the 57mm (6-pounder) gun that was finally coming off the production lines. Production of the up-gunned Churchill Mark III began in the spring of 1942, and the new gun's armour-piercing performance made the Mark III a far more potent tank than its predecessors.

Churchill Mark IV

Despite the effort that had gone into perfecting the welded turret, there were doubts about the future supply of suitable-quality weldable plate. A cast turret was hastily designed to ensure that production could continue in the event of a complete supply failure. This cast turret version was designated Churchill IV, but was otherwise virtually identical to the Mark III.

'Tanks for Russia'

The Marks III and IV formed the vast majority of the Red Army's lend-lease Churchills. Both types were shipped on the Arctic Convoys of 1942 and 1943,

Churchill Mark III

A Churchill Mark III in the winter of 1943/44. The type was phased out of service during 1944 as Guards tank regiments re-equipped with JS-2s.

Infantry Tank Mark IV, Churchill Mark III

Crew: 5
Weight: 39.12 tonnes (38.5 tons)
Length: 7.44m (24ft 5in)
Width: 3.25m (10ft 8in)
Height: 2.49m (8ft 2in)
Engine: 261kW (350hp) Bedford 12-cylinder
Speed: 24km/h (14.9mph)
Range: 140km (88 miles)
Armour: 102mm/16mm (4in/0.62in)
Armament: 1 x 57mm (2.24in) 6pdr Ordnance Quick-Firing (OQF) gun, 1 x coaxial 7.92mm (0.31in) Besa MG, plus 1 x 7.92mm (0.31in) Besa MG in front hull
Radio: Wireless Set No. 11

Churchill Mark IV
Churchill Mark IV, 36th Guards Heavy Tank Regiment, at Kursk, July/August 1943.

Infantry Tank Mark IV Churchill Mark IV
Crew: 5
Weight: 39.12 tonnes (38.5 tons)
Length: 7.44m (24ft 5in)
Width: 3.25m (10ft 8in)
Height: 2.49m (8ft 2in)
Engine: 261kW (350hp) Bedford 12-cylinder
Speed: 24km/h (14.9mph)
Range: 140km (88 miles)
Armour: 102mm/16mm (4in/0.62in)
Armament: 1 x 57mm (2.24in) 6pdr Ordnance Quick-Firing (OQF) gun, 1 x coaxial 7.92mm (0.31in) Besa MG, plus 1 x 7.92mm (0.31in) Besa MG in front hull
Radio: Wireless Set No. 11

the probable totals being:

- Mark III – 151 sent, 24 lost, 127 received.
- Mark IV – 105 sent, all of which arrived safely.

Although these represented a significant improvement in comparison with the initial shipment of Mark IIs, the Red Army was still critical of the Churchill's reliability and its mobility in snow or icy conditions. Some attempts were made to improve its performance by modifying the tracks, but these were no more than partially successful. However, some favourable conclusions were drawn. One report commented that: 'The [Churchill] Mk IV tank has weaker armament than the KV-1 and KV-1S, but superior armour. The Mk IV carries three times as much ammunition for its machine guns as the KV. At 950 metres the AP shell from the 57mm gun goes through one side of a Panzer III and out of the other, penetrating a total of 60mm of armour. The Mk IV has lower power/weight ratio, and therefore a lower maximum speed, than the KV-1 and KV-1S, but its average speed is equal. The Mk IV and KV are equivalent in their operational range.'

Plans for future shipments of Churchills were cancelled in favour of increased deliveries of the Valentine infantry tank that was much preferred by the Red Army.

Red Army Churchills

The allocation of the handful of Churchill Mark IIs to reach the Red Army is unknown, but the Marks III and IV were issued to the following regiments:

Kursk, July 1943
A Churchill IV of 5th Guards Tank Army passes a destroyed SdKfz 232 armoured car.

- **15th Guards Heavy Tank Regiment** – Formed on 26 October 1942 in the Moscow Military District from 137th Tank Brigade. It was initially assigned to I Guards Mechanized Corps, but was removed from the corps in July 1943 and thereafter served as an independent infantry support regiment. It was disbanded in February 1944 to provide cadres for new heavy assault gun regiments.
- **36th Guards Heavy Tank Regiment** – Formed in March 1943 in the Moscow Military District. Unusually, it was organized as an ordinary tank regiment with a total of 31 Churchills instead of the standard heavy tank regiment's establishment of 21 tanks. It was assigned to XVIII Tank Corps in June 1943 and took part in the fighting around Prokhorovka. In the subsequent reorganization of 5th Guards Tank Army, it was removed from XVIII Tank Corps and deployed in the infantry support role until mid-1944. In June/July 1944, it re-equipped with JS-2 heavy tanks before joining IX Tank Corps in October 1944, where it served for the rest of the war.
- **48th Guards Heavy Tank Regiment** – Formed in November 1942 in the Moscow Military District. It first saw action in the infantry support role with 21st Army at Stalingrad in January 1943. It was transferred to V Guards Tank Corps in June 1943, before going into Stavka reserve in the Moscow Military District. During the first half of 1944, it re-equipped with JS-2 heavy tanks before being assigned to VIII Guards Mechanized

Universal Carrier Mark I
This carrier retains its Boys anti-tank rifle in the front gunner's position, but has a DP light machine gun on an AA mount in the rear compartment.

Universal Carrier Mark I
Crew: 5
Weight: 3.81 tonnes (3.75 tons)
Length: 3.65m (12ft)
Width: 2.06m (6ft 9in)
Height: 1.57m (5ft 2in)
Engine: 63kW (85hp) Ford V8
Speed: 48km/h (30mph)
Range: 250km (150 miles)
Armour: 10mm/7mm (0.39in/0.28in)
Armament: 1 x 7.7mm (0.303in) Bren gun. Many lend-lease carriers seem to have been shipped with a Boys anti-tank rifle in addition to the Bren gun.

Corps, where it served for the rest of the war.

- **59th Guards Heavy Tank Regiment** – Formed in July 1943 in the Volga Military District and assigned to IX Mechanized Corps. There is a degree of uncertainty about its equipment, but it is most likely to have formed with Churchills and been re-equipped with JS-2 heavy tanks at some time in 1944.

Universal Carrier

In the 1920s, the British Army accepted the first Carden-Loyd machine gun carriers – simple, open-topped machines powered by Ford Model T engines. The cheapness of these little AFVs made them attractive to the chronically underfunded British Army of the interwar years, and their development culminated with the introduction of the Universal Carrier in 1940.

Production of the Universal Carrier and its variants was undertaken on a vast scale: factories in Britain, Canada, the USA, Australia and New Zealand turned out roughly 81,700 vehicles during the war years, with a further 31,300 completed in the postwar period. At least 2600 were sent to the Red Army, and were mainly used as armoured personnel carriers (APCs), reconnaissance and command vehicles. The Russians criticized the type's battlefield mobility, as its narrow tracks did not perform well in deep snow and mud.

UK-SUPPLIED LEND-LEASE AFV WEAPONS

7.7mm (0.303in) Bren Gun

The Bren was a licence-built version of the Czechoslovak ZGB 33 light machine gun. This, in turn, was a modified version of the ZB vz. 26, which had performed exceptionally well in a series of British service trials in 1935. The Bren's name was derived from Brno, the Czech city where the Zb vz. 26 was designed (in the Zbrojovka Brno Factory) and Enfield, site of the Royal Small Arms Factory. The Bren featured a distinctive top-mounted curved box magazine, conical flash hider and quick-change barrel. It proved to be an outstanding weapon and was adopted for AFV use in addition to its primary role as the infantry's standard light machine gun.

The Bren armed the Universal Carriers shipped to the Red Army and was also the AA armament of most British and Canadian-supplied tanks. These tanks usually carried the Bren stowed inside the turret – when needed, it was fitted to the collapsible Lakeman AA mount.

David Fletcher of the Bovington Tank Museum commented that Tom Lakeman, the designer of the AA mount, was a Royal Tank Regiment officer, generally regarded as slightly mad, who devised all kinds of strange machine-gun mountings. The Lakeman mount comprised a set of collapsible arms and springs, the idea being to reduce the weight of the weapon when used against aircraft. In practice, it was generally more trouble than it was worth, with (allegedly) an alarming tendency to collapse as the Bren was firing.

Bren Gun

A cut-away diagram of the Bren, showing the feed mechanism and the standard 30-round box magazine. A 100-round drum magazine was also produced in limited quantities (primarily for use in the AA role.)

7.92mm (0.31in) Besa machine gun

The Besa was the British version of the Czech ZB-53 machine gun, which was adopted by the Czech army for AFV and infantry use as the TK vz. 37. In British service, it was purely an AFV weapon, which rapidly gained a reputation for reliability when it entered service in 1939. The vast majority of British tanks sent to Russia mounted Besas as their secondary armament.

Boys Anti-Tank Rifle

This weapon was named after its designer, Captain Henry Boys, who died shortly before it was approved for service in November 1937. It was the standard British infantry anti-tank weapon of the early war period, but was increasingly ineffective against anything other than armoured cars and light tanks after 1940. Boys anti-tank rifles seem to have been included with

'O Group'
The crews of Red Army Universal Carriers receive their orders. Both carriers are armed with Boys anti-tank rifles.

the majority of Universal Carriers supplied to the Red Army.

Ordnance QF 2-pounder

The 2-pounder was originally designed as a tank gun in 1934 to replace the obsolete 3-pounder gun. In January 1935, the 2-pounder was approved for future British tanks and first saw service in the A9 cruiser tank. Thereafter, it was the main armament of most British tanks until the 6-pounder became available in 1942.

In British service, the 2-pounder was found to be effective against the German and Italian AFVs of 1940, few of which had armour thicker than 30mm (1.18in), but struggled to penetrate the better-protected German tanks and assault guns that began to appear from 1941 onwards. In part, this was due to the fact that the 2-pounder fired only simple solid steel AP shot that tended to break up on hitting German face-hardened armour. The situation only began to improve in May 1942, when APCBC rounds became available.

In 1942, the Red Army carried out firing trials of a Valentine III's 2-pounder gun against a captured Panzer 38(t) with frontal armour of 25mm (0.98in), plus a further 25mm (0.98in) of appliqué armour and 30mm (1.18in) of side armour. It was found that: 'At 250 metres, the 2dr penetrates the first 25mm plate of the front armour, but does not penetrate the second. The front plate develops a crack 250mm long. At 400 metres, it can only form a 7mm deep dent in the first armour plate. Closing in to 200 metres, the Valentine fires at the front plate of the turret and penetrates. A hole is formed, 50mm in radius. Cracks run though the first armour plate, 200 mm around the breach. Five bolts holding the front armour plate in place are torn off. Firing again, from 600 metres, the shot forms a crack from the top to the

Valentine
The Valentine was generally popular with Soviet tank crews who appreciated its low silhouette, exceptional reliability and good protection.

bottom of the front armour plate. Moving on to the side, the first shot penetrates the turret all the way through. One hole on the left side, 55mm entrance diameter, 70mm exit diameter. One hole on the right side, 38mm entrance and 38mm exit diameter. Another shot at 600 metres penetrates the turret, as well as the ammunition racks.

'At 800 metres, the Valentine penetrates the side of the turret, forming two cracks, 600 and 400mm long. Ten bolts securing the armour plate on are torn off. Another shot from 800 metres penetrates the side of the upper hull, forming two 300mm cracks, and causing spalling.

'Moving to the front of the tank again, the Valentine fires a shot at the upper sloped plate at 400 metres. A section of the armour, 300mm by 140mm, is broken off. Another shot at the lower sloped plate breaks off a piece 100mm by 150mm and penetrates the fuel tank.

'Conclusions: AP rounds do not penetrate the frontal armour. The reason for this is the poor quality of the shot which are completely destroyed on impact. The 30mm side armour can be penetrated from 800–1000 metres.'

There are a couple of points that are not immediately obvious from the report – the 38(t) was a good light tank, but many production batches were completed with armour that had been over-hardened to the point that it had become dangerously brittle. This very hard armour shattered shot that failed to penetrate, but was also prone to cracking and spalling, with potentially lethal consequences for the crew.

Ordnance QF 6-pounder

Even as the 2-pounder entered service, it was recognized that a more powerful gun would soon be needed to deal with the next generation of AFVs. A 57mm (2.24in) gun was chosen, as the calibre had been adopted by the Royal Navy as long ago as 1884 and tooling was readily available. Woolwich Arsenal began design studies in 1938, and the new gun was scheduled to replace the 2-pounder from mid-1940. The massive losses of equipment in the Dunkirk evacuation and the subsequent invasion scare forced continuation of 2-pounder production until late 1941. The first 6-pounder-armed tanks (Churchill Marks III and IV, Valentine Mark IX and Crusader Mark III) began to enter service in 1942. Both the Churchill and the Valentine were shipped to the Red Army from late 1942 onwards.

Another Soviet test pitted the Churchill Mark IV's 6-pounder against a captured Tiger. The report noted:

'Target: turret. Armour thickness: 82 mm. Range: 800 metres. Result: penetration. Entrance hole 82mm in diameter, exit hole, 75mm in diameter.

'Target: turret. Armour thickness: 82mm. Range: 1,000 metres. Result: dent 90mm deep, 90mm in diameter. The hit cracked the inner face of the turret wall and formed a 10mm bump.

'Target: turret. Armour thickness: 82mm. Distance: 1,000 metres. Result: dent 120mm by 80mm, 70mm deep. Bump on the inside.

'Target: side. Armour thickness: 82mm. Range: 1,000 metres. Result: penetration, entrance hole 70mm in diameter, exit hole 115mm in diameter.

'Target: side. Armour thickness: 82mm. Distance: 625 metres. Result: penetration, breach diameter 58mm.'

Ordnance QF 3-inch howitzer

This tank howitzer was introduced to provide smoke and HE fire support for 2-pounder-armed AFVs. British and Commonwealth AFVs armed with the howitzer were identified by the suffix CS (Close Support). The Red Army received a number of Matilda CS tanks after raising concerns about the lack of an HE round for the 2-pounder.

Matildas of 5th Mechanized Corps

In October 1942 5th Mechanized Corps was mainly equipped with British lend-lease tanks – 78 Matilda IIs, 117 Valentine tanks and just two T-34s.

US LEND-LEASE AFVS

Lend-lease deliveries from the USA were on a truly massive scale – besides 12,000 AFVs (including 7,000 tanks) they included a total of 427,284 trucks and 35,170 motorcycles – 'soft-skin' vehicles that provided crucial mobility and logistic support for the Red Army.)

Light Tank M3

The M3 was essentially an updated version of the Light Tank M2, incorporating thicker armour, a modified suspension and a new gun recoil system. The type entered service with the US Army in February 1941, and the first lend-lease M3s arrived in Russia in the spring of 1942. These M3s never seem to have been referred to by the British nickname of 'Stuart' – in Russian service, the type was generally known as the M3l or M3 light.

The Red Army appreciated the armour-piercing performance of the M3l's 37mm (1.46in) gun, which they judged to be better than that of both the 2-pounder that armed British-supplied tanks and the Russian 45mm (1.77in) gun. However, they were critical of the tank's height, which made it dangerously conspicuous, and its rubber track pads, which gave poor traction in deep snow or mud. Locally produced metal 'spurs' were fitted to the tracks and marginally improved cross-country performance.

The later M3A1 was also criticized

M3A1

A Red Army M3A1 in a wintry setting – in common with many other British and US-supplied AFVs, it did not cope well with the extremes of the Russian climate.

M3 Stuart
The Russians felt that the sponson-mounted machine guns of early-production M3s were virtually useless as they had no proper sights.

M3

Crew: 4
Weight: 12.7 tonnes (12.5 tons)
Length: 4.53m (14ft 10in)
Width: 2.24m (7ft 4in)
Height: 2.64m (8ft 8in)
Engine: 186.4kW (250hp) Continental W-670-9A radial
Speed: 58km/h (36mph)
Range: 110km (70 miles)
Armour: 44mm/10mm (1.73in/0.39in)
Armament: 1 x 37mm (1.45in) gun, plus 5 x 7.62mm (0.3in) Browning machine guns (1 x AA, 1 x coaxial, 1 in front hull and 2 in hull sponsons)

M3A1

Crew: 4
Weight: 12.9 tonnes (12.7 tons)
Length: 4.53m (14ft 10in)
Width: 2.24m (7ft 4in)
Height: 2.39m (7ft 10in)
Engine: 186.4kW (250hp) Continental W-670-9A radial
Speed: 58km/h (36mph)
Range: 217km (135 miles)
Armour: 51mm/13mm (2in/0.5in)
Armament: 1 x 37mm (1.45in) gun, plus 3 x 7.62mm (0.3in) Browning machine guns (1 x AA, 1 x coaxial and 1 in front hull)

M3A1 Stuart
Although very cramped even by Russian standards, the M3A1 was lower than the M3 and benefited from slightly thicker armour.

M3 Medium Tank

In Russian service, the vulnerable M3 became known as 'A grave for seven brothers'.

Medium Tank M3

Crew: 7
Weight: 27.9 tonnes (27.46 tons)
Length: 5.64m (18ft 6in)
Width: 2.72m (8ft 11in)
Height: 3.12m (10ft 3in)
Engine: 298.28kW (400hp) Wright (Continental) R975 EC2 radial
Speed: 39km/h (24mph)
Range: 190km (120 miles)
Armour: 51mm/13mm (2in/0.5in)
Armament: 1 x 75mm (2.95in) M2 or M3 limited traverse hull gun, 1 x 37mm (1.45in) gun in turret, plus 4 x 7.62mm (0.3in) Browning machine guns (1 x cupola, 1 coaxial, and 2 in front hull)

by the Russians, who felt that the newly fitted turret basket and power traverse mechanism unacceptably reduced the crew space in what was already a very cramped tank. An estimated 1240 M3/ M3A1 tanks were used by the Red Army, but the offer of M5 light tanks was turned down in favour of increased deliveries of M4 mediums.

Medium Tank M3

From late 1941 until well into 1943, 1386 M3 medium tanks were shipped to the Soviet Union, with 410 lost in transit. As with many other lend-lease tanks, the Red Army was not too impressed. One report noted that: 'Both the size and design of the hull are not modern. The tank is too tall, and, except for the sloped frontal armour, it is poorly protected against anti-tank fire. The tank comfortably accommodates the crew of seven and it also can carry ten infantrymen armed with submachine guns in summer conditions. While carrying troops, all tank guns can fire. The ten infantrymen can disembark through the side doors in 25–30 seconds.'

Presumably, the rather bizarre idea of cramming infantry inside the tank was due to the configuration of its high, sloping engine decks, which made it impractical to carry tank riders externally. Although firing the tank's guns with infantry aboard may have been possible for demonstration purposes, it seems unlikely under combat conditions – imagine cursing loaders shoving infantrymen out of the way as they tried to reach the ammunition racks.

A further report dated January 1943 condemned the basic design, which meant that taking up a hull down position made it impossible to use the 75mm (2.95in) gun or hull machine guns. In this situation, only the turret-mounted 37mm (1.46in) gun and machine guns could fire, which was totally inadequate for a medium tank.

The height of the tank was also a major issue, as it made it a conspicuous target for hostile anti-tank guns and, just like the M3 light tank, it burned all too readily when penetrated.

With almost 1500 T-34s being built per month, Soviet use of the M3 medium tank declined after mid-1943. However, the type remained in service on secondary fronts, such as in the Arctic during the Petsamo–Kirkenes Offensive in October 1944.

Medium Tank M4 Sherman

The Red Army knew the M4 as the *Emcha* – derived from the resemblance of an open-topped figure 4 to the

Medium Tank M4A2 Sherman
Crew: 5
Weight: 31.8 tonnes (31.3 tons)
Length: 5.92m (19ft 5in)
Width: 2.62m (8ft 7in)
Height: 2.74m (9ft)
Engine: 280kW (375hp) General Motors 6046 diesel
Speed: 48km/h (30mph)
Range: 240km (150 miles)
Armour: 108mm/13mm (4.25in/0.5in)
Armament: 1 x 75mm (2.95in) M3, plus 1 x 12.7mm (0.5in) AA machine gun and 2 x 7.62mm (0.3in) Browning machine guns (1 x coaxial, and 1 in front hull)

M4A2 Sherman Tank
An M4A2 in worn winter camouflage, Narva, northern Estonia, winter 1944/45.

M4A2 76(W) Sherman

M4A2 76(W), 1st Mechanized Corps, 2nd Guards Tank Army, Berlin, May 1945.

M4A2 76(W) Sherman

Crew: 5
Weight: 33.3 tonnes (32.77 tons)
Length: 6.3m (18ft 6in)
Width: 2.62m (8ft 7in)
Height: 2.97m (9ft 9in)
Engine: 280kW (375hp) General Motors 6046 diesel
Speed: 48km/h (30mph)
Range: 161km (100 miles)
Armour: 108mm/13mm (4.25in/0.5in)
Armament: 1 x 76mm (3in) M1A2, plus 1 x 12.7mm (0.5in) AA machine gun and 2 x 7.62mm (0.3in) Browning machine guns (1 x coaxial and 1 in front hull)

Cyrillic letter *che* or *cha*. The Russians insisted on diesel-powered M4s, at least partly to ease fuel supply problems, as most of their own tanks had diesel engines. Another reason was that Soviet-produced petrol had a very low octane rating that quickly damaged Western petrol engines designed for higher-octane fuel. Diesel also posed a lower fire risk if a tank was hit and penetrated by enemy fire, although postwar analysis showed that ammunition fires were the greatest threat to tank crews. The Russians felt that their M4A2s were markedly less prone to ammunition fires than the T-34. The first lend-lease M4A2s arrived in Russia in late 1942, and were regarded as a major improvement on the M3 Medium. The majority of these early vehicles had factory-fitted appliqué armour on the hull sides to give improved protection to the ammunition racks. The initial 2007 Shermans received by the Red Army were armed with the 75mm (2.95in) gun, but the remaining 2095 had the more potent 76mm (3in) gun.

The battlefield survivability of the 2095 M4A2 76(W)s was vastly improved by incorporating wet ammunition stowage – hence the 'W' suffix in the designation. This involved replacing the conventional ammunition racks with double-walled stowage boxes. The gap between the walls of the boxes was filled with water, treated with ethylene glycol to prevent freezing, and 'Ammudamp', a solution containing rust inhibitors. If the boxes were penetrated, the water would douse the resulting ammunition fire.

This wet stowage, and the transfer of most of the ammunition from the hull sponsons to boxes under the turret, drastically reduced the Sherman's readiness to catch fire when hit. The 76mm (3in)-armed tanks were fitted with a 6-round ready rack in the turret surrounded by 7.9 litres (1.74 gallons) of water and a box on each side of the drive shaft, one holding 30 rounds and the other 35, containing a total of 131 litres (28.8 gallons) of water.

The first 76mm (3in)-armed Shermans arrived in Russia in the late summer of 1944. They were so highly regarded that they eventually formed the entire tank strength of some elite formations, notably the 1st, 3rd and 9th Guards Mechanized Corps.

SU-57

SU-57 was the Soviet designation of the T48 Gun Motor Carriage. This was a tank destroyer produced by mounting the 57mm (2.24in) gun M1 – a US licence-built version of the British 6-pounder anti-tank gun – on a modified M3 halftrack. A total of

SU-57
16th Separate Tank Destroyer Brigade, Lower Dnieper Offensive, October 1943.

SU-57
Crew: 5
Weight: 8.6 tonnes (8.46 tons)
Length: 6.42m (21ft)
Width: 1.96m (6ft 5in)
Height: 2.3m (7ft 6in)
Engine: 95kW (128hp) White 160AX
Speed: 72km/h (45mph)
Range: 320km (200 miles)
Armour: 16mm/6.4mm (0.62in/0.25in)
Armament: 1 x 57mm (2.24in) M1 gun

M15A1

The M15A1 carried 200 rounds of 37mm (1.46in) ammunition and 1200 rounds for the twin Browning machine guns.

M15A1 Combination Gun Motor Carriage

Crew: 7
Weight: 9 tonnes (8.86 tons)
Length: 6.42m (21ft 1in)
Width: 2.5m (8ft 2in)
Height: 2.64m (8ft 8in)
Engine: 110kW (148hp) White 160AX
Speed: 72km/h (45mph)
Range: 320km (200 miles)
Armour: 16mm/6.4mm (0.62in/0.25in)
Armament: 1 x 37mm (1.46in) AA Gun M1, plus 2 x 12.7mm (0.5in) Browning machine guns

650 were supplied to the Red Army, who deployed them in tank destroyer brigades, each with three 20-strong battalions.

M15A1 Combination Gun Motor Carriage (CGMC)

The origin of this self-propelled AA gun can be traced back to the T1A2 Multiple Gun Motor Carriage (MGMC) project, which comprised a 37mm (1.46in) AA gun on an M2 halftrack. A prototype was completed and redesignated as the T28, but failed its acceptance trials due to excessive recoil; the type was rejected for service in 1942.

A requirement for a mobile AA system for service in North Africa led to the rapid reinstatement of the project based on the larger M3 halftrack as the T28E1, armed with a 37mm (1.46in) AA gun and two water-cooled 12.7mm (0.5in) M2 Browning machine guns. A total of 80 vehicles were completed before production switched to the M15 with the same armament in an armoured mount.

The weight of the guns and armour pushed the M3 chassis to its limits; after 680 had been completed during 1943, the type was replaced in production by the M15A1. This was armed with the 37mm (1.46in) AA gun and two air-cooled 12.7mm (0.5in) M2HB Browning machine guns in a lighter armoured mount. A total of 1652 were produced in 1943/44, 100 of which were supplied to the Red Army.

M17 Multiple Gun Motor Carriage (MGMC)

The M17 was a combination of the M5 halftrack and the M45 Quadmount. The latter was a turret developed by the W.L. Maxon Corporation in response to a US Army requirement for a light AA weapons system. Prototypes armed with twin 12.7mm (0.5in) M2HB Browning machine guns were tested successfully and immediately accepted for service as the M33. Experiments showed that the turret could be adapted to mount four M2HBs; this configuration was standardized as the M45. The new turret was mounted on a variety of vehicles, including the M5 halftrack that became the M17 MGMC. The type entered service in December 1943 and 1000 vehicles were shipped to the Red Army.

M2 Halftrack

The M2 was the earliest US armoured halftrack to see widespread service in all Allied armies. The design was based on French Citroën-Kégresse vehicles that had been evaluated by the US

M17 Multiple Gun Motor Carriage
Weight: 8.94 tonnes (8.8 tons)
Length: 6.49m (21ft 4in)
Width: 2.17m (6ft 5in)
Height: 2.3m (7ft 6in)
Engine: 95kW (128hp) International Harvester RED-450-B
Speed: 68km/h (42mph)
Range: 320km (200 miles)
Armour: 16mm/6.4mm (0.62in/0.25in)
Armament: 4 x 12.7mm (0.5in) Browning machine guns

M17
The powered traverse and elevation of the M45 Quadmount made it a significantly more effective AA system than the M15A1's manually operated M54 turret.

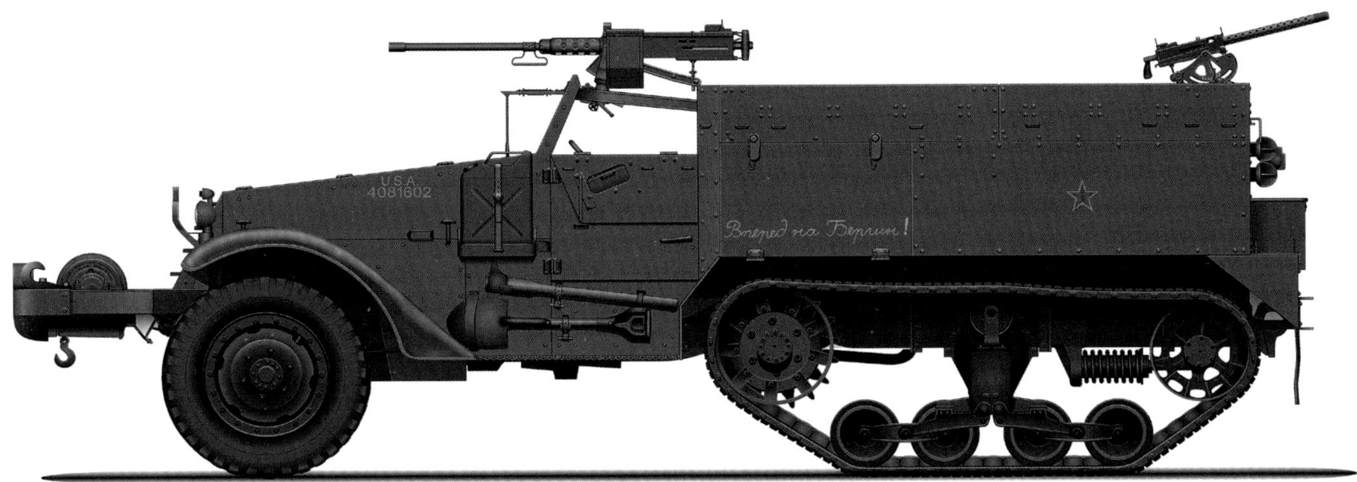

M2 Halftrack
Both the M2's machine guns were mounted on a skate rail running around the inside of the hull giving a full 360° traverse.

M2 Halftrack
Crew: 2, plus 7 infantrymen
Weight: 8.7 tonnes (8.56 tons)
Length: 5.96m (19ft 7in)
Width: 2.2m (7ft 3in)
Height: 2.26m (7ft 5in)
Engine: 110kW (148hp) White 160AX
Speed: 72km/h (45mph)
Range: 350km (220 miles)
Armour: 12mm/6mm (0.47in/0.25in)
Armament: 1 x 12.7mm (0.5in) Browning machine gun, plus 1 x 7.62mm (0.3in) Browning machine gun

ordnance department in the 1930s, but used standard American truck components to speed up production and reduce costs.

The prototype used a modified M3 scout car hull and the Timken rear bogie assembly from a Ford Marmon-Herrington T9 halftrack truck. This prototype was too underpowered for service use, but the installation of the more powerful White 160AX engine improved the type's performance sufficiently for it to be adopted by the US Army as the M2.

An estimated 800 M2s were sent to the Soviet Union, serving mainly as artillery tractors, command and reconnaissance vehicles.

M3A1 Scout Car

In 1937, the White Motor Company began design studies for a vehicle to succeed the T9/M2 scout car. An initial 64 vehicles were completed under the designation M3, before production switched to the enlarged M3A1 in 1940.

Almost 21,000 of these versatile 4x4s were built between 1940 and 1944; 3300 were supplied to the Red Army, which primarily used them as command vehicles, personnel carriers and liaison vehicles.

The type remained in Soviet service until 1947, and may have influenced the design of the postwar BTR-40 armoured personnel carrier.

Overwatch duties

The gunner of an M3A1 covers the advance of the rest of his detachment.

M3A1 Scout Car

This example was used as a command vehicle by General Pavel Rotmistrov, commander-in-chief of Fifth Guards Tank Army.

M3A1 Scout Car

Crew: 2, plus 6 infantrymen
Weight: 5.62 tonnes (5.53 tons)
Length: 5.626m (18ft 5in)
Width: 2m (6ft 8in)
Height: 1.99m (6ft 6in)
Engine: 82kW (110hp) Hercules JXD
Speed: 80km/h (50mph)
Range: 400km (250 miles)
Armour: 13mm/6mm (0.5in/0.25in)
Armament: 1 x 12.7mm (0.5in) Browning machine gun, plus 1 x 7.62mm (0.3in) Browning machine gun

US-SUPPLIED AFV WEAPONS

7.62mm (0.3in) Browning M1919A4 machine gun
The M1919 was an air-cooled derivative of the water-cooled M1917 Browning. It was a highly reliable weapon that was fitted to almost all US-supplied AFVs as a hull, coaxial or pintle-mounted. weapon.

12.7mm (0.5in) Browning M2HB heavy machine gun
Like the M1919, the M2HB was an air-cooled derivative of an earlier water-cooled Browning, in this case the M1921. The HB suffix refers to the heavy barrel used in all land service 12.7mm (0.5in) Brownings to allow sustained fire without dangerous overheating. It was fitted to many US-supplied tanks as a pintle-mounted AA weapon, and was the main armament of most US halftracks shipped to the Red Army.

37mm (1.46in) Gun M6
The M6 was a modified version of the 37mm (1.46in) M3 anti-tank gun that formed the main armament of most versions of the M3 light tank and the secondary armament of the M3 medium tank. Anti-tank performance was roughly similar to other 37mm (1.46in) and 40mm (1.57in) guns, but the M6 was more versatile as it was issued with HE and canister ammunition as well as armour-piercing rounds.

75mm (2.95in) Gun M2/M3
These guns were derived from the French Canon de 75 modèle 1897 field gun of World War I, which was also adopted by the US Army and used well into World War II as the 75mm (2.95in) M1897 field gun.

They fired the same range of ammunition as the French field gun, together with a number of US-designed rounds, which eventually included M72 AP, M61/A1 APCBC-HE, M48 HE, M64 white phosphorus, and M89 hexachloroethane (HC) smoke. Although they were not

Below: 7.62mm (.3in) M1919A4 Machine Gun
The Browning M1919A4 had a rate of fire of 400-600rpm and an effective range of 1,400 metres (1,500 yards).

Bottom: 12.7mm M2HB Heavy Machine Gun
First produced in the 1930s, the M2HB is still used in updated form today by many armed forces around the world.

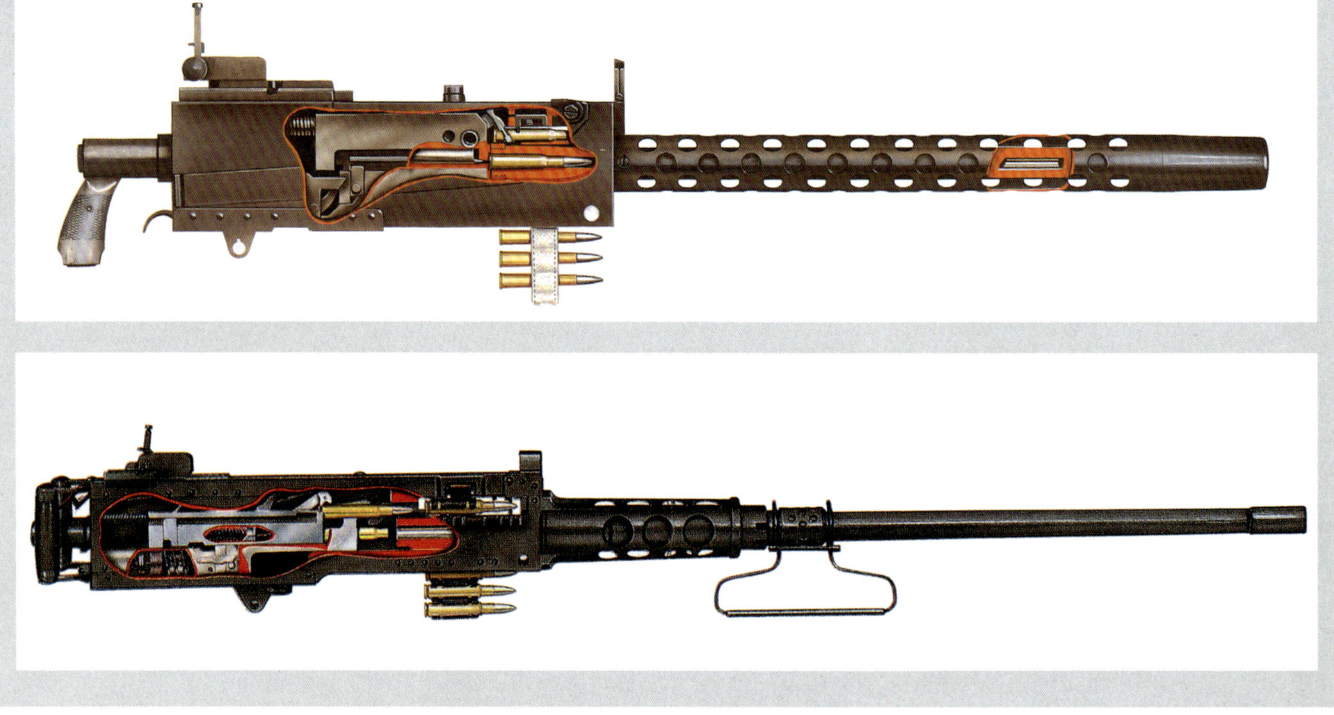

outstanding anti-tank weapons, the M2 and M3 were highly effective when firing HE in the infantry support role.

76mm (3in) gun M1

The need for a more powerful tank gun was recognized even before the 75mm (2.95in) M2/M3 guns saw action. The specification for the M4 medium tank that was issued in September 1941 included provision for a variety of guns, including a high-velocity 76.2mm (3in) gun. By August 1942, the design of the M1 had been finalized, although it took another year to develop a suitable turret for the gun that would satisfactorily fit the M4.

Combat experience emphasized a number of problems that had been encountered during firing trials, notably that of muzzle blast throwing up clouds of dust and revealing the tank's position (besides obscuring the 'fall of shot'). This was largely solved by fitting a muzzle brake on later-production guns, which were designated M1A1C and M1A2.

37mm (1.46in) AA gun M1

The M1 originated with design studies undertaken as early as 1921,

Su-57s on the road
SU-57s of the anti-tank battery, 4th Motorcycle Regiment, 6th Tank Army, travel through Romania, Summer 1944.

but the financial crisis of the late 1920s forced work to be suspended until 1934. The type entered service with the US Army in 1938. Almost 7300 were produced before it was replaced by licence-built versions of the Bofors 40mm (1.57in) gun.

The M1 formed the main armament of the M15A1 Combination Gun Motor Carriage (M15A1 CGMC). A total of 100 of these self-propelled AA guns were supplied to the Red Army.

'In the deep mid-winter'
A Hurricane en-route to Vayenga. Its engine is protected from the worst of the cold by a close-fitting quilted cover as winter temperatures in northern Russia averaged -14°C (7°F).

LEND-LEASE AIRCRAFT

Official Soviet sources consistently downplayed the importance of Western aircraft and criticized their performance, rating most as inferior to their Russian counterparts. In part, this was seen as essential propaganda for home consumption, but many of the problems that did occur were down to the operational conditions on the Eastern Front. British and US aircraft designed to be flown from well-equipped airfields did not fare well on Russia's primitive airstrips in extreme winter and summer temperatures. Equally, Red Air Force attempts to operate these aircraft on Russian-produced low-octane fuels drastically reduced their performance and serviceability.

The fuel problem was tacitly acknowledged; there were constant Soviet requests for deliveries of high-octane aviation fuel, and a total of 1,086,432 tonnes (1,197,587 tons) was shipped to Russia, including 506,597 tonnes (558,428 tons) of 99 or higher octane.

The best estimate of the major types of aircraft supplied under lend-lease is:

- Hawker Hurricane 2897
- Supermarine Spitfire 1338
- Handley Page Hampden 32
- Bell P-39 Airacobra 4700
- Bell P-63 Kingcobra 2397
- Curtiss P-40 2100
- A20 Boston 3000
- B-25 Mitchell 862

Hawker Hurricane

Even in its 'hour of glory' during the Battle of Britain, the Hurricane was barely adequate in combat against the Bf 109E. The more powerful Hurricane II improved matters, but was thoroughly outclassed by the Bf 109F that began entering service in October 1940.

Nevertheless, various sub-types of the Hurricane II and later Marks remained in production until 1944. A significant number of these were shipped to Russia, the breakdown being:

- 218 Mark IIA, 22 of which were lost before arrival.
- 1884 Mark IIB, 278 lost before arrival.
- 1182 Mark IIC, 46 lost before arrival, 117 rejected.
- 60 Mark IID, 14 rejected.
- 30 Mark IV.

In all, 3374 Hurricanes were supplied, of which 346 were lost before delivery, 2897 accepted by the Russians and 131 rejected.

The first Hurricane IIBs arrived in Russia in September 1941, flown by 151 Wing RAF deployed to Vayenga near Murmansk. The RAF flew bomber escort missions until early October while training Russian pilots and ground crews to operate the Hurricanes. The aircraft were then formally handed over to the Red Air Force, which had mixed feelings about them and those that followed.

Many Russian pilots felt that the Mark IIB's armament of twelve 7.7mm (0.303in) Browning machine guns were inadequate – some units replaced them with two 20mm (0.79in) ShVAK cannon and two 12.7mm (0.5in) UB machine guns.

Eventually, all surviving machine-gun-armed Hurricanes (about 1200) were rearmed for the ground-attack role with four 20mm (0.79in) ShVAK cannon, two 7.7mm (0.303in) ShKAS machine guns and six RS-82 rockets. Besides improving firepower, the new

Crash landing

A Hurricane IIB of the 609th Fighter Regiment forced down near the Finnish airfield at Tilksjarvi, Eastern Karelia, April 1942.

Hurricane IIB

A Hurricane IIB as operated by 151 Wing RAF at Vayenga, near Murmansk during September and October 1941, before being handed over to the 72nd Composite Regiment, VVS.

Hurricane Mark IIB
Type: Single-seat fighter-bomber
Length: 9.84m (32ft 3in)
Wingspan: 12.19m (40ft)
Height: 4m (13ft 1.5in)
Wing area: 23.92m² (257.5ft²)
Empty weight: N/k
Loaded weight: 3480kg (7670lb)
Maximum take-off weight: 3950kg (8710lb)
Powerplant: 1 × Rolls-Royce Merlin XX liquid-cooled V-12, 883kW (1185hp)
Maximum speed: 547km/h (340mph)
Range: 965km (600 miles)
Service ceiling: 10,970m (36,000ft)
Rate of climb: 14.1m/s (2780ft/min)
Wing loading: 121.9kg/m² (29.8lb/ft²)
Armament: 12 x 7.7mm (.303in) Browning machine guns

armament also eased the strain on the supply chain, as the Russians no longer had to rely on replacement guns and components from Britain.

The same criticism could hardly be levelled at the Mark IIC – its four 20mm (0.79in) Hispano cannon delivered twice the weight of fire of the Yak-3's armament of one 20mm (0.79in) ShVAK cannon and two 12.7mm (0.5in) machine guns.

Supermarine Spitfire

In October 1942, Stalin wrote to Churchill specifically requesting urgent deliveries of Spitfires. The first Spitfire VBs were sent in the spring of 1943, but the Red Air Force units which received them were unimpressed. Many of the aircraft had already seen considerable service with the RAF and, despite reconditioning, were virtually worn out.

After receiving new VBs, Russian pilots were less critical. The type's performance and firepower were good, although getting used to the wing-mounted armament was difficult. Almost all Russian-built fighters had closely grouped engine-mounted guns, which required little adjustment. In contrast, the Spitfire's widely spaced guns required careful harmonization by unit armourers to ensure that they would hit the target at normal air combat ranges.

A total of 143 Mark VBs were sent to Russia. These were followed by 1183 of the markedly superior Mark IX. However, the VVS found that all Spitfires were difficult to operate from the primitive grass airstrips in forward

Spitfire IX
A two-seat trainer conversion of a Spitfire IX produced by No.1 Aircraft Depot, Leningrad, 1945.

Spitfire Mark IX
Type: Single-seat fighter
Length: 9.47m (31ft 1in)
Wingspan: 9.9m (32ft 6in)
Height: 3.86m (12ft 8in)
Wing area: 21.46m² (231ft²)
Empty weight: 2309kg (5090lb)
Loaded weight: 3354kg (7400lb)
Maximum take-off weight: 3950kg (8710lb)
Powerplant: 1 × Rolls-Royce Merlin 66 liquid-cooled V-12, 1283kW (1720hp)
Maximum speed: 650km/h (404mph)
Range: 698km (434 miles)
Service ceiling: 12,954m (42,500ft)
Rate of climb: 24.1m/s (4745ft/min)
Wing loading: 149kg/m² (30.6lb/ft²)
Armament: 2 × 20mm (0.79in) Hispano Mark II cannon (120rpg), 2 x 12.7mm (0.5in) Browning M2 machine guns (250rpg) plus up to 2 x 110kg (250lb) and 1 x 230kg (500lb) bombs

areas; their narrow-track undercarriages meant that they were dangerously unstable while taxiing over rough ground. A further risk was that the Spitfire could easily be mistaken for the Bf 109 under combat conditions, and 'friendly fire' incidents were all too common.

Eventually, the majority of Soviet Spitfires were transferred to PVO Strany home defence units that operated from better-equipped airfields, where they could receive more thorough maintenance. A further factor may have been that the Spitfire's Merlin engine could not tolerate the low-octane Russian-produced fuel, which was often all that was readily available to the VVS. As late as the summer of 1944, it took Stalin's personal intervention to ensure that sufficient high-octane fuel was made available for the VVS units supporting Operation Bagration.

Handley Page Hampden

Following the virtual destruction of Arctic Convoy PQ17, it was decided that air cover was essential for the following convoy, PQ18. This was scheduled to include 32 Hampden torpedo-bombers operating from bases near Murmansk to counter any sortie by major German surface units. The Hampdens of 144 Squadron RAF and 445 Squadron RAAF deployed to Vayenga near Murmansk in September 1942, but seven were lost and two more damaged en route. The squadrons flew several sorties from Vayenga without making contact with the enemy before

Hampden T.B. Mark I

A Hampden T.B. Mark I of the 24th Mine and Torpedo Bomber Regiment, VVS VMF Northern Fleet, based at Vayenga, 1942.

Handley Page Hampden T.B. Mark I
Type: Four-seat torpedo-bomber
Length: 16.32m (53ft 7in)
Wingspan: 21.09m (69ft 2in)
Height: 4.55m (14ft 11in)
Wing area: 62.1m² (668ft²)
Empty weight: 5789kg (12,764lb)
Loaded weight: N/k
Maximum take-off weight: 10,206kg (22,500lb)
Powerplant: 2 × Bristol Pegasus XVIII 9-cylinder radials, 754kW (1000hp) each
Maximum speed: 397km/h (247mph)
Range: 2768km (1720 miles)
Service ceiling: 5790m (19,000ft)
Rate of climb: 4.98m/s (980ft/min)
Wing loading: N/k
Armament: 1 x 7.7mm (0.303in) fixed forward-firing Browning machine gun plus 5 x flexible 7.7mm (0.303in) Vickers K machine guns (one in nose and two each in dorsal and ventral positions) plus 1 x 457mm (18in) Mark XII torpedo and up to 2 x 230kg (500lb) bombs

handing over their aircraft to the Russians and returning to Britain in October.

It seems likely that about 20 Hampdens were incorporated into the VVS VMF (Naval Aviation) and modified to take Russian 45-36AN torpedoes. In at least some aircraft, the dorsal gun position was replaced by a manually operated UTK-1 turret armed with a single 12.7mm (0.5in) UBT machine gun.

Amused by the Hampden's distinctive fuselage shape, Soviet naval pilots dubbed the type 'Balalaika'. They flew their first sorties in December 1942, attacking German shipping along the Norwegian coast. However, losses to German flak and fighters were such that the Hampdens were phased out of service from April 1943 in favour of Douglas A-20G torpedo-bombers.

Curtiss P-40 Warhawk/ Tomahawk/Kittyhawk

In Russian service, the various P-40 variants were generally referred to as Tomahawks (for versions equivalent to the P-40B and P-40C) and Kittyhawks (for types equivalent to the P-40D and all later variants). A total of 247 P-40Bs and Cs, together with 2178 P-40Es, Ks, Ls and Ns were supplied between 1941 and 1944.

The early-production P-40B/C versions were reported to be inferior to Soviet-produced: '...M-105P-powered production fighters in speed and rate of climb.' However, they were praised for their good short-field performance, manoeuvrability, range and endurance. Many VVS units stripped down these early P-40s to improve performance, in some cases removing the wing guns altogether, preferring to rely on the twin 12.7mm (0.5in) engine-mounted machine guns. Russian pilots liked the type's range, which was superior to that of most Soviet fighters, although they still preferred the P-39. One recalled that: 'At first it felt unpleasant to sit waist-high in glass, as the edge of the fuselage was almost at waist level. But the bullet-proof glass and armoured seat were strong and visibility was good.'

A major criticism of the type was its poor climb rate and high maintenance requirements. To improve their chances of survival, VVS pilots had to fly the P-40 at War Emergency Power settings in fighter versus fighter combat. Although this brought their acceleration and speed closer to that of their German counterparts, it could burn out engines in a matter of weeks.

There were also problems with the low-grade Russian-produced fuel and oil that contributed to the short operational life of their Allison engines. In common with most other Western aero-engines, these were designed to be run on higher-octane fuel than anything produced by Soviet refineries. As replacement Allisons were hard to obtain, a fair number of worn-out P-40s were refitted with Klimov engines, but these performed relatively poorly and were relegated to rear area use.

As better Russian-built fighters became available, P-40s were gradually transferred to PVO Strany home defence units and the VVS VMF. Nikolay

P-40C

A P-40C of the 154th Fighter Regiment, VVS VMF, Red Banner Baltic Fleet, Leningrad, early 1942.

P-40C

Type: Single-seat fighter
Length: 9.66m (31ft 8in)
Wingspan: 11.38m (37ft 4in)
Height: 3.76m (12ft 4in)
Wing area: 21.92m² (235.94ft²)
Empty weight: 2880kg (6350lb)
Loaded weight: 3760kg (8280lb)
Maximum take-off weight: 4000kg (8810lb)
Powerplant: 1 x Allison V-1710-33, 775kW (1040hp)
Maximum speed: 565km/h (351mph)
Range: 1050km (650 miles)
Service ceiling: 8840m (29,000ft)
Rate of climb: 11m/s (2100ft/min)
Wing loading: 171.5kg/m² (35.1lb/ft²)
Armament: 6 x 7.7mm (0.303in) Browning machine guns (four in wings, two in nose)

Golodnikov of the VVS VMF 2nd Guards Fighter Regiment recalled:

'Actually, the P-40 could engage all Messerschmitts on equal terms, almost to the end of 1943. If you take into consideration all the characteristics of the P-40, the Tomahawk was equal to the Bf 109F and the Kittyhawk was slightly better. Its speed and vertical and horizontal manoeuvre were good and fully competitive with enemy aircraft. Acceleration rate was a bit low, but it was OK once you got used to the engine. We considered the P-40 to be a decent fighter.'

Bell P-39 Airacobra

The P-39 was one of the first aircraft to be designed as a weapons system, with its layout dictated by the requirement to carry the 37mm (1.46in) M4 cannon. The result was a highly unusual fighter with its engine mounted behind the cockpit, driving the propeller via a long transmission shaft.

Although this gave space in the nose for the cannon, two 12.7mm (0.5in) machine guns and the nose wheel of the tricycle undercarriage, it caused a host of problems. These included fiendishly awkward engine maintenance – ground crews had to strip off several fuselage panels and often remove the rear cockpit canopy, plus the pilot's seat and back armour, just to carry out routine servicing. More seriously, it proved impossible to fit anything other than a very basic single-stage,

Bell P-39Q

The P-39Q flown by the VVS ace Aleksandr Pokryshkin of 16th Guards Fighter Regiment in which he scored the majority of his victories.

Bell P-39Q Airacobra
Type: Single-seat fighter
Length: 9.2m (30ft 2in)
Wingspan: 10.4m (34ft)
Height: 3.8m (12ft 5in)
Wing area: 19.8m² (213ft²)
Empty weight: 2955kg (6516lb)
Loaded weight: 3433kg (7570lb)
Maximum take-off weight: 3800kg (8400lb)
Powerplant: 1 × Allison V-1710-85, 894kW (1200hp)
Maximum speed: 626km/h (389mph)
Range: 840km (525 miles)
Service ceiling: 10,700m (35,000ft)
Rate of climb: 19.3m/s (3805ft/min)
Wing loading: 169kg/m² (34.6lb/ft²)
Armament: 1 x 37mm (1.46in) M4 cannon, 4 x 12.7mm (0.5in) Browning M2 machine guns plus a maximum bombload of 230kg (500lb)

single-speed supercharger that made the type sluggish at altitudes above 5200m (17,000ft).

The RAF was impressed by the Airacobra's claimed performance figures. In September 1940, Britain ordered 386 P-39Ds, armed with a 20mm (0.79in) Hispano cannon and six 7.7mm (0.303in) Browning machine guns. The RAF eventually ordered 675 P-39s. However, when the first aircraft were issued to 601 Squadron in September 1941, it was obvious that they had an inadequate rate of climb and high-altitude performance for the air war being fought over Western Europe. They were promptly replaced by Spitfires, and Britain transferred about 200 P-39s to the Soviet Union.

These aircraft were the first P-39s to reach Russia, followed by 4500 examples of later variants, especially the N and Q models. Soviet pilots found that the type was ideally suited to the sort of air combat being fought over the Eastern Front, where it proved to be a sturdy, low-altitude fighter. They admired the devastating effect of the 37mm (1.46in) cannon, but disliked the low rate of fire (less than three rounds per second), its low velocity and limited ammunition supply (only 30 rounds).

A total of 1,232,991 of the cannon's 0.61kg (1.34lb) HE rounds were supplied to the VVS – these were sufficiently powerful to destroy most German fighters and medium bombers with a single hit. Five of the ten highest-scoring Soviet pilots made the majority of their kills flying P-39s. Alexander Pokryshkin logged 47 of his 59 victories in P-39s. This total excludes his six shared victories, at least some of which were achieved with the P-39.

Bell P-63 Kingcobra

The P-63 prototype first flew on 7 December 1942 and was essentially an enlarged and more powerful P-39. By the time the first production aircraft were delivered in October 1943, the USAAF did not want them, as they were judged to be distinctly inferior to the P-51 Mustang. The type was then offered to the Russians, who were already successfully operating large numbers of P-39s, and was enthusiastically accepted. A total of 3303 P-63s were completed by the time production ended in 1945, of which at least 2397 (and possibly as many as 2672) had been supplied to the VVS.

It seems likely that the 4th Guards Fighter Regiment converted to P-63s in 1944 and flew them in action over East Prussia and Berlin. Hans-Ulrich Rudel, the *Luftwaffe*'s most highly decorated pilot, recalled that he frequently encountered '…American types of aircraft, especially Airacobras, Kingcobras and Bostons' over the Courland Pocket in 1944/45.

In the Far East, P-39s and P-63s provided air cover for the Soviet invasion of Manchuria in August 1945, flying escort and ground attack missions. Soviet P-63s scored their first air victory of the invasion on 15th August, when Lieutenant Miroshnichenko shot down a Nakajima Ki-43 Hayabusa fighter off the coast of North Korea.

Kingcobras remained in front-line service with the VVS until about 1950,

Soviet ceremonial
A P-39 unit receives a banner denoting its newly-awarded Guards status.

Bell P-63A Kingcobra
Type: Single-seat fighter
Length: 10m (32ft 8in)
Wingspan: 11.7m (38ft 4in)
Height: 3.8m (12ft 5in)
Wing area: 23m² (248ft²)
Empty weight: 3100kg (6800lb)
Loaded weight: 4000kg (8800lb)
Maximum take-off weight: 4900kg (10,700lb)
Powerplant: 1 × Allison V-1710-117, 1340kW (1800hp)
Maximum speed: 660km/h (410mph)
Range: 725km (450 miles)
Service ceiling: 13,100m (43,000ft)
Rate of climb: 12.7m/s (2500ft/min)
Wing loading: 173kg/m² (35.48lb/ft²)
Armament: 1 x 37mm (1.46in) M4 cannon, 4 x 12.7mm (0.5in) Browning M2 machine guns plus a maximum bombload of 680kg (1500lb)

after which they were used to train pilots converting to the new MiG-15 jet fighter.

The P-63 was chosen for this role as it had a tricycle undercarriage similar to that of the Mig-15, whereas all Soviet-built piston-engined fighters had tail-wheel landing gear.

Douglas A-20 Boston

The VVS was impressed by reports of the excellent performance of the A-20. Test pilots reported that it: '… has no vices and is very easy to take off and land … The aeroplane [is] … extremely pleasant to fly and manoeuvre.'

The first aircraft arrived in Russia

in February 1942: most of the early deliveries were A-20B (665 aircraft) and A-20C (690 aircraft). VVS bomber pilots loved the aircraft. One recalled that: '…they were really fast… neither Messerschmitts [Bf-109s] nor LaGGs [LaGG-3s] could catch up with them.'

They also appreciated its survivability – the type flew well on one engine – but even so, low-level bombing raids inevitably entailed heavy losses from flak and fighters.

The type's one real failing lay in its defensive armament: the early models

A-20C

A winter-camouflaged A-20C torpedo bomber of 1st Guards Mine and Torpedo Bomber Regiment, VVS VMF, Red Banner Baltic Fleet.

A-20G

An early-production A-20G, with the original limited traverse twin 7.62mm (.3in) dorsal guns replaced by a manually operated UTK-1 turret armed with a single 12.7mm (.5in) UBT machine gun.

Douglas A-20G

Type: Three-seat light bomber
Length: 14.63m (48ft)
Wingspan: 18.69m (61ft 4in)
Height: 5.36m (17ft 7in)
Wing area: 43.1m² (464ft²)
Empty weight: 7708kg (16,693lb)
Loaded weight: 10,964kg (24,127lb)
Maximum take-off weight: 12,338kg (27,200lb)
Powerplant: 2 × Wright R-2600-23 Twin Cyclone radials, 1200kW (1600hp) each
Maximum speed: 510km/h (317mph)
Range: 1521km (945 miles)
Service ceiling: 7225m (23,700ft)
Rate of climb: N/k
Wing loading: N/k
Armament: 9 x 12.7mm (0.5in) Browning M2 machine guns (6 x fixed forward-firing, 2 in dorsal turret, 1 x ventral); maximum bombload of 1800kg (4000lb)

carried four fixed forward-firing and three flexible 7.62mm (0.3in) Browning machine guns, two in the dorsal position and one firing through a ventral hatch. Soviet aircrews felt that the weak rear-firing armament left them unnecessarily vulnerable to German fighters.

Various solutions were tried before it was found that the dorsal gun position could be replaced with a manually operated UTK-1 turret armed with a single 12.7mm (0.5in) UBT machine gun. As many as 830 Soviet A-20s were eventually rearmed in this way. From 1943, the VVS began receiving the new A-20G.

This eliminated concerns about armament, as the glazed nose was replaced by a solid nose with either four 20mm (0.79in) cannon and two 12.7mm (0.5in) M2 Browning machine guns or six M2s. Most also had a power-operated dorsal turret armed with two M2s and another in the ventral position. The type's firepower led the VVS to deploy it as a ground-attack aircraft, rather than as a light bomber, but it proved to be too vulnerable to German light flak. All surviving aircraft were withdrawn from ground-attack operations by November 1943, and many were rebuilt to incorporate a glazed nose and bomb aimer's position.

A-20Gs were also issued to the VVS VMF (Naval Aviation) as torpedo-bombers. These aircraft were fitted with external racks to carry two Russian 45-36AN torpedoes, and most had an additional fuel tank installed in the bomb bay. The type operated in support of the Black Sea, Baltic and Northern Fleets until the end of the war.

North American B-25 Mitchell

The first of a total of 862 B-25s were sent to Russia in the spring of 1942. Soviet pilots liked the handling and range of these D models, which were issued to the ADD (Long Range Aviation) to supplement its Il-4s and Pe-8s. Initial operational experience revealed one failing with the defensive armament: the lack of a rear gun position. Theoretically, this shouldn't have been a problem, as the B-25D had power-operated dorsal and ventral turrets, each with twin 12.7mm (0.5in) Browning M2 machine guns. However, the remote-controlled retractable ventral turret gave constant trouble. Its periscopic sight had a limited field of view and vibrated so badly when the guns were fired that it was almost impossible to aim accurately.

German fighters quickly learned to exploit this weakness by attacking from astern and below; many Russian B-25Ds were modified to mount a single flexible 12.7mm (0.5in) UBT machine gun in the tail to give some protection against these attacks. From 1944, the ADD began to receive more heavily armed B-25Js with twin Browning M2s in the tail.

From September 1942, the Mitchells were used in night interdiction raids against a variety of targets, but as the war progressed, they increasingly switched to strategic bombing, including attacks on Warsaw, Breslau, Konigsberg, Tilsit, and Berlin.

Despite intensive operational use, 497 B-25s survived the war, and the type remained in service with the ADD until 1949.

LEND-LEASE AIRCRAFT WEAPONS

7.62mm (0.3in) and 7.7mm (0.303in) Browning machine guns

These were the US and British models of the AN/M2 aircraft version of the 7.62mm (0.3in) Model 1919A4 machine gun. They were significantly lighter than the M1919A4, with a markedly higher rate of fire (1200–1500rpm). The 7.62mm (0.3in) version armed many of the US aircraft supplied to Russia.

The 7.7mm (0.303in) Browning was based on the 1930 Pattern belt-fed Colt-Browning machine gun. It was adopted by the RAF as the Browning .303 Mk II in the 1930s. The type was licence-built by Vickers Armstrong and BSA in hydraulically operated and hand-fired versions (for fighters and bombers respectively). The majority of British-supplied lend-lease aircraft were armed with these machine guns.

Vickers K machine gun

The Vickers K (also known as the Vickers Gas Operated – VGO) was designed in the 1930s to replace the RAF's obsolescent Lewis machine guns. The Vickers K armed many British bombers in the immediate pre-war period, and was not phased out of RAF and Fleet Air Arm service until the end of the war.

12.7mm (0.5in) Browning machine guns

The water-cooled 12.7mm (0.5in) Browning Model 1921 AA machine gun provided the basis for the development of all US 12.7mm (0.5in) aircraft guns. The first such guns were produced in small numbers in the 1920s, and were finally standardized as the .5 Browning AN/M2. (AN indicates 'Army/Navy' as the gun was developed jointly for use by both services.) The gun was air-cooled, lighter than the ground-fired M2HB, and had a higher rate of fire.

20mm (0.79in) Hispano Mk. II

The Hispano originated with the Hispano-Suiza Type 404 Moteur Canon that was developed in the early 1930s and entered service with the Dewoitine D.501 fighter in 1935.

The gun's performance was so outstanding that it was selected for licence production for the RAF. Early-production cannon designated Hispano Mk. I were limited by their 60-round drum magazines, which gave at best 10 seconds' firing time.

A further problem was the fact that the Hispano had been designed for mounting in the Hispano-Suiza 12Y aero-engine, firing through the propeller shaft. It operated reliably in this well-supported mounting, but constantly jammed when fitted in far less rigid wing mountings in the Spitfire.

The solution lay in the adoption of a belt-feed system that had been trialled by Hispano-Suiza in 1939/40. It was finally developed into a workable system by the Molins Machine Company, which was able to reduce stoppages to an average of one in every 1500 rounds. Belt-fed cannon entered service as the Hispano Mk. II in 1941 and armed most RAF fighters until the mid-1950s.

37mm (1.46in) Automatic Gun, M4

This cannon was designed by John Browning and armed the Bell P-39 Airacobra and P-63 Kingcobra fighters. It was a compact design and light for its calibre, but had a relatively low muzzle velocity and rate of fire, which made it less than ideal for its intended bomber destroyer role. Despite this, lend-lease P-39s and P-63s were popular with the VVS, which used them as effective low-level fighters from 1942 until the end of the war.

CHAPTER 6

Naval Weapons

The Soviet Navy was formally established in 1918 as the 'Workers' and Peasants' Red Fleet' (Raboche-Krest'yansky Krasny Flot – RKKF). At the time, what remained of the former Imperial Russian Navy was rapidly deteriorating. Work had virtually stopped in the shipyards, where vessels rotted at their moorings.

The few nominally operational vessels were crippled by shortages of equipment and trained manpower. Desertion was rife and few officers remained: many had been killed in the Red Terror, others had joined the anti-Communist 'White' forces, and more had simply resigned. Much of the Black Sea Fleet had been taken over by the Whites, and Communist atrocities were even eroding the morale of the Kronstadt seamen who had been instrumental in Lenin's seizure of power. The Kronstadt garrison would finally erupt in revolt in 1921, which was only suppressed after Lenin ordered an assault by 60,000 troops.

In the later 1920s, many older naval vessels were scrapped, leaving the Baltic Fleet with three old battleships, two cruisers, ten destroyers, and a few submarines. A small Black Sea Fleet was also maintained, together with thirty flotillas of small craft on Russia's inland waterways. The earliest Soviet naval construction programmes concentrated

Opposite:
85mm (3.35in) 90-K AA Gun
The crew of a 90-K on the Kirov-class cruiser *Kalinin*. The 90-K replaced the notoriously unreliable 100mm (3.9in) B-34 guns which originally armed the Kirov-class.

Naval gunfire support
The 305mm (12in) main armament of the *Parizhskaya Kommuna* bombarding Axis positions in the Crimea, 1942.

on submarines and light surface forces, but these were sufficient to allow the formation of the Pacific Fleet in 1932 and the Northern Fleet in 1933. Stalin's plans went much further than this. In 1936, he authorized the construction of 16 new capital ships to counter growing German naval strength.

Tacitly recognizing the lack of Soviet design capability for such an ambitious construction programme, Stalin agreed to seek help from Western naval architects. Italian designers Ansaldo of Genoa proposed a class of battleships similar to that of the *Littorio* then under construction. Further requests for hybrid battleship-aircraft carrier designs were sent to US companies. Gibbs & Cox responded with a series of designs for vessels up to 73,000 tonnes (71,850 tons) mounting 12 x 406mm (16in) guns and carrying up to 30 aircraft.

The lack of professionalism in the RKKF was worsened by Stalin's purges, whose victims included eight out of nine admirals. The purge badly affected the Navy, whose officers and men were suspected of exploiting their opportunities for foreign contacts. This may have influenced the decision to abandon attempts to use foreign design teams and to ensure that the new battleships were entirely 'Soviet-made'. The first three units of this Sovetskiy Soyuz-class were laid down in 1938/39, but none were ever completed.

Technical limitations

The battlefleet was intended to be strengthened by 16 of the new Kronshtadt-class battlecruisers, but overwhelming technical difficulties convinced even Stalin that Soviet shipyards were incapable of producing capital ships on this scale. The battlecruiser programme was gradually reduced to just two vessels that were laid down in November 1939, but

RKKF Strength 22 June 1941				
	Baltic Fleet	Black Sea Fleet	Northern Fleet	Pacific Fleet
Battleships	2	1	-	-
Cruisers	2	5	-	-
Flotilla leaders	2	3	-	2
Destroyers	17	14	8	5
Submarines	71	44	15	85
Escort vessels	7	2	7	6
Gunboats	2	4	-	-
Minesweepers	30	12	2	18
MTBs	67	78	-	145
Patrol boats	33	24	14	19
Aircraft	656	625	116	500

Soviet naval strength

The figures represent a mix of some pre-World War I ships – the battleships, some cruisers and the Novik-class destroyers – together with modern vessels built in Russia and Europe, such as the Italian-built destroyer *Tashkent* and the partially completed German heavy cruiser *Lützow*. A further 219 vessels including three battleships, two battlecruisers, two heavy and seven light cruisers, 45 destroyers, and 91 submarines were under construction.

construction was halted by the German invasion and both were scrapped after the war.

The German invasion

The opening stages of Operation 'Barbarossa' were disastrous for the Baltic Fleet. The loss of Lithuania, Latvia and Estonia forced a hasty evacuation of its forward bases, during which it suffered heavy losses from mines and air attack. Thereafter, it was blockaded in Leningrad and Kronstadt, where its surface units supplemented the city's AA defences and bombarded German positions. The ships took significant losses from air attacks and artillery fire, notably the old battleship *Marat*, which sank at its moorings when its bows were blown off by Stukas, although it was later raised and returned to service as a floating battery.

For much of the war, Soviet naval operations in the Baltic were confined to submarine sorties. Until the end of 1944, these only sank small numbers of German and Finnish vessels, but during 1945, they torpedoed and sank the former liners *Wilhelm Gustloff* and *Steuben*, together with the freighter *Goya*. All three ships were crowded with German military personnel and civilians being evacuated from the Courland Pocket and East Prussia. The total fatalities in these three sinkings may well have exceeded 19,000.

The Black Sea Fleet also suffered badly throughout 1941 and 1942 with the loss of its bases at Odessa and Sevastopol. German air attacks were responsible for most of its losses during this period; by 1943, its remaining major surface units were in such poor condition that they were practically non-operational.

Although the RKKF's total manpower increased from 290,000 in June 1941 to 600,00 by May 1945, its professionalism suffered badly as a result of the heavy losses of 1941/42. These were worsened by the deployment ashore of almost 390,000 seamen, mostly as infantrymen. Many were thrown into actions such as the defence of Odessa and Sevastopol without any field training, which simply served to inflate already massive casualty lists.

MAJOR WARSHIP CLASSES

Gangut-class battleships

The four Gangut-class battleships (*Gangut*, *Petropavlovsk*, *Sevastopol* and *Poltava*) were Russia's first dreadnoughts, which entered service with the Imperial Navy's Baltic Fleet in 1914/15. They saw virtually no action during World War I before being taken into the RKKF and renamed in the 1920s:

- *Gangut* became *Oktyabrskaya Revolyutsiya* (1925)
- *Petropavlovsk* became *Marat* (1921)
- *Sevastopol* became *Parizhskaya Kommuna* (1921)
- *Poltava* became *Frunze* (1926)

Although *Frunze* remained in commission until 1940, she had been badly damaged in 1919 by a fire in her forward boiler room, which gutted much of her hull.

Various plans to rebuild her were considered, but she was gradually stripped to provide spare parts for her sister ships and was finally scrapped in 1949.

The remaining three ships were reconstructed to varying degrees between 1928 and 1940. *Parizhskaya Kommuna* became the flagship of the Black Sea Fleet in 1930 and carried out a number of naval gunfire support

Volga Flotilla, Battle of Stalingrad
Crewmen boarding a Project 1125 Bronkater armoured river gunboat. The forward T-34 turret is just visible, together with the PB-5 machine gun turret on the conning tower and the aft M-8-M 82mm Katyusha salvo rocket launcher.

RKKF Strength 1944/45				
	Baltic Fleet (1 Jan 1945)	**Black Sea Fleet (May 1944)**	**Northern Fleet (1 Jan 1945)**	**Pacific Fleet (10 Aug 1945)**
Battleships	1	1	1	-
Cruisers	2	4	1	2
Flotilla leaders	2	-	1	1
Destroyers	10	6	17	12
Submarines	28	29	22	78
Escort vessels	5	13	12	19
Gunboats	10	3	-	-
Minesweepers	73	27	36	52
MTBs	78	47	40	204
Patrol boats	220	113	59	49
Aircraft	781	467	721	1618

Late-war strength
In the final year of the war Soviet naval strength was concentrated in light ships, patrol boats and submarines that could operate in the coastal waters of the Black Sea and Baltic.

missions against Axis targets in the Crimea in 1941/42. Thereafter, she saw no further action, as she was judged to be too vulnerable to German air attacks. She reverted to her original name in 1943 and remained in service until 1956, when she was scrapped.

Marat and *Oktyabrskaya Revolyutsiya* undertook only a single shore bombardment mission in the opening stages of the Winter War before both ships had their AA armament modernized during the winter of 1939–40. *Oktyabrskaya Revolyutsiya* was fitted with additional AA guns in February/March 1941.

Neither vessel saw combat again until 8 September 1941, when they fired on German troops from positions near Kronstadt and Leningrad. *Marat* was sunk at her moorings on 23 September by two near-simultaneous hits by 1000kg (2200lb) bombs dropped by the Stukas of III/StG 2. These detonated her forward magazine, which blew off her fore turret, besides wrecking her bridge and forward funnel. More than 320 crewmen were killed, and the ship gradually sank in 11m (36ft) of water.

The aft section of the ship was later refloated and served as a floating battery. Initially, only the two rearmost turrets were operable, but the second turret was repaired by the autumn of 1942, and she fired 1971 305mm (12in) shells during the Siege of Leningrad. In 1943, she reverted to her original name, but was finally renamed *Volkhov*, after the nearby river, in November

Sevastopol
Sevastopol in the Black Sea during the late 1940s in her final configuration with British Type 290 and Type 291 air-warning radars. Although all the surviving Gangut-class battleships were totally obsolete by this time, Stalin insisted that they should be kept in service as a matter of national prestige.

Sevastopol
Displacement: 24,800 tonnes (24,400 tons)
Length: 181.2m (594ft)
Beam: 26.9m (88ft)
Draught: 8.99m (29ft 6in)
Engines: 10 x steam turbines totalling 38,776kW (52,000hp)
Speed: 44.6km/h (24.1 knots)
Range: 5900km (3200 nautical miles) at 19km/h (10 knots)
Armament as built (Main): 12 x 305mm (12in) **(Secondary):** 16 x 120mm (4.7in) ; (AA): 1 x 76mm (3in) (TT): 4 x 450mm (17.7in)
Armament after 1941 refit (Main): 12 x 305mm (12in) **(Secondary):** 12 x 120mm (4.7in) **(AA):** 3 x 76.2mm (3in), 16 x 37mm (1.5in) and 12 x 12.7mm (0.5in)
Armour: 125–225mm (4.9–8.9in) belt, 12–50mm (0.47–1.97in) deck, 76–203mm (3–8in) turrets, 75–150mm (3–5.9in) barbettes, 100–254mm (3.9–10in) conning tower
Complement: 1149

1950. She remained in service as a stationary training ship until 1953, when she was scrapped.

Oktyabrskaya Revolyutsiya was badly damaged on 21 September 1941 by three bomb hits that knocked out two of her turrets. She was under repair until November 1942, when she resumed fire support missions in defence of the Leningrad defensive perimeter. She was the last Soviet battleship to fire shots in anger in support of the Vyborg–Petrozavodsk Offensive on 9 June 1944. After the war, she remained on the active list until 1954, when she was reclassified as a training ship before being scrapped in 1956.

Kirov-class cruisers

The six Kirov-class cruisers were the first large naval vessels to be entirely built in Soviet shipyards after the Russian Revolution. The design was based on that of the Italian Navy's Raimondo Montecuccoli-class cruisers, but suffered from an attempt to pack in too much armament on a limited displacement. Their triple 180mm (7.1in) turrets gave constant trouble. They were very cramped, which slowed their rate of fire from a theoretical six rounds per minute to roughly a third of this figure. Accuracy was also poor, as there was considerable blast interference between the closely mounted guns in each turret.

The first two pairs of ships (*Kirov*, *Voroshilov*, *Maxim Gorky* and *Molotov*) were deployed on shore bombardment and supply missions with the Baltic and Black Sea Fleets throughout the war, while the last pair (*Kaganovich* and *Kalinin*) were still under construction for the Pacific Fleet at the Amur Shipbuilding Plant and saw no combat. All six ships survived the war and lingered until the 1970s in training and other secondary roles before being scrapped.

Leningrad-class destroyer leaders

This class of six large destroyers were completed between 1936 and 1940. All were completed well behind schedule, as deliveries of engines and guns were badly delayed. Neither were ready when the lead ship *Leningrad* was laid down in 1932; the engines were delivered a

Kirov
Kirov first saw action against Finnish coastal batteries during the Winter War. She acted as the flagship for the evacuation of Tallinn in August 1941, before taking refuge in Kronstadt. She gave gunfire support during the Siege of Leningrad and bombarded Finnish positions in mid-1944 during the Vyborg–Petrozavodsk Offensive, but played no further part in the war. *Kirov* was reclassified as a training cruiser in 1961 and scrapped in 1974.

Kirov-class cruisers
Displacement: 7890 tonnes (7765 tons) (standard), 9436 tonnes (9287 tons) (full load)
Length: 191.3m (627ft 7in)
Beam: 17.66m (57ft 11in)
Draught: 6.15m (20ft 2in)
Engines: Steam turbines totalling 84,600kW (113,500hp)
Speed: 66.56km/h (35.94 knots)
Range: 6940km (3750 nautical miles) at 33km/h (18 knots)
Armament (Main): 9 x 180mm (7.1in)
(Secondary): 6 x 100mm (3.9in)
(AA): 6 x 45mm (1.77in), 4 x 12.7mm (0.5in)
(TT): 6 x 533mm (21in)
(Mines): 96–164
(Depth charges): 50
Armour: 50mm (2in) belt, deck, turrets and barbettes, 150mm (5.9in) conning tower
Aircraft: 2
Complement: 872

Moskva
The Leningrad-class destroyer leader *Moskva* was commissioned into the Black Sea Fleet in 1938. She took part in Vice Admiral Oktyabrsky's raid on the Romanian port of Constanta on 26 June 1941 and was damaged by the fire of the destroyer *Regina Maria.* She attempted to withdraw, but sank after running into a Romanian minefield.

Leningrad-class destroyer leaders
Displacement: 2185 tonnes (2150 tons) (standard), 2623 tonnes (2582 tons) (full load)
Length: 127.5m (418ft 4in)
Beam: 11.7m (38ft 5in)
Draught: 4.06m (13ft 1in)
Engines: Steam turbines totalling 44,740kW (60,000hp)
Speed: 74.6km/h (40.28 knots)
Range: 3900km (2100 nautical miles) at 37km/h (20 knots)
Armament (Main): 5 x 130mm (5.1in)
(AA): 2 x 76.2mm (3in) and 2 x 45mm (1.77in)
(TT): 8 x 533mm (21in)
(Mines): 68–115
(Depth charges): 52
Complement: 311

year later, but her main armament was not fitted until 1935. Construction was also plagued by the poor quality of many components: up to 90 per cent of some items failed to pass quality control inspections.

As the class entered service, it was found that they were poor seaboats, as their massive bridge structures made them top-heavy. They were also very wet in anything other than calm seas as there was an excessive concentration of weight forward caused by three 130mm (5.1in) turrets closely grouped around the bridge.

Minsk was sunk in Kronstadt Harbour by Stukas of StG 2 on 23 September 1941, but was salvaged and recommissioned in June 1943. Two more of the class (*Moskva* and *Kharkov*) were sunk in the Black Sea – the first by mines off Constanta, Romania, in June 1941 and the second by Stukas off the Crimea in October 1943.

The remaining three (*Leningrad, Baku* and *Tblisi*) survived the war and were scrapped or expended as targets in the early 1960s.

Soobrazitelnyy-class destroyer

The Soobrazitelnyy class were less vulnerable to battle damage than earlier Soviet destroyers due to their unit machinery (four boilers instead of three) and a strengthened hull. However, even by Russian standards, they were very cramped and unpopular with their crews.

Some of the class were upgraded by the middle of the war; these had their two single 130mm (5.1in) bow guns replaced by a fully enclosed twin

Soobrazitelnyy-class destroyer
Displacement: 1727 tonnes (1700 tons) (standard), 2279 tonnes (2243 tons) (full load)
Length: 112.5m (369ft 1in)
Beam: 10.2m (33ft 6in)
Draught: 3.98m (13ft 1in)
Engines: Steam turbines totalling 44,740kW (60,000hp)
Speed: 74.6km/h (40.28 knots)
Range: 2760km (1490 nautical miles) at 35km/h (19 knots)
Armament (Main): 4 x 130mm (5.1in)
(AA): 2 x 76.2mm (3in), 3 x 45mm (1.77in) and 4 x 12.7mm (0.5in)
(TT): 6 x 533mm (21in)
(Mines): 58–96
(Depth charges): 30
Complement: 271

Soobrazitelnyy
Soobrazitelnyy was commissioned into the Black Sea Fleet in 1941. She survived the disastrous raid on Constanta and was active throughout the war. Her final wartime deployment was as part of the naval detachment patrolling the Crimean coast during the Yalta Conference in February 1945.

L-3

In common with the rest of the L-class, *L-3* carried its 20 mines in two stern galleries. Later submarines in the class had two additional stern torpedo tubes.

Leninets-class submarine minelayers
Displacement: 1219 tonnes (1200 tons) (surfaced), 1356.42 tonnes (1335 tons) (submerged)
Length: 81m (265ft 9in)
Beam: 7.5m (24ft 7in)
Draught: 4.08m (13ft 8in)
Engines: Diesel/electric 1193kW (1600hp) diesel, 932kW (1250hp) electric
Speed: 26km/h (14 knots) surfaced, 17km/h (9 knots) submerged
Range: 13,700km (7400 nautical miles) at 17km/h (9 knots)
Armament (TT): 6 x 533mm (21in), 12 x torpedoes 20 x mines
(Guns): 1 x 100mm (3.9in), 1 x 45mm (1.77in)
Complement: 53

130mm (5.1in) B-2LM turret. However, this turret shared the problem of the earlier open, shielded single mounts – a maximum elevation of 45 degrees that meant that it could not be used in the AA role. At the same time, the superstructure was enlarged, increasing crew space, and the AA armament was slightly upgraded.

SUBMARINES AND PATROL BOATS

Leninets-class submarine minelayers

This was a class of 25 submarine minelayers completed between 1931 and 1941. The design was based on that of the British submarine L55, which was sunk in action against Bolshevik destroyers in the Gulf of Finland in 1919. L55 was salvaged by the Russians in 1928, repaired and used as a training submarine before being scrapped in 1960.

The majority of the class scored modest successes (primarily by minelaying). However, on the night of 16/17 April 1945, L-3 torpedoed the German evacuation transport *Goya*, crammed with an estimated 7200 troops and refugees en route from Gotenhafen (Gdynia) to Kiel. *Goya* sank in barely four minutes, with the loss of 7000 passengers and crew.

S-class submarine

The S-class originated with a German-designed submarine that was completed at Cádiz in 1932. Three modified submarines were built in 1934/35 as prototypes of the S-class, which went into production in 1936. A total of 56 were completed between 1936 and 1948, 16 of which were lost to enemy action.

Malyutka-class (M-class) coastal submarines

The M-class, which began entering service in 1933, were the first prefabricated Soviet submarines.

S-class submarine
Displacement: 853 tonnes (840 tons) (surfaced), 1067 tonnes (1050 tons) (submerged)
Length: 77.8m (255ft 3in)
Beam: 6.4m (21ft)
Draught: 4.4m (14ft 5in)
Engines: Diesel/electric 2982kW (4000hp) diesel, 820kW (1100hp) electric
Speed: 36.1km/h (19.5 knots) surfaced, 11.7km/h (6.3 knots) submerged
Range: 11,000km (6000 nautical miles) at 17km/h (9 knots)
Armament (TT): 6 x 533mm (21in) – 4 x bow, 2 x stern – 12 x torpedoes
(Guns): 1 x100mm (3.9in), 1 x 45mm (1.77in)
Complement: 50

S-13
On 30 January 1945, *S-13* sank the 23,118-tonne (25,484-ton) former cruise ship *Wilhelm Gustloff*, carrying almost 10,500 refugees and troops from Gotenhafen (Gdynia) to Kiel. An estimated 9600 died. On 10 February 1945, she torpedoed the 13,300-tonne (14,660-ton) former liner *Steuben*, carrying about 5200 troops and refugees from Pillau to Swinemünde. *Steuben* sank in 20 minutes with the loss of at least 4500 passengers and crew.

Sections were produced at the Gorky Shipyard on the Volga and were then transported by rail to Leningrad for assembly and fitting out. The 109 completed by 1945 served mainly with the Baltic and Black Sea Fleets; 33 were lost.

G-5 class motor torpedo boats (MTBs)

The G-5 entered production in 1933. It was a single-step, hydroplaning design with a whaleback upper hull, largely made of duralumin. This offered significant weight savings, but caused serious maintenance problems due to duralumin's galvanic corrosion in salt water. In service, it was found that G-5s had to be hoisted ashore for anti-corrosion treatment after a maximum of 15 days in the water.

The type was powered by two de-rated Mikulin aero-engines, giving it a good top speed, but imposed a minimum speed of 33km/h (18 knots), which made mooring a tricky business.

G-5 (early production)
An early-production G-5 with a single 12.7mm (0.5in) DShK machine gun.

G-5 (late production)
A later G-5, armed with two 12.7mm (0.5in) DShK machine guns and launch rails for 24 x 82mm (3.2in) rockets.

G-5 class MTB
Displacement: 16.26 tonnes (16 tons) (standard)
Length: 19.1m (62ft 8in)
Beam: 3.5m (11ft 6in)
Draught: 0.82m (2ft 8in)
Engines: 2 × Mikulin GAM-34BS petrol engines, 630kW (850hp) each
Speed: 98km/h (53 knots)
Range: 407km (220 nautical miles)
Armament: 2 x 533mm (21in) torpedoes
(AA): 1 or 2 x 12.7mm (0.5in) DShK machine guns
Complement: 7

To save weight, the torpedoes were carried in rear-facing troughs. On firing, they were pushed backwards by steel rams to enter the water tail-first. Trip-wires linking the torpedoes and the ram heads would start the torpedo motors once pulled taut during release, and the boat would make a sharp turn to clear the torpedoes.

A total of roughly 300 G-5s were completed between 1933 and 1941. At the time of the German invasion, 293 G-5s were in service (60 with the Baltic Fleet, 92 with the Black Sea Fleet, 135 with the Pacific Fleet and six with the Caspian Flotilla). A total of 73 were lost in action and at least 31 were scrapped after becoming unserviceable. Low-rate production continued during the war and by 1945, 24 were in still in service with the Baltic Fleet, 134 were with the Pacific Fleet and six were still on the strength of the Caspian Flotilla.

D-3-class MTBs

The limitations of the G-5 MTBs prompted design studies of larger, more seaworthy, MTBs. Following trials of G5-derived boats of various sizes, the stern torpedo troughs were abandoned in favour of deck-mounted torpedo-launching racks. A wooden-hulled design was selected for production as the D-3 class.

A total of 119 were built by 1944, but the type was plagued with shortages of sufficiently powerful engines, which led to 56 of them being completed as gunboats/subchasers.

Bronekater armoured river gunboats

In the mid-1930s, the Russians developed two classes of armoured river gunboats armed with tank turrets. The Project 1124 medium gunboats were fitted with two 76.2mm (3in) KT-28

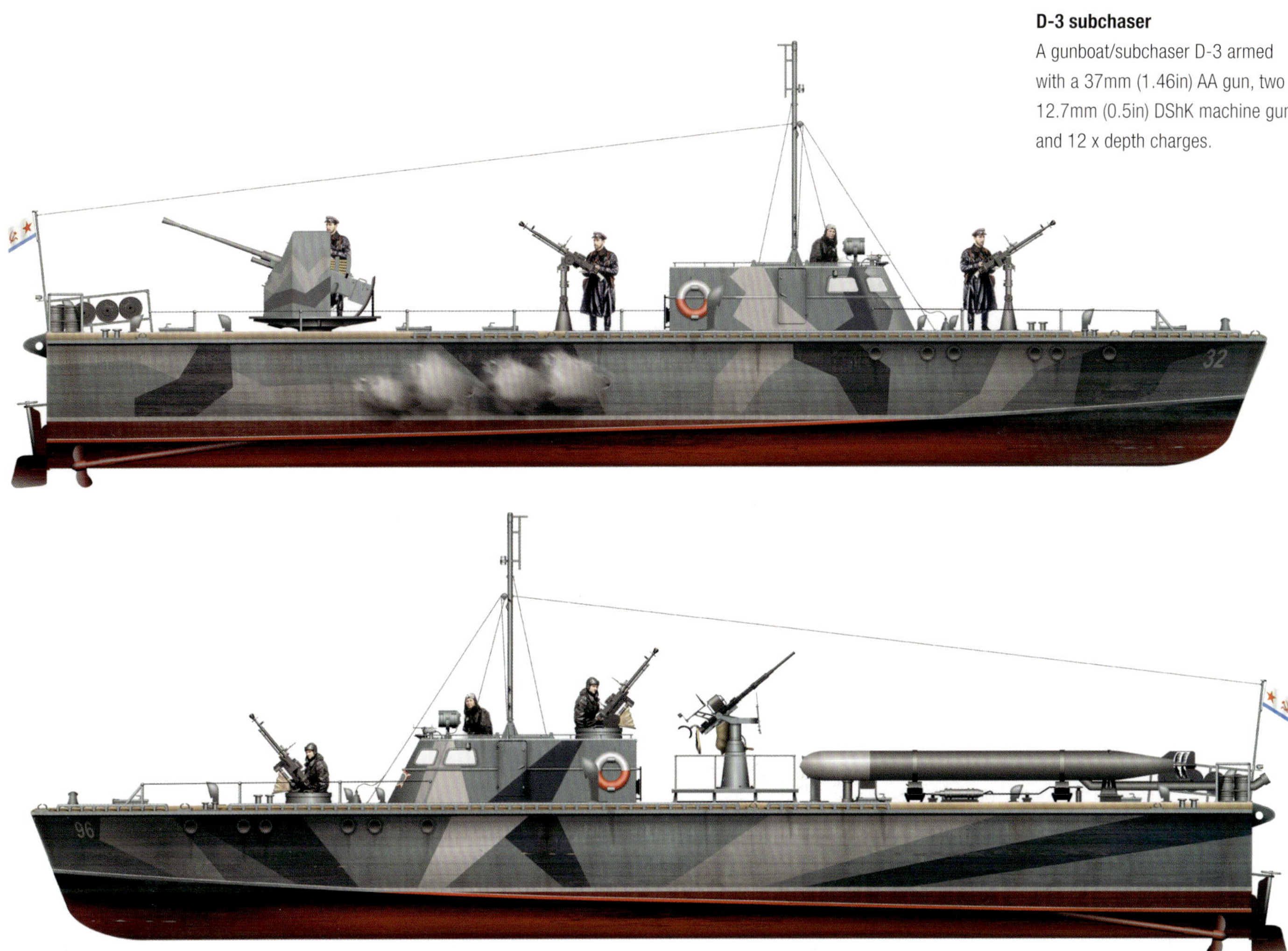

D-3 subchaser

A gunboat/subchaser D-3 armed with a 37mm (1.46in) AA gun, two 12.7mm (0.5in) DShK machine guns and 12 x depth charges.

D-3 gunboat

One of the original D-3s in a typical disruptive camouflage scheme.

D-3 class MTB

Displacement: 32.1 tonnes (31.6 tons) full load
Length: 21.6m (70ft 10in)
Beam: 3.9m (12ft 7in)
Draught: 1.35m (4ft 5in)
Engines: 3 × Mikulin GAM-34F petrol engines, 559kW (750hp) each
Speed: 68km/h (37 knots)
Range: 1018km (550 nautical miles) at 14.8km/h (8 knots)
Armament: 2 x 533mm (21in) torpedoes
12 x depth charges
(AA): 2 x 12.7mm (0.5in) DShK machine guns
Complement: 10

turrets as used to arm the T-28 medium tank, together with one or two 12.7mm (0.5in) DShK machine guns in an AA turret on top of the conning tower.

The smaller Project 1125 gunboats were very similar, but mounted only a single 76.2mm (3in) turret and three PB-5 sub-turrets (again as used on the T-28), each armed with a single 7.62mm (3in) DT machine gun. Both types had a thinly armoured conning tower and waterline armoured belt.

As T-34 turrets became available, they replaced the old KT-28 turrets, offering anti-tank anti-fixed positions capabilities. From 1942 onwards, some boats had their aft turrets replaced by a 24-rail 82mm (3.2in) rocket launcher or a 16-rail 132mm (5.2in) rocket launcher. A total of 97 Project 1124 boats and 151 Project 1125 boats were completed between 1936 and 1944.

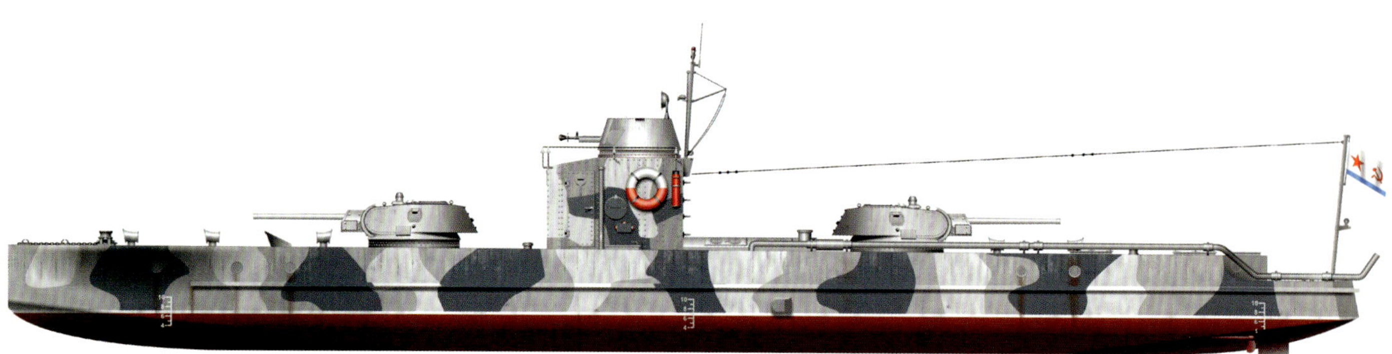

Project 1124

A mid-war Project 1124 Bronekater with a main armament of 2 x T-34 turrets. An open-topped turret with 2 x 12.7mm (0.5in) DShK AA machine guns is mounted on the conning tower.

Project 1124
Displacement: 53 tonnes (52.2 tons)
Length: 25.3m (83ft)
Beam: 4.04m (13ft 3in)
Draught: 0.85m (2ft 9in)
Engines: 2 x GAM-34BS petrol engines, 559kW (750hp) each
Speed: 36km/h (19.4 knots)
Range: 640km (340 nautical miles)
Armament: 2 x T-34 turrets, 2 x 12.7mm (0.5in) DShK machine guns, plus up to 10 mines
Armour: 7–45mm (0.28–1.77in)
Complement: 17

Project 1125

A mid-production Project 1125 with a T-34 Model 1941 cast turret and three PB-5 sub-turrets each armed with a single DT machine gun.

Project 1125
Displacement: 27.2 tonnes (26.8 tons)
Length: 22.65m (74ft 4in)
Beam: 3.5m (11ft 6in)
Draught: 0.52m (1ft 8in)
Engines: 1 x GAM-34BS petrol engine, 560kW (750hp)
Speed: 36km/h (19.4 knots)
Range: 463km (250 nautical miles)
Armament: 1 x T-34 turret, 3 x 7.62mm (0.3in) DT machine guns, plus up to 6 mines
Armour: 7–45mm (0.28–1.77in)
Complement: 13

SOVIET NAVAL WEAPONS

The RKKF's ships were armed with a bewildering variety of weapons, ranging from obsolete 'museum pieces' to ultra-modern designs. This section covers the commonest types – complete coverage would fill an entire book.

GUNS

305mm/52 (12in) Model 1907

These guns formed the main armament of the Gangut-class battleships. Although it seems likely that they never fired against naval targets during World War II, they were highly accurate weapons. They had also armed the World War I Imperatritsa Mariya-class battleships, one of which hit the Turkish cruiser *Midilli* at a range of 21,000m (68,900ft) in April 1916.

Modified versions of these guns were also used as coastal artillery; the most famous of these were the two batteries defending Sevastopol, generally known as Maxim Gorky I and Maxim Gorky II.

180mm/60 (7.1in) B-1-K Model 1931 and 180mm/57 (7.1in) B-1-P Model 1932

The Model 1931 was based on the old 203mm/50 (8in) Model 1905 and formed the main armament of the cruiser *Krasnyi Kavkaz*. In service, the gun showed so many problems (mainly associated with very rapid barrel wear) that it was extensively redesigned as the Model 1932 before being cleared for use aboard the new Kirov-class cruisers.

The guns were also widely used as coastal artillery, with the last batteries remaining in service until the 1990s.

130mm/50 (5.1in) B13 Model 1936

The design began life as a submarine deck gun, but was adapted for use aboard destroyers (and a host of other vessels) when it was found to be too large for the Pravda-class submarines. Production began in 1935 to arm the much-delayed flotilla leader *Leningrad*, but early guns were virtually unserviceable due to extremely rapid barrel wear. This problem was eventually resolved, but the type suffered from an unreliable breech mechanism throughout its service life. It remained in production until 1954, by which time 1199 guns had been completed.

120mm/50 (4.7in) Model 1905

These guns were a Vickers design; the first examples were shipped to Russia in 1905. They armed many Russian ships built between 1905 and 1913, including the Gangut-class battleships. 110 guns were still in service in 1941.

100mm/51 (3.9in) B-24 Model 1936

The Model 1936 was designed to meet a requirement for a modern 100mm (3.9in) gun to arm small surface vessels and submarines. By 1941, 76 were in service. Although no more than five more were made

Gunnery practice

The crew of the 100mm (3.9in) B-24 deck gun of a Black Sea Fleet submarine about to open fire. (For most of the war, Axis air superiority made surfaced attacks suicidal.)

during the war, low-rate production continued until 1950, by which time an additional 63 had been made for submarines.

100mm/56 (3.94in) B-34 Model 1940

Prototypes of various 100mm (3.9in) AA guns had been tested with uniformly poor results throughout the late 1930s, but in 1940 the latest design was rushed into production as the B-34. It initially formed the secondary armament of the Kirov-class cruisers, but the breech and fuse-setting mechanisms were so unreliable that 85mm (3.35in) 90-K AA guns were fitted to the last two Kirovs.

85mm/52 (3.35in) 90-K

The dire problems encountered in producing a reliable 100mm (3.94in) AA gun led to a quick-fix solution created by combining the Army's 85mm (3.35in) AA Gun Model 1939 (52-K) with the naval 34-K 76.2mm (3in) gun mount. This worked well and production began in 1942, although it was not officially accepted into service until June 1946. A total of at least 600 guns were completed by the time production ended in the1950s.

76.2mm/55 (3in) 34-K Model 1935

This AA gun was based on a Rheinmetall design of 1930 that was produced under licence for the Red Army as the 76.2mm (3in) AA Gun Model 1931 (3-K). Impressed with the weapon's performance, the Navy requested its own version. The initial production version proved impossible to elevate in rough seas; a new mounting had to be designed, which entered production in 1936. A total of 285 of these single mounts were completed by the end of 1941.

Design of a twin turret mount began in 1936, but was plagued with problems and production did not begin until 1939.

45mm/46 (1.77in) 21-K and 45mm/68 (1.77in) 21-KM

These guns were developed from the Red Army's 45mm (1.77in) anti-tank guns. The 21-K was the first to enter service in 1934 based on the Model 1932 anti-tank gun, while the 21-KM used the longer barrel of the Model 1942 anti-tank gun. Both types saw extensive service despite their limited effectiveness as AA weapons. This was due to their semi-

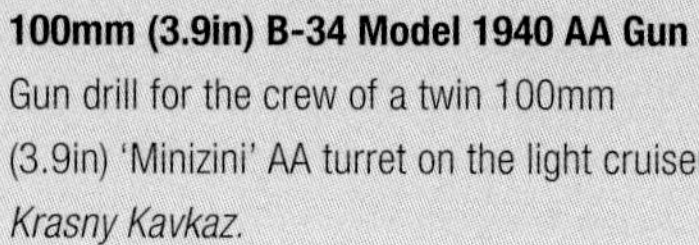

100mm (3.9in) B-34 Model 1940 AA Gun

Gun drill for the crew of a twin 100mm (3.9in) 'Minizini' AA turret on the light cruiser *Krasny Kavkaz.*

37mm/67 (1.46in) 70-K
With a rate of fire of 150rpm the automatic 70-K was far superior to the Soviet Navy's earlier semi-automatic 45mm light AA guns.

automatic action, which restricted their rate of fire, and the fact that neither was issued with time-fused ammunition, meaning that they had to score direct hits to destroy their targets.

37mm/67 (1.46in) 70-K

This gun was a navalized version of the Red Army's 37mm (1.46in) 61-K that was designed in 1938 and accepted into service in 1940. It was put into volume production and began to replace the semi-automatic 45mm/46 21-K guns on most Soviet warships from 1942 onwards. The type became the RKKF's main light AA gun, with 1641 weapons completed between 1941 and 1945. It remained in production until 1955, by which time 3113 had been built.

TORPEDOES

450mm (17.7in) 45-36NU

This was developed from an Italian 450mm (17.7in) torpedo design that had been purchased in 1932. The type armed Novik-class destroyers and could also be fired from submarine 533mm (20.9in) tubes using a special adaptor.

553mm (21in) 53-38U

This was the most widely used Soviet-designed 533mm (21in) torpedo, which entered service in 1939 and armed large surface vessels, MTBs and submarines. Most had standard impact fuses, but magnetic fuses became available from 1942 onwards.

Anti-Submarine Warfare (ASW) Weapons

Soviet ASW techniques remained primitive throughout the war. None of the RKKF's ships had Asdic/sonar until 1941, and most received it only from 1943 onwards. Despite dropping a total of 88,000 depth charges, the Russians sank no more than seven U-boats during the war. However, many of these depth charges were used against magnetic mines rather than submarines.

SOVIET TANK PRODUCTION

Improved Soviet war production was achieved at the expense of civilian living standards and with the help of Lend-Lease supplies. Soviet factories were ordered to concentrate on the production of low-cost, low-maintenance AFVs, in contrast to German attempts to gain decisive qualitative superiority by producing costly and sophisticated designs such as the Panther. All major Soviet types were incrementally upgraded while simplified and refined manufacturing processes increased production.

Tank Production by Type and Year	1941	1942	1943	1944	1945	TOTAL
Light Tanks						
T-40	41	181	–	–	–	222
T-50	48	15	–	–	–	63
T-60	1818	4474	–	–	–	6292
T-70	–	4883	3343	–	–	8226
T-80	–	–	120	–	–	120
Sub-total	**1907**	**9553**	**3463**	**–**	**–**	**14,923**
Medium Tanks						
T-34	3014	12,553	15,529	2995	–	34,091
T-34/85	–	–	283	11,778	7230	19,291
T-44	–	–	–	–	200	200
Sub-total	**3014**	**12,553**	**15,812**	**14,773**	**7430**	**53,582**
Heavy Tanks						
KV-1	1121	1,753	–	–	–	2874
KV-2	232	–	–	–	–	232
KV-1S	–	780	452	–	–	1232
KV-85	–	–	130	–	–	130
IS-2	–	–	102	2252	1500	3854
Sub-total	**1353**	**2533**	**684**	**2252**	**5001**	**8322**
Total Tanks	**6274**	**24,639**	**19,959**	**17,025**	**8930**	**76,827**
Assault Guns						
SU-76	–	26	1928	7155	3562	12,671
SU-122	–	25	630	493	–	1148
SU-85	–	–	750	1300	–	2050
SU-100	–	–	–	500	1175	1675
SU-152	–	–	704	–	–	704
ISU-122/ISU-152	–	–	35	2510	1530	4075
Sub-total	**–**	**51**	**4047**	**11,958**	**6267**	**22,323**
Total AFVs	**6274**	**24,690**	**24,006**	**28,983**	**15,197**	**99,150**

SOVIET TANK STRENGTH (MONTHLY, ALL THEATRES)

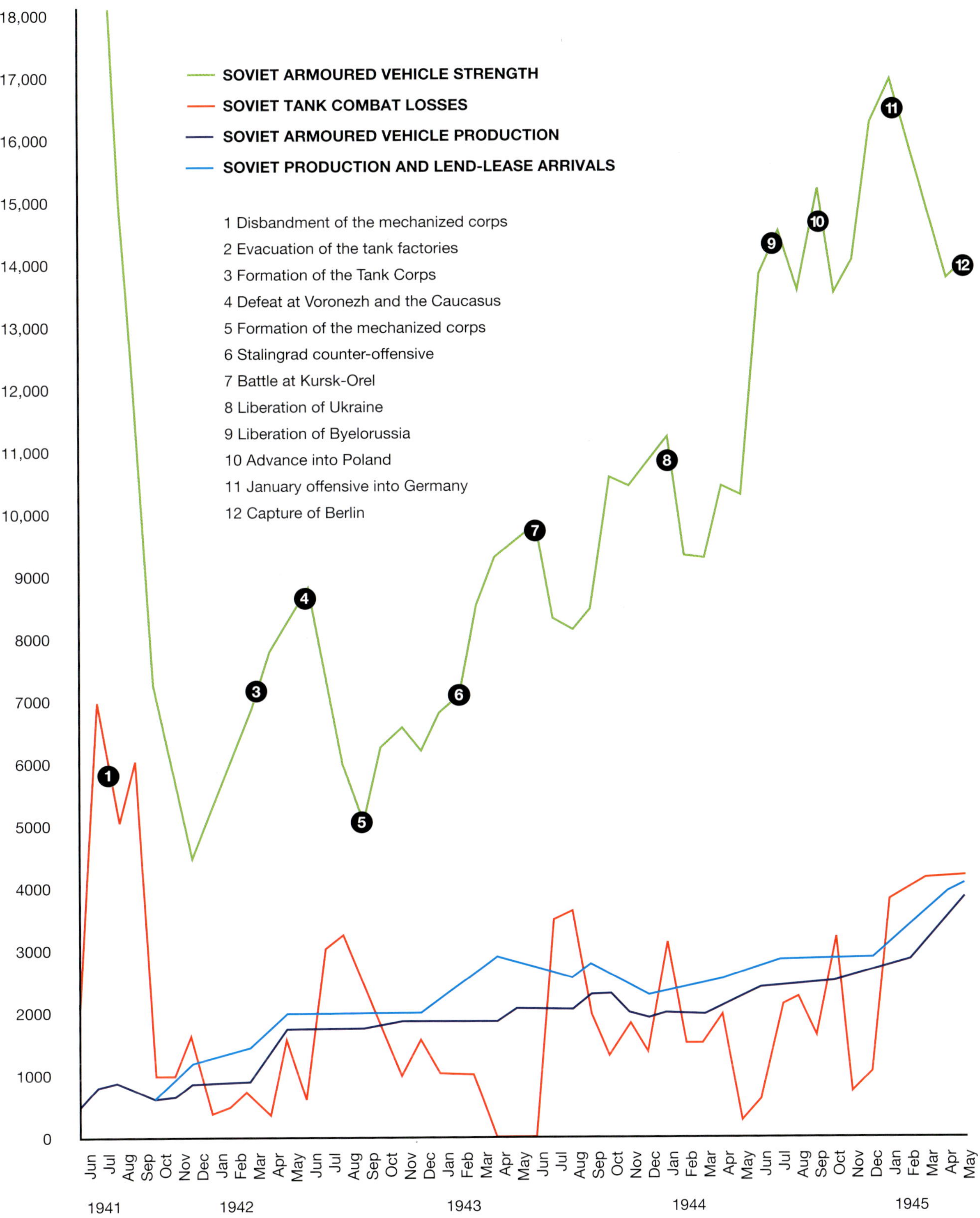

LEND-LEASE ARRIVALS: AFVS

The total of Lend-Lease AFVs supplied to the Red Army equalled approximately 16 per cent of Soviet wartime tank production and 12 per cent of self-propelled gun production.

British & Canadian AFVs, Lend-Lease (1941–45)	Sent	Lost	Arrived
Brit Inf Tk Mk II Matilda	1084		
– Matilda Mk III	113		113
– Matilda Mk IV	915	221	694
– Matilda Mk IV CS	156	31	126
Brit Inf Tk Mk III Valentine	**2394**		
– Valentine Mk II	161	25	136
– Valentine Mk III	346	–	346
– Valentine Mk IV	520	71	559
– Valentine Mk V	340	113	227
– Valentine Mk IX	836	18	818
– Valentine Mk X	74	8	66
– Valentine Bridgelayer	25	–	25
Brit Inf Tk Mk IV Churchill	301		
– Churchill Mk II	45	19	26
– Churchill Mk III	151	24	127
– Churchill Mk IV	105	–	105
Cromwell	6	–	6
Tetrarch	20	–	20
Universal Carriers	1212	not known	–
Canadian Valentine Mk VII	1388	180	1208
Canadian Universal Carriers	1348	not known	–
Total Tanks	**5193**	**710**	**4483**
Total Universal Carriers	**2560**	**224**	**2336**
Total AFVs	**7753**	**934**	**6819**

American AFVs, lend-lease (1942–45)	Sent	Lost	Arrived
M3/M3A1 Stuart	1676	–	–
M5 Stuart	5	–	–
M24 Chaffee	2	–	–
Total Light Tanks	**1682**	**443**	**1239**
M3 Lee medium tank	1386	–	–
M4A2 Sherman (75mm/2.9in)	2007	–	–
M4A2 Sherman (76mm/3in)	2095	–	–
Total Medium Tanks	**5374**	**417**	**4957**
M26	1	–	–
M31B2 ARV	115	–	–
M15A1 MGMC SP AA	100	–	–
M17 MGMC SPG AA	1000	–	–
T48 SPG (SU-57)	650	–	–
M18 tank destroyer	5	–	–
M10 3in GMC TD	52	–	–
M2 halftrack	342	–	–
M3 halftrack	2	–	–
M5 halftrack	421	–	–
M9 halftrack	413	–	–
Total Halftracks	**1158**	**54**	**1104**
Universal Carrier T16	96	–	–
Total AFVs	**8310**	**914**	**7396**

Soft Vehicles, Lend-Lease	1941	1942	1943	1944	1945	Total
Towing Vehicles					–	–
Studebaker	–	3800	34,800	56,400	19,200	114,200
GM	–	1400	4900	400	–	6700
International	–	900	1800	100	300	3100
Chevrolet	–	2700	13,100	25,100	6800	47,700
Ford	–	400	500	–	100	1000
Dodge 3/4	–	–	4300	10,700	4600	19,600
Trucks	**520**				**71**	**559**
Ford-6	–	7600	18,600	29,000	5800	61,000
Dodge 11/2 ton	–	8000	1500	100	–	9600
Dodge 3 ton	–	–	1400	300	–	1700
Bedford	–	1100	–	–	–	1100
Ford Marmon	200	300	–	–	–	500
Austin	200	300	–	–	–	500
Light Vehicles	151				24	127
Willys	–	5400	13,900	14,300	6200	39,800
Bantam	–	500	100	–	–	600
Chevrolet	–	–	–	–	200	200
Special Auto	1212				–	–
Dodge Staff Car	–	–	–	100	100	200
Ford Amphibian	–	–	–	1900	300	2200
GM Amphibian	–	–	–	–	300	300
Trailer	–	–	–	600	200	800
Mack Diesel	–	–	–	–	900	900
Other	–	–	200	300	–	500
Total	**400**	**32,400**	**95,100**	**139,300**	**45,000**	**312,200**

LEND-LEASE ARRIVALS: AIRCRAFT

In addition to aircraft, a significant quantity of spares and raw materials were sent to Russia. Britain alone supplied £1.15bn worth of aircraft engines. Raw materials were arguably even more important – more than half of all Soviet aircraft were produced using aluminium supplied by the Allies.

Types of aircraft supplied:	
Fighters	**Pcs.**
Bell P-39 Airacobra	4,700
Hawker Hurricane	3,374
Bell P-63 Kingcobra	2,397
Curtiss P-40	2,100
Supermarine Spitfire	1,338
Republic P-47 Thunderbolt	203
North American P-51 Mustang	10
Bombers	
Douglas A-20 Boston	3,000
North American B-25 Mitchell	862
Handly-Page Hampden	32

Types of aircraft supplied:	
Flying boats	
Consolidated PBN-1	138
Consolidated PBY-6A	48
Vout OS2U Kingfisher	20
Observation aircraft	
Curtiss O-52 Owl	19
Transport aircraft	
Douglas C-47 Dakota	707
Training aircraft	
North American AT-6 Teksan	82

BIBLIOGRAPHY

Bellamy, Chris. *Absolute War: Soviet Russia in the Second World War.* Macmillan, 2007.

Bonn, Keith, E. *Slaughterhouse: The Handbook of the Eastern Front.* Aberjona Press, 2005.

Budzbon, Przemyslaw. *Soviet Navy at War 1941–1945.* Arms and Armour Press, 1989.

Hooton, E.R. *War over the Steppes: The Air Campaigns on the Eastern Front, 1941–45.* Osprey Publishing, 2016.

Merridale, Catherine. *Ivan's War: The Red Army 1939–1945.* Faber and Faber Ltd., 2006.

Orgill, Douglas. *T34 Russian Armour* (Purnell's History of the Second World War, Weapons Book, No.21). Macdonald & Co. Ltd, 1971.

Perret, Bryan. *Iron Fist: Classic Armoured Warfare Case Studies.* Brockhampton Press, 1999.

Porter, David. *The Essential Vehicle Identification Guide: Soviet Tank Units 1939–1945.* Amber Books, 2009.

Porter, David. *Order of Battle: The Red Army in WWII.* Amber Books, 2009.

Porter, David. *Visual Battle Guide: Fifth Guards Tank Army at Kursk, 12 July 1943.* Amber Books, 2011.

Winchester, Charles D. *Hitler's War on Russia.* Osprey Publishing, 2007.

Zaloga, Steven J. & Grandsen, James. *Soviet Tanks and Combat Vehicles of World War Two.* Arms and Armour Press, 1984.

Zaloga, Steven J. & Grandsen, James. *The Eastern Front, Armour, Camouflage and Markings, 1941 to 1945.* Arms and Armour Press, 1989.

Zaloga, Steven J. & Ness, Leland S. *Red Army Handbook 1939–1945.* Sutton Publishing Ltd., 1998.

Index

References to photographs are in *italics*.